# unzipped souls

unzipped souls

TEMPLE

UNIVERSITY

PRESS

PHILADELPHIA

WILLIAM

MINOR

# unzipped souls

A

Jazz

Journey

through the

Soviet Union

Temple University Press, Philadelphia 19122
Copyright © 1995 by William Minor

Published 1995

Printed in the United States of America

♾ The paper used in this book meets the requirements of the American National Standard for
Information Sciences — Permanence of Paper for Printed Library Materials, ANSI Z39.48-1984

Text design by Tracy Baldwin

Library of Congress Cataloging-in-Publication Data

Minor, William, 1936-
    Unzipped souls : a jazz journey through the Soviet Union / William Minor.
        p. cm.
    Includes index.
    ISBN 1-56639-324-8
    1. Jazz — Soviet Union — History and criticism. I. Title.
ML3509.S7M56 1995
781.65'0947 — dc20                                                                   94-37345
                                                                                      MN

From these woods a good way out along the hill
there now came a sound that was new to us. . . .
Which of these calls seemed the more mysterious,
it is not possible to say. Their quality was very
different by virtue both of their difference in
distance and of a distinct though indefinable
difference in the personality of the callers.

James Agee, *Let Us Now Praise Famous Men*

# contents

# acknowledgments

For much of my life I assumed that when that great day came and a work of substance of mine was published, I would keep the acknowledgments page sweet and short, taking most of the credit for myself because, after all, I was the one who wrote the book. I've since discovered that such narcissism is impossible. A world of people contributed to the making of *Unzipped Souls,* and I would like to thank them now.

First, all those, both West and East, who granted information, interviews, conversation, and friendship: people who will appear throughout the following pages. Among the U.S., Canadian, and British contributors, I'd like to thank Howard Mandel, S. Frederick Starr, Ted Levin, Laurel E. Fay, Naomi Marcus, Ted Everts, Steve Boulay, John Ballard, Bruce Granath, Phyllis Schwartz, Herb Belkin, John Orysik, Veronica Crauford, David Friesen, Larry Ochs, Bob Murphy, Phil Crumley, Anna Markael, Richie Cole, Louis Scherr, Igor Butman, David Azarian, Gennadi Loktionov, and especially Leo Feigin, who recognized the true nature of this work from the start.

In the former Soviet Union I would like to thank Michael Dubilet, Yuri Saulsky, Zhanna Braginskaya, Irina Novikova, Alexei and Larisa Batashev, Igor Illarionov, Igor Schmidt, Gela Charkviani, Evgeny Orchinnikov, Alexander Kahn, Vladimir Feyertag, Kolya Dmitriev, Tatiana Didenko, Anthony and Jeanne Marhel, Germann and Inna Lukianov, Igor Bril, Alexander Oseychuk, Viktor Dvoskin, Sergei Karsaev, Aziza Mustafa-Zadeh, Elza Mustafa-Zadeh, Anatoli Vapirov, Yuri Kuznetsov, Igor Egikov, Irina Vorontsova, Andrei Kondakov, Alexei Kanunnikov, Tamaz Kurashvili, Konstantin Kokhreidze, and Konstantin Ketischvili. Plus the ghosts of Alexander Herzen, Alexander Pushkin, Fyodor Dostoevsky, Daniil Kharms, Anna Akhmatova, and Osip Mandelstam — who accompanied me along the way.

**ix**

I am grateful to the editors of magazines and journals who printed material from these chapters in its initial form: Pawel Brodowski at *Jazz Forum,* Bill Smith at *Coda,* W. Royal Stokes and Mike Joyce at *JazzTimes,* John Ephland and Dave Helland at *Down Beat,* Alice Hummer at the *Christian Science Monitor,* and Mary Heath at the *Massachusetts Review.* Several radio and TV stations took an interest in the music represented here and allowed me to talk about and present it. I would like to thank Morton Marcus at KUSP (Santa Cruz), Barbara Rose Schuler and David Gitin at KAZU (Pacific Grove), Phil Siena at WCNI (New London), Allan McKay at KUNR (Reno), Janis Lohnquist and Ron Montana at the Community Channel 2-B (San Jose), and Alexei Kovalev and Sonya Holsted at Voice of America in Washington, D.C.

I would also like to express my gratitude to the USSR Composers Union, the Community Foundation for Monterey County, and Monterey Peninsula College for financial assistance that made this trip possible; and to friends and colleagues who offered encouragement or assistance, or who just put up with me throughout the writing: Dick and Sara Maxwell, Marat and Sasha (and Mary) Akchurin, John Detro, Lincoln Curtis, Matthew Friday, Steve Turner, Ray March, Eleanor Szazy, Vern Neal, George Lober, Nina Whiting, Martha Casanave, Linda Allen, Jane Haines, Mark and Elizabeth Hopkins, Rosemary Matson, Andre Stepanovsky, Lou and Amy Bernstein, and our neighbors, Alex and Lara, who kept those good Russian sounds going long after the trip.

I'd like to thank everyone at Temple University Press who had a hand in making this book possible, and especially my adamant editors Micah Kleit and Janet Francendese, who kindly worked to curb, even when they could not cure, my "Russian" excesses. Thanks also to production editor Debby Stuart. I am also grateful to that wonderful woman, my mother, and that stalwart fan, my sister Emily, who actually remained in one place long enough to read some of the manuscript. And once again, this work is dedicated to my (lifelong) traveling companion, Betty, and to all the members of our family: Tim, Steve, Janice, Yoko, Blake, and Emily—without whom this book, and my life, would not be plausible.

unzipped souls

"A concert set is just too short, too *small*," Odessa pianist Yuri Kuznetsov told me after I'd heard him play forty-five minutes straight shot, no interludes, no chasers — at a jazz festival in Riga. "I can't express my entire soul at a festival, for my soul is vast and requires more time to reveal all its vivacity, its poetry. I need more time to express myself from *a* to *ia* [*a* to *z*]."

This gargantuan *War and Peace* (or what in this country we might call "Texas") syndrome provided the missing link in cultural continuity for me when my wife and I undertook our nine-thousand-kilometer, six-republic, nine-city, two-major-festivals jazz journey through the former Soviet Union — assembling more than a thousand minutes of taped interviews with musicians, fans, and critics; and a stash of fine photographs, posters, press releases, and nearly more phonograph records than I could carry. Don't worry. This is not a book of facts, although I hope there are more than a few of the right ones in it. This is a book that pays homage to those unique, gifted, dauntless "unzipped souls" who play jazz music in what was once the USSR — music made in the past, present, and possibly even future under trying conditions with a richness, precision, and depth of feeling that reaches far back into the Russian past and prevails to the present day in the artistry of a pianist such as Yuri Kuznetsov.

In her introduction to the Russian writer Alexander Herzen's memoirs, *Ends and Beginnings,* Aileen Kelly comments on the extended form the author's recollections take, "the work's dazzling multiplicity of genres, styles and modes: comedy, satire, sober analysis, lyrical and philosophical digressions." I discovered this same range when I heard Yuri Kuznetsov play his "small" forty-five-minute suite, a work that included every musical element from jazz scat to classical trills, quick bop runs and rapturous falsettos, chants lifted straight from the Orthodox service, some form of universal bluegrass, a smattering of Kurt Weil, Estonian and Ukrainian folk tunes, and a jolting sailor's horn-pipe complete with cries of "Odessa! Rah, Odessa!" — in homage to Yuri's hometown.

In homage to Russian cultural continuity in general, I have adopted its broad approach to the material that makes up this book: a novel of discovery filled with firsthand encounters, observations, assessments; a fusion of personal experiences; travel pieces; musical analysis; and profiles of original, talented, and courageous people in both the United States and the USSR. Originally, I had set out to study specific national elements that made up the music I had come to admire, but I discovered that nearly everything I experienced on the trek served as a component of jazz in the Soviet Union, for the music was a natural extension of this vast and amazing culture as a whole.

In 1989, four years after Mikhail Gorbachev was installed as general secretary, émigré writer Vassily Aksyonov published *In Search of Melancholy Baby,* in which he describes his first encounter with American jazz. An adolescent in the early 1950s, Aksyonov listened to homemade records cut on X-ray plates scavenged from hospital garbage cans, crude vinyl transcriptions of Willis Conover's Voice of America broadcasts. For Aksyonov, the music epitomized America, and his own Russian youth, "for its refusal to be pinned down, its improvisatory nature." Jazz was "more than music. It was a platonic rendezvous with freedom."

Reading this, I recalled the excitement I experienced myself when, growing up near Detroit — a grand town, then and now, for the music — I'd first heard and seen masters such as Roy Eldridge, Charlie Parker, and Art Tatum. As a freshman at the University of Michigan, I'd sat in the front row of a hall, dragged there by a friend to witness some upstart from California named Dave Brubeck's recording of "Jazz Goes to College." West Coast music was as alien and exotic to me then as the names Lompoc, Azusa, and Cucamonga on the Jack Benny radio show. So later I could imagine the excitement — intensified by even greater distance and cultural disparity — of Soviet teenagers huddled close to each revolution of their crude discs, what Aksyonov calls "Jazz on Bones," the barely visible grooves etched upon chest cavities and spinal cords. These teenagers committed Dizzy Gillespie's and Charlie Parker's solos to memory, note by note — the sweetness of hidden water and stolen bread.

Aksyonov writes of his surprise when he discovered that jazz was "a rare guest in its homeland"; this rich form of native expression was not *the* music of America. I thought again of those Soviet adolescents for whom it was. I envied those lonely Soviet jazz aspirants, for I had begun to feel that, in America today, artists in too many fields had settled for a nearly senescent adherence to formula, popular approval (our own form of censorship), or deliberately promoted impersonality. I admired the Soviet artists' dangerous devotion, the courage required to undertake any creative endeavor so far from its source and, given the political climate of their day, so unlikely to reap external acceptance or reward.

"Now's the time," I sang to myself, sitting down at the piano, pecking at Charlie Parker's tune, a six-note blues riff repeated until it drops to a dominant seventh, then a diminished chord, a brief G-minor flourish, and resolves itself, at home again — the reiteration infectious, the culmination clean. I played the riff again, infatuated with its carpe diem urgency, and then, stuck by my limitations as a pianist, got up to play a tape of "Now's the Time" by alto saxophonist Frank Morgan.

Morgan is not Russian, and, aside from this brief and spontaneous moment of celebration, he did not really figure into my sudden desire to travel to the USSR, to attempt to hear and see, firsthand, what sort of jazz was being made there, but he's a good place to start. Morgan was what a musician of any nation might aspire to be. His music, with its hard-won force and tenderness can, like that of the classic Russian masters — Mussorgsky, Rachmaninoff, Scriabin, Shostakovich — tear your heart apart. He can imbue the tunes of our own culture, even its syrupy ballads, with the warmth, sincerity, and confidentiality of a club vocalist. A master of the entire jazz vocabulary — pinched tones, overt wail, deflated or abruptly designated notes — Morgan, on ensemble-stated classics such as Miles Davis's "Half Nelson" or Theolonious Monk's "Well, You Needn't," can run off the best of worry-bead lines, his playing so liquid he seems to slide through the changes as if they weren't there, like those Chinese sages who emerged from torrential rivers unscathed because they'd simply followed all the natural vortexes.

Frank Morgan proved an appropriate figure to help me celebrate my decision to go to the USSR, then an exciting if precarious social enterprise, and see for myself if the extraordinary events taking place might produce the sort of creature Morgan is — an alchemist transforming the self-conscious stuff of his own culture into art.

I let his reading of Parker's tune play out and then sat down to make some plans. (How was I ever going to get *this* one past my wife?) I had one last thought about Morgan, with whom I shared a love of jazz, approximate age, and, perhaps, a sense of life restored. My circumstance was not nearly as extreme as his. A one-time heroin addict, Morgan had emerged as perhaps *the* top alto artist after having spent three decades in prison, star of the "Warden's Band" at San Quentin but, as far as the outside world was concerned, a forgotten, buried man. I had nothing so colorful by way of circumstance to offer (and I sure as hell can't play like him), yet Frank Morgan held out hope for all those who wish to start over again, and I did.

## part one

*Homework*

# Now's
# the
# Time

"Why Russia?" my wife asked.

Good question . . .

I knew next to nothing of the sort of life an American tourist was likely to encounter on the road — that is, not in the company of Intourist spokespeople and homogeneous sightseeing. I'd read the available travel literature, and precious little of it was encouraging. Hedrick Smith (*The Russians*, 1976), Andrea Lee (*Russian Journal*, 1979), David K. Shipler (*Russia: Broken Idols, Solemn Deams*, 1983), and Colin Thubron (*Where Nights Are Longest: Travels by Car through Western Russia*, 1984) all commented on the lack of "cheer," the drabness, uniformity, and impenetrability of Soviet life. Their observations themselves became somewhat monotonous, describing suffocating restrictions encountered at every turn, down to the confiscation of books (or, in Thubron's case, manuscripts) — a litany of harsh social criticism.

I took refuge in the thought that all this commentary had been written before 1985, when Gorbachev came to power. The headlines since 1988 and growing larger and more fantastic as 1989 drew to a close told a different story: "Human Chain Formed across Baltic States," "Communist Party Backs Gorbachev's Reforms," "KGB Chief Criticizes Role of Street Police," "Soviets OK Use of Strikes for First Time," "Communists OK Multiparty Plan," "Soviet Lawmakers Endorse Private Ownership of Farms," "Lithuanian Popular Front Wins," "Reform Candidates Winning Soviet Elections." Not to mention the photographs of children playing in what was left of the Berlin Wall.

Now's the time.

I had discovered and bought Soviet jazz recordings released as early as 1986 on East Wind Records of Hartford, Connecticut, and I especially liked one album, appropriately titled *Aspiration,* by pianist Vagif Mustafa-Zadeh, a man of immense talent who had died in his early forties, according to the liner notes, at one with his powers. I fell into a game all too easy for Westerners to play on their first encounter with this music. I urged my friends to listen to the record. Appreciating the speed and dexterity, they'd guess, "Oscar Peterson? Phineas Newborn?"

"No," I said. "Vagif Mustafa-Zadeh."

"Who's he?"

"A pianist from Azerbaijan."

"Where's that?"

We'd all bend over a map. In spite of familiarity with things Soviet, I thought I too had better check to make sure the republic had not moved, or been moved, in the interim.

Despite early doses then and incessant doses now of *perestroika,* the agony of change or painful restructuring, people in the West seem stumped by the phenomenon of Soviet jazz. "Soviet *what?*" is a fairly common response. Even critics, who should know better, have a tendency to dismiss this unique music too easily, paying it the dubious compliment of saying that it sounds just like somebody else, usually an American "original," leaving the impression that Soviet jazz is derivative and culturally deprived. When the Ganelin Trio — represented on one of the East Wind recordings, *Poi Sequé* — toured the United States, critic Patricia O'Haire compared their music to Chinese water torture, saying the latter was preferable, a "jolly game" compared to the Soviet musical variety sent to the United States, claiming that the sounds "tossed" at the audience from a JVC (Victor Company of Japan) jazz concert stage were "as incomprehensible as the Cyrillic alphabet is to Western eyes." Even a perceptive critic such as the *Village Voice*'s Gary Giddins, who found the music "diverse, well-played, witty, theatrical," wrote it off as "familiar . . . Eurofree jazz . . . caricature." Such attitudes smacked to me of those early Cold War years when both the USSR and the United States claimed to have invented ice cream, motherhood, potash fertilizer, the automobile, and electricity.

Listening closely to Vagif Mustafa-Zadeh in *Aspiration,* I heard much more than a clone. I heard less Oscar Peterson and more a man with a unique background following his own cultural imperatives. I had no means, at the time, by which to comprehend terms in the liner notes such as *"chargia"* and *"bayati shiraz"* folk harmonies, "pizzicato *dutar,*" "bowed *kyamanch*" and "Moogam," but I think whoever wrote them was trying to tell me to look beyond what I was accustomed to, even in what was quite familiar, such as the rapid locked-hand, adventurous, blues-inflected, assertive rhythm of Denzil Best's "Bemsha Swing."

My favorite pieces were those based on Azerbaijani folk songs — "In the

Garden" and "Dark Eyebrows" — in which the pianist was joined by his vocal-ist wife, Elza. In the first piece, a unison piano/vocal "scat," her guttural, musty syllables played off against Vagif's dazzling two-handed patterns and vivid dramatic interweavings, the overall texture mournful, nearly elegiac yet at the same time vividly alive. "Dark Eyebrows" contained words I could not understand, but, again, the piece displayed an attractive polyphony, a charm-ing complexity that put me in mind of a fine oriental carpet. I listened again and again to the combination of solid swing, to which the intricate work of bassist Tamaz Kurashvili and drummer Vladimir Boldyrev lent themselves handsomely. The percussive assertiveness was joined with rapid-fire ornamen-tation and liquid-quick finger work, dangerously self-satisfied but sinuous, sultry, and joyous.

From the back of the album stared the face of Vagif Mustafa-Zadeh; his body tilted at a decisive angle, inserting itself into the picture on its own terms, declaring its originality, his own voice and person. The Russian writer Dos-toevsky, more than a century ago, declared that no nation or society could be "developed to order, on the lines of a programme imported from abroad," that such ideas, "no matter how fertile," could only take root and prove useful if they met a nation's own needs, a statement with implications that went be-yond philosophical ideas and music. I did not think the Soviet jazz I had heard up to that time would have caused Dostoevsky untoward concern. The word *fusion* has become meaningless in the hands of U.S. musical publicists, but Vagif Mustafa-Zadeh had found the right hybrid: an impassioned assimilation and transformation of the best the cultures he had been exposed to and grown up with had to offer — just as jazz itself had been that sort of music, with its fusion of classical, field holler, brass band, hymnal, blues, pop dance, minstrel, and ragtime strains.

I realized that, just as for Frank Morgan, with his thirty years of rehearsal time in San Quentin and the dedication and desire he'd mustered for that, circumstances are responsible for our "sound." We are what surrounds us.

"Why Russia?" my wife, Betty, continued to ask.

Why indeed? I considered the circumstances responsible for my attach-ment to this music. Soviet jazz did not materialize, suddenly and full grown, out of nowhere — nor did I, or my interest in the USSR in general. So how did a typical American product of the Cold War years come to discover the rich, warm life beneath the icy conception of Russia and the Russians with which we were inoculated?

Of Dutch, Scotch-Irish, and English stock, I enjoyed a fairly typical middle-class American childhood. I even grew up on a street named Pleasant and, while it did not always live up to such expectations, it frequently came close. (Author Vassily Aksyonov, four years older than I, was at this time living with his mother, a political prisoner in exile, in Magadan, Siberia.) I had absolutely no blood or geographical ties to Russia, and by rights I should have fallen prey to the fear and suspicion of, even hostility toward, the Soviet Union bred in a generation that came of age during the McCarthy era. Somehow I escaped it.

I do recall cowering beneath blankets, safe from enemy planes, during the Hot War years, 1941–1945. My father reminded us each evening at dinner that, situated as we were near Detroit (the auto plant yards no longer filled with splashy Mercuries and Buicks, but green tanks now, uniform and frightening), we were targeted for extinction and just might be lucky enough to make it through dessert. I recall seeing films in which Russian soldiers in white parkas braved glacial temperatures and unfair military odds in the defense of hero cities such as Kiev, Sevastopol, Leningrad, Stalingrad, and Odessa. These people were depicted as proud, admirable, and infinitely self-sacrificing. Subversive books such as Maurice Hindus's *Red Bread* stood on the family bookshelf. They were more than likely gifts from my "goddam no-good do-gooder" Uncle Bill, as my father called him, a relative with heavy socialist leanings whom I loved.

I probably worried my sixth-grade teacher, Miss Larsen—a woman of considerable charm on whom I had a crush—and I think I sacrificed any feeling she might have reciprocated when, assigned a paper on a foreign country in which we would most like to live, I chose Russia. I had taken a decidedly unhealthy interest in the return of southern Sakhalin and the Kurile Islands to the by then dreaded USSR. Why those photographs of people enshrouded in snow and bitter cold appealed to me so much I will never know. My native Michigan weather was bad enough. I took my skates to school each day, along with my goalie stick. I had actually chosen to play goalie. Perhaps this fledgling streak of masochism, a love of suffering for the sake of suffering itself, is what attracted me to the Russians.

It certainly wasn't politics, about which I couldn't have cared less. The ideological sparring between my father and uncle had rendered politics senseless to me. Safe at home on Pleasant Street, I tried instead to imitate an uncle who played piano (the socialist played clarinet and alto sax) and was no more Slavic than anyone else in the family. When I took up piano myself, this man chastised me for my dead left hand, decrying this tendency among the "moderns." Edging me from the stool, his body poised at a jaunty angle to the piano, he punished me with his solid stride, an ambidexterity worthy of Fats Waller or James P. Johnson.

With a budding interest in the visual arts, at eighteen I went to the Pratt Institute in Brooklyn. Contrary to the popular notion of the mid-1950s, this was an extremely exciting time in the arts: Philip Guston taught us how to render pump handles in charcoal by day and introduced the world to abstract expressionism in galleries by night. Visual artists were closely allied then with jazz musicians, and I still recall vividly the night when, as a frightfully unprepared house pianist at a place called the 456 Club, I saw one of my admired teachers, the sculptor Cal Albert, come strolling through the door with Hal Overton. In the words of Orrin Keepnews on the original Riverside liner notes, Overton's "considerable formal musical training and sensitive affection for Monk's work" were responsible for the arrangements for Theolonious Monk's 1959 Town Hall concert. Again I found myself vacating a piano bench in great haste, but I did switch to guitar and jam with Overton, along with our drummer, a kid from Jersey, and a tall black bass player from Harlem who, in those days of smoke-infested bars, rushed to the exit at the end of every set in quest of oxygen.

Those were great jazz days, or nights, for me: having a beer with Chet Baker and Gerry Mulligan at Basin Street; hearing whoever happened to be at Birdland; digging Marian McPartland at Hickory House (the amazing Joe Morello on drums), Billy Taylor at the Embers, Cozy Cole on Forty-second Street; acquiring the tremulant autograph of Pee Wee Russell at Eddie Condon's one night. After classes, trudging the forlorn gray slum-clearance streets with a giant sketchboard beneath my arm, I began to march in step toward some imagined guillotine when I heard Berlioz's *Symphonie Fantastique* blaring straight and proud from the cold-water pad I shared with another student. And on Sunday mornings I listened in rapture to the raucous sounds emerging from the black Baptist church at the end of our street, a joyful noise that shook that wooden building as if it were being shredded by an earthquake.

My roommate was a promising young painter—faculty members purchased his works. He read lots of books, and quit reading each of them at about page 38. But he talked a lot about the little he'd read, and I got curious enough to try reading myself. I eventually made my way past page 38 of *The Brothers Karamazov.* What a shock this book was! I had never before considered the possibility that one could be brutally honest with life and still believe in and be able to live it. One could face up to the full measure of infamy, injury, and insult that constitutes life—and survive? I'd heard some of this attitude in jazz, especially the blues, but I'd never expected to read it. A single mad Russian author had invaded the sanctuary I'd so carefully assembled beneath those World War II blankets (on Pleasant Street, no less) and proceeded to rape and pillage my soul and mind with all the incivility of that mother whom Ivan Karamazov describes as having forced her own child to eat excrement, or the Turks who tossed babies in the air and then skewered them on the points of their bayonets, just for kicks.

Set alongside Dostoevsky, jazz proved to be my salvation, the only thing that, although carting its full share of suffering, didn't strike me — at the time — as being in total cahoots with absurdity. Paul Desmond sweetly playing "Audrey" sent me off to sleep each night. Romance could, on occasion, be a solace too. A couple of years later, I somehow managed to persuade a former childhood sweetheart, Betty, to marry me, and we set off on our travels. We lived on Clement Street in San Francisco, an area where we were more likely to hear Russian than English on the street, and I began to study Russian language and literature seriously. I taught English and Soviet Russian literature in Wisconsin in the late 1960s and later returned to California. I was now attempting to persuade Betty to accompany me to the USSR, under the pretext that Gorbachev was turning the nation of 250 million people around.

Betty and I had earlier spent nearly a year in Greece, traveling under somewhat primitive (financially restrained) conditions, so I now tried tempting her with what was, I thought, a pleasing concession. I would apply for sabbatical leave from the college where I was teaching and spend the first few months on necessary research. We would then go back to Greece at the beginning of May, making our way up the islands along the Turkish coast to Istanbul, explore that unique city for a couple of days and set sail, across the Black Sea, to Odessa — where I imagined our entry into the Soviet Union would be dramatic. Why Odessa? Because I had seen that baby carriage bump its way down steps when the tsarist police opened fire in Eisenstein's movie *Potemkin*. I wanted to go proudly *up* those stairs that the carriage had so awkwardly descended.

I didn't have the faintest idea whether a stitch of this scenario was plausible, but the thing seemed right and had to be done. We'd give ourselves about two months of traveling time in the USSR, sampling a wide range of cities, interviewing a host of musicians and critics. The Soviet Union! On the map the place looked formidable (lots of Siberia) and, in the fall of 1989, still forbidding. Yet I discovered that every sort of group tour imaginable existed: "citizen diplomacy" excursions tailored to environmentalists, alcoholics (a CASW — Creating a Sober World — tour, two years of sobriety required), veterans of World War II, evangelists, police officers, wine lovers, teachers, journalists. And every sort of standard packaged tour from "White Nights" in Leningrad/Vilnius/Minsk/Moscow to a twenty-day cruise down the Volga for $2,835. But I didn't care to go that route, even if I'd had the money, which I didn't. No jazz journeys were listed, so we would have to go on our own.

I wrote to S. Frederick Starr, whose book *Red and Hot: The Fate of Jazz in the Soviet Union* was the Bible of Western books on the subject, partly because it was the only one until émigré Leo Feigin, living in London, took up where Starr left off (around 1980), adding his New Testament, *Russian Jazz: New*

*Identity. Red and Hot* was a remarkable piece of scholarship that read like a novel. Detached, witty, insightful, thorough, it was rife with history, vital information, anecdotes, intriguing personalities. In contrast, Feigin's book professed an actual creed, a "new aesthetic" that took Soviet jazz out of the realm of "light entertainment" and into that of a "serious art form," heralding a musical revolution that embraced both jazz and modern classical music to become "the richest music in the world." I read both testaments religiously (how else?) and decided to write Starr. Leo Feigin produced Leo Records, the only outfit other than East Wind then providing Soviet jazz recordings.

Starr's encouraging reply suggested that I bury myself in the language and make contact with the International Research and Exchange Board (IREX) at Princeton. He gave me the name of an "old friend" there, and the names of three top jazz critics in the USSR: Vladimir Feyertag in Leningrad, Valter Ojakäär in Tallinn, and Alexei Batashev, whom he described as "the Sol Hurok of jazz in Moscow and a delightful guy."

I had taken the first steps to convert this dream of a jazz journey to the Soviet Union to reality. I listened devotedly now to groups like the Ganelin Trio—pianist Vyacheslav Ganelin, alto saxophonist Vladimir Chekasin, and drummer Vladimir Tarasov—the one group fairly well known in the West. I found it hard to associate them with the monster nation, this throwback to the Dark Ages I'd been reading about. The music was anguished enough, just as existence is, but I did not hear a furtive cry for freedom. What I heard was freedom itself: something logical and inevitable in the development of their suites, even though the music does not present itself that way. The music is almost solely emotive, nearly rankling in its insistence on creating, within its chosen context, just about any kind of musical effect it desires. Chekasin alone was a master of intonation, creating a host of colors and aims from wild to comic, his playing fleet and fiesty, nervous, questing, lithe, liquid, skittery, bashing, cute—capable of sudden crushes and cuts, both a send-up of and salute to the available musical vocabulary.

I was intrigued, frightened, and delighted by the very ingenuity and freshness of the Ganelin Trio. How could such art spring from the stale, oppressive state I had been reading about? Could these people be so different from ourselves? Once, riding in a car in San Francisco, I listened as an American colleague kept needling a visitor from the USSR about the plethora of public political propaganda in his country. The Soviet visitor pointed to the many immense billboards that line the freeway with garish messages promoting suntan lotion, Cutty Sark, Club Med, various airlines, and he had the audacity to suggest that there was no difference between our being bombarded with images of what we were supposed to live up to and that to which he was exposed.

"But that's not propaganda," the American driver argued, pointing to a massive sign that showed a woman in a bikini floating on an inflatable rubber raft in Las Vegas.

"What is it then?" the Russian visitor asked.

"That's advertising!"

We become what surrounds us. All the more reason to keep a good eye on it. And all the more reason, if you truly wish to see and know a place, to go there and find out. I felt compelled to go to the Soviet Union now and experience, firsthand, the relationship between these musicians and whatever sort of world they lived in. But before I could begin to make plans, luck stepped in and brought one of the new Soviet jazz musicians I had discovered to my own shores.

# A Man
# from
# Mars

Tolstoy said that he once spent twenty minutes dusting his room without having a single thought in his head. For him, this was a crime. He was embarrassed — caught with the trousers of his consciousness down, so to speak — and equated the state to not existing, being dead. Years later the incident gave rise to the theory of *ostranenie,* or defamiliarization, which Soviet literary critic Viktor Shklovsky has described as destroying the habitual logic of associations, a deliberate cultivation of the unexpected, of dissonance — the world of everyday reality becoming more perceptible in the process, objects restored from mere "recognition" to actual "seeing."
All well and lofty and good, but what does any of this have to do with Soviet improvisational pianist Sergei Kuryokhin? Well, everything. Journalist Howard Mandel had already written a *Down Beat* article on the "Russian Martian," citing ROVA Saxophone Quartet's Larry Ochs's comment on the crowd that had flocked to hear the Ganelin Trio concert in San Francisco: "They heard the Martians landed and came to hear them play."

Yet from the moment I walked into the Kuumbwa Jazz Center in Santa Cruz on the night of Sunday, October 23, 1989, I was plunged not into a "Martian" world but just good old Russian defamiliarization. For one thing, it seemed I'd come on the wrong night. I'd been informed just the day before that Soviet improvisational pianist Sergei Kuryokhin was in town for a solo piano venture, yet the stage was filled with various wood flutes and saxophones, some violinists, a contra bass clarinetist, a cellist, inverted lamp shades, a slender rose-packed glass vase perched atop an amp, a giant Chinese gong, assorted sound specialists, a synthesizer (both machine and human performer), and a host of other electronic devices, the most intriguing of which seemed to be a red ice chest with enough cords running from its back to resemble brain circuitry or a map of the New York subway system. In the midst of this a boy charged about, energetic yet fey as a street urchin, sporting a striped long-sleeved t-shirt, shocks of brown hair drumming on his forehead, crying out in thick Slavic syllables for his translator.

That boy was thirty-five-year-old Sergei Kuryokhin.

"Sharp! Sharp! He wants it *sharp*. It should be very sharp in contrast," the translator advised the group of musicians on stage, as she charged from the back of the hall.

American critics at the time were fond of pointing out the new Soviet music's debt to everyone from Archie Shepp to John Cage to the Art Ensemble of Chicago. In my own revisionist fervor, I felt the land that had produced Mussorgsky, Scriabin, Stravinsky, and Shostakovich probably did not have much to apologize for musically, even in the area of jazz, which Kuryokhin once said he found "aesthetically dead" anyway. Inconsistency is Kuryokhin's virtue, for he had also said that he'd once been "stunned" by the jazz keyboard mastery of McCoy Tyner, heard on VOA broadcasts. He simultaneously proclaimed the piano an "anachronism" that no longer interested him (he was then enamored of saxophones — an instrument he plays at).

The pianist (and antipianist) has also claimed that his improvisational method ideally requires a choir, a zoo, a symphony orchestra, a gypsy camp, a circus, a lot of synthesizers, and a host of other stuff he felt, not so long ago, he'd never have. His translator at Kuumbwa, Naomi Marcus, told me that Kuryokhin, who once played piano for morning ballet classes and exercise sessions for athletes, was now supplied with a full military band for his happenings, complete, as he wished, with epaulettes. At a breakthrough concert at the Great October Concert Hall in January 1988, he employed that band, plus a chorus of pigs and chickens, saxes perched on scaffolding, and trumpets in the balcony.

Indeed, the session I'd stumbled into was beginning to resemble the setting Berlioz imagined for his *Funeral and Triumphal* symphony, originally scored for a modest chorus of 2,000 men, 1,500 children and 500 women with an orchestra of 400 performing a work expressing every one of the ideals nurtured by the human heart. Yet the Kuumbwa Jazz Center stage also resembled one of those frantic family reunions we are all too familiar with: an event fraught with every sort of independent impulse and gesture, except these musicians were strangers to one another, being coached by a man who couldn't say "sharp" in English.

Part of the group the pianist was working with is called Ut Gret, one with its own but compatible ideology of "pan-idiomatic free improvisation" and a range of instruments to prove it, from steel guitar to koto. While the contra bass clarinet grackled over what sounded to me like lush Rachmaninoffian lyricism, the interplay was invaded by two violins, a cello, and a flute.

"Now we play very simple . . . one note *C*," Kuryokhin said, "one note *C*, up to absolutely incredible . . . like echo."

I'd stumbled into a rehearsal, the boy Kuryokhin at its heart. He kept rising from the piano bench as if he'd just made contact with a whoopee cushion, his wild gestures denoting universal enthusiasm but not necessarily conveying any specific instruction.

"Many . . . many," he cried, jumping up and prancing around. This must have meant "more, more," for the words solicited more vital timbres, more of everything: a cello bouncing to the leader's staccato bent, squeezed violins, suggestions of sneezing, wheezing, of ripped paper bag or sliced throat, some basal synthetic sound at the center of it all — a carnival of tonalities that left one residing in shock and awe.

"How about guitar?" Kuryokhin cried and, getting that, "Give me something radical in middle."

A light vamp and some straight blues on piano lasted about a millisecond, then turned bacchanal.

"Next part," Kuryokhin cried. "One, two, tree, four . . . after that . . . this . . . loud!" The pianist made a grand swooping gesture, from the ground up.

"What you've just seen and heard is a rehearsal of the third set," one of the Ut Gret group announced, in English. The rehearsal ended as impulsively as it had begun.

"I don't know how much of this we're all going to remember by 10:30, but . . . ," one member of the musical coalition said, passing by me.

"They're like lists, his directions," another replied.

When I try to describe Sergei Kuryokhin's music, the words become as varied and unique as the music itself. His work contains percussive force (a legacy from McCoy Tyner?), relentless insistence (repetition, at times, devoid of increment), a punishingly short attention span, incredible speed (the result, no doubt, of that virtuosity and technical brilliance he has called "the Russian disease"), a host of anything-goes associations, naiveté, anxiety, collision, conflict, wit, humor, arch romanticism, self-mockery, audience mockery. The music can be tedious at times, pretentious, funning without philosophy; musical objects fighting to dominate a listener's attention cancel each other out, technique used for the sake of technique alone (surprisingly uniform for all its busyness), an amazing continuity of movement — and, at least on the night I heard him, considerable joy.

Sergei Kuryokhin was born in Murmansk in 1954. He liked operetta at an early age, and he laces his performances with it. The family moved to Leningrad in 1971, where Kuryokhin played with a rock band, and he also spices performances with King Crimson. He was kicked out of two conservatories, and proud of it, but he did manage, when he attended classes, to study piano and conducting. He encountered jazz by way of McCoy Tyner, Anthony Braxton, Cecil Taylor, and Monk and has worked with excellent Soviet saxophonists Anatoli Vapirov and Vladimir Chekasin. Kuryokhin's first recording, *The Ways of Freedom* on Leo Records, was released in the West in 1981, with a stipulation that read, "Sergei Kuryokhin does not bear any responsibility for publishing this tape." This was no idle dadaist joke, but the result of political expediency. Until just a few years ago, Kuryokhin had by no means enjoyed official status.

When I first heard him, Kuryokhin was not an American avant-garde clone but a unique cultural entity. "We could talk about Russian spiritual tradition," he has said. "I'm a nationalist-chauvinist, you know. . . . The mechanism of the influence of tradition is hidden somewhere in the subconscious." Kuryokhin also echoes his fellow countryman Scriabin's desire for "action in total harmony," stating that "all areas of art are equal." Some musicians care little about literary and artistic traditions, but Kuryokhin is not one of them.

Whatever his antecedents, he was mostly himself when he officially walked on stage at the Kuumbwa Jazz Center in California. The emcee introduced him as a "key premier keyboard artist," commenting that "it's amazing that he's made it to the United States; incredible that it's here in Santa Cruz." This premier pianist then set about divesting us of "tasteful predilection," to defamiliarize, restoring us from "recognition" to "seeing." He did so by employing the whole arsenal of musical means available, slow, cautious, and classical at the start, moving from mock drawing-room piano and lush musing to stern rapid-fire street urchin survival, employing an encyclopedia of pianistic devices, a nerve-twittering attack of clusters that converted his hands to hummingbird wings.

Not content with the piano's exterior, he scraped and plucked at interior strings, then slapped his own sides like a seal, flapped his arms, offered wheezing vocalizations: sheep's bleat, rasp of sandpaper, small noises like someone winding a watch or unwrapping a stick of gum, unnerving in their near silence. Mock sullen Volga boatmen folk tunes evolved to stride or nodded off to sleep through the weight of sentimentality. Bop riffs were mixed with the Gershwin of *Rhapsody in Blue;* a mocking Liszt *Liebesträume* was overdubbed with laughter.

Kuryokhin was joined by Andrew Voigt, formerly of the ROVA Saxophone Quartet, in a rich exchange, from liquid piano and pretty sax to high-kicking cancan to a wild gypsy dance that, caught up in the dervish swirl, made me want to pick up tables with my teeth. The performance ended with an overdose of lush Russian lyricism and rolling sax R&B, beyond pathos and heroics, moving into that sincerity of the comical that Kuryokhin claims alone cannot be doubted — along with improvisational freedom.

Sergei Kuryokhin once wandered the streets of Leningrad with hippie hair, a bright and witty manner, scat singing in time to a Walkman, "his dog, his pet," a "baby of the cassette boom," an unofficial artist running the risk of "parasitism." Back in the USSR he is now, quite simply, a star. He fills the four-thousand-seat Great October Concert Hall, leads his group appropriately dubbed Pop Mechanics, scores movies for Lenfilms. "Lots of our friends' fates haven't been so sweet as his," I was told by his translator. "He's an original. An original in the modern world."

I left the Kuumbwa Jazz Center delighted with and impressed by this "Martian."

# The
# Breakthrough

I tracked our mailman, Will, up and down streets — Walnut, Laurel, Cedar, Willow — finally sighting him on Granite. I'd known the moment I discovered the pink slip in the mailbox, giving notice of attempted delivery of a registered package, that at long last I had made contact with someone within the Soviet Union.

"They got jazz in Russia? Really?" Will said when I finally caught up with him and explained why I was so excited over the small, cassette-sized postal packet adorned with a giant stamp of Vladimir Ilyich Lenin staring up at me from one side, and a silver satellite disk floating alongside a blood-red planet and the words "Mezhdunarodnyi kosmicheskii proekt 'Fobos'" (International Space Project 'Phobos') on the other.

It was fall of 1989, and I had been waiting for more than six months for a reply to my letter to Michael Dubilet, chair of the Jazz Club in Dnepropetrovsk, a city on the Dnieper River in Ukraine, above Odessa. Actually I'd been waiting for almost a year for word from anyone in the USSR and even from people connected with Soviet jazz in the United States. After my exciting introduction to this music live, by way of Sergei Kuryokhin, I became a veritable Dervish of entrepreneurial effort, the epitome of Yankee energy and ingenuity. I was determined to get to the Soviet Union and applied for just about every grant that might allow me to do so: at IREX, the Guggenheim and Soros foundations, the National Endowment for the Humanities, the United States Information Agency. A friend told me about a friend of his affiliated with the International Foundation for the Survival and Development of Humanity (*Bozhe moi!* My God, what an organization that must be!). Yet I couldn't land a grant from any one of these groups, and some didn't even bother to reply.

From a list of people who had worked on U.S.-USSR initiatives, I wrote the distinguished pianist Dr. Billy Taylor. I wrote Willis Conover, the man responsible for the Voice of America (VOA) broadcasts that made such an impact on young Vassily Aksyonov. I even wrote Aksyonov himself, now living in Washington, D.C. I wrote twice to the Moscow critic Frederick Starr had mentioned in his letter, Alexei Batashev. I did not receive a reply from any of these people.

Silence descended like snow over the Gulag.

I waited and waited.

"Why Russia?" Betty continued to ask.

To supplant the frustration and boredom of expectation, I memorized all the terms required for survival in the USSR: *beriozka* (state stores for foreigners), *blat* (mutual favors or influence used to get what you need), *vlasti* (those in power), *fartsovshchiki* (blackmarketeers), *vranyo* (leg pulling or lies), *vzyatka* (the take), plus phrases such as *Skoro budet* (It will be here soon) and, should the longed-for not occur, *Nu, byvaet* (Well, it happens — resignation in the face of defeat). Unfortunately, all these terms reinforced the impression of a society steeped in suspicion, doubt, and paranoia — states of mind I did not need, at the time, to become any more familiar with myself.

I found consolation in John Steinbeck's *Russian Journal,* an account of his 1948 excursion to the USSR with photographer Robert Capra. "It occurred to us that there were some things that nobody wrote about Russia, and they were the things that interested us most of all," Steinbeck wrote. He pledged not to go in with a chip on his shoulder, to be neither "critical nor favorable" but just find a good story. And if he couldn't do that, he'd have a story too, he said, "the story of not being able to do it." That was exactly the way I felt. But how could I make the necessary contacts; how could I get there?

I discovered another *Down Beat* article by Howard Mandel reporting on a 1988 summer jazz festival he'd attended in Moscow. Presuming it was an annual affair, why not plan our trip around this event? I wrote the consulate general in San Francisco, who wrote back saying that, as far as this festival was concerned, "information is not available." Another letter I wrote to a musicologist involved in U.S.-USSR initiatives came back with a note saying he was dead.

The silence deepened. I was beginning to doubt that such a thing as *glasnost* existed. Paranoia sneaks in like a thief. Somebody was deliberately trying to keep me out of the USSR. Had Soviet musicians, in their desire to find out more about American jazz, in their desire to get closer to its source, been as frustrated as I had become attempting to get close to them? And then, just as I began to despair of hope beyond hope, a miracle arrived — this packet from Dnepropetrovsk!

I had written to Michael Dubilet on official college stationery, after a woman apparently in the know about such things advised me that Russians adored official stationery of any sort, and that I probably would never receive a reply unless I used it. My letter had been sent after I'd read one of Michael's own in *Jazz Notes,* newsletter of the Jazz Journalists Association, an organization I'd just joined. My luck was turning perhaps, along with my timing. After thanking our mailman, Will, profusely, I ran home and opened the packet delivered to me. It contained a letter, a cassette tape, several newspaper reviews in Russian, and two badges making me an honorary member of the Dnepropetrovsk Jazz Club.

Michael's letter was typed on somewhat spongy paper, stamped at the top with the jazz club's name and logo: "Molodezhny klub 'MRIIA' — klub liubitelei dzhazovoi muzyki" (Youth Club "MRIIA" — a Club for Fans of Jazz). The contents of his letter were couched in that highly original brand of English that, from the first time I read it in *Jazz Notes,* I regarded as Michael's own. He said he would "with my pleasure" send me "different informations about Soviet jazz," along with a tape with "honogramms by musicians of our jazz-club." What "honogramms" were was anybody's guess, but I could sense the urgency behind his quest, the deep curiosity and need to know, not unlike my own. He discussed two large festivals held in Dnepropetrovsk; monthly concerts to which "leading jazzmen" in the USSR were invited; and told me that every Thursday evening they had "jazz-sound recording" and every Saturday a jam-session. Michael Dubilet wished "to get the information about American jazz from the first hands. . . . Certainly, the scales of our own jazz club's work are not comparable with the range of activity . . . which excites the deep envy about your seething jazz-life."

Next, I read the articles. One was an interesting interview with a pianist named Andrei Kondakov, from Petrozavodsk, north of Leningrad; another was about a local pianist, Oleg Kosko; a third about a pianist from Odessa named Yuri Kuznetsov. I jotted down all of these names. I also gained insight into the machinations of a jazz club in the USSR: through affiliation with the Philharmonic Society, a cut-rate subscription to a series of six jazz concerts guaranteed (or so the article said) artists of national prominence seats in advance, and assurance of no "overcharging." There were scalpers in the Soviet Union?

I was ready now for the tape — one which, unfortunately, proved to be quite homegrown, much of the music sluggish, terribly self-conscious ("Sorry for bad quality of tape and for mistakes if there are any," Michael had written). The music was imitative, yet I wasn't really all that concerned about quality now. I was amazed and pleased that jazz was being played in a city whose single distinction for me heretofore had been its hydroelectric dam. I assumed that I would hear my share of pros in Moscow and Leningrad, but attending jam sessions, proudly wearing my two Dzhaz klub badges, digging firsthand what the home folks were up to in this city on the Dnieper — that appealed to me. And that's what I planned to do.


A second breakthrough came when a friend from Palo Alto called to tell me that "some Russians" were scheduled to give a jazz concert at Stanford University in November. These Russians turned out to be a group led by pianist Igor Bril, whose recordings I had. The Stanford event was billed as "From Glasnost to Glad Notes," prematurely euphoric perhaps, but I could understand why the Soviet musicians must be elated to make this trip.

The biggest surprise was the announcement that acting as master of ceremonies and slated to give two lectures on Soviet jazz at the university would be the "foremost critic in the Soviet Union," none other than Alexei Batashev, who'd answered none of the letters I'd sent. Here was an opportunity to meet the man whose voice I'd heard on Igor Bril's *Live at the Village Gate* CD, announcing each number with a flourish and a strong accent. In fact, in the second unanswered letter I'd written, I mentioned that he'd already been in my living room, so to speak, so I felt I knew him somehow.

On the evening of the concert, before a packed house, a Stanford student who'd had a hand in arranging the Russians' visit launched the occasion as a "historical event." He then introduced the eminent critic Alexei Batashev — tall, nattily dressed, a good-looking Groucho Marx with a large space between his two front teeth when he smiled, which was often. Batashev sported a slight potbelly and wore a felt bow tie so large it resembled a giant black moth which seemed to have suddenly taken up residence beneath his chin. From the moment he bounded on stage to the moment he reluctantly left it, he was fully at home, digging his entrepreneurial chores.

"Good morning," he said. It was eight o'clock in the evening. "Because in my home town it is now Monday morning." He introduced the participants: Bril, alto saxophonist Alexander Oseychuk, bassist Viktor Dvoskin, and a young drummer named Eugene Rayboy. The leader proved to be a short, bald, shy man who settled in immediately behind the piano, his left hand perched in the air concert-style, his head bowed close to the keyboard as he tapped out the intro to his own composition, "In Hope and [in] Joy." Oseychuk, elegantly tall and slender, his suit as well-styled as his full head of hair that extended to his shirt collar, was a strikingly handsome man with a flat nose. When he was not playing, he tenderly cradled the bottom of his alto sax with his right hand, as if holding a child. Viktor Dvoskin remained seated throughout the evening, his stance rigid as the silhouette of a classical cellist, unsmiling, chin thrust forward and up. He was intent, as if "reading" his own solos, the stiff physical presence at odds with the wild, magical sounds emerging. Rayboy, the kid of the group and the only one not in suit and tie, wore a short-sleeved shirt. He weaved, bobbed, and dipped his shoulders in time behind his drum kit, yet not really providing that large a bed of percussion in his wake: that deluge of effects a drummer such as Al Foster, Tony Williams, or Danny Richmond provides a soloist to move around in.

Batashev announced "the most beautiful ballad in classical jazz repertoire: 'My One . . . and . . . *On*-ly . . . *Luf*.'" After an extended Oseychuk cadenza, the Russian adoration of melody took hold, the passion for ornamentation and embellishment. Vibraphone player Bobby Hutcherson, the first American guest to appear, changed all that. He danced on stage ever hip in a blue sport coat with a bright green handkerchief protruding from the top pocket like some obscene flower, a white Nehru blouse beneath the jacket. He immediately put Dvoskin and then the entire group to work, sizzling, playing not just with his hands and head (or even heart) but with his entire body: assaulting his instrument, backing away from it as if spent by his own explosive efforts, then just as suddenly attacking it again. Dvoskin grinned (he liked this), Hutcherson playing four-mallet comping behind Bril, who, after another long solo, seemed to run short of ideas — unlike the inexhaustible Hutcherson, a musical event in himself.

Then a second American guest came on: Joe Henderson, the Stoic, the Beatific, the Buddha. In contrast to his composure, he was lavishly introduced by Batashev. "And nowwww, ladies and gentlemen, a *real*-ly ggggrreat tenor sax player: *Jo*-seph Henderson!" Henderson moved slow and cool, tapping off a tune, falling into the driving rhythm with quick invention, as gracefully and smoothly as an Olympic diver springs from a board into wholly receptive waters.

Batashev announced "a small saxophone summit," explaining that, since Henderson didn't know any of Oseychuk's tunes, they would play one of Henderson's. Off they went, slowly, Latin, Oseychuk's smooth, precise Benny Carter float full of fine fresh intervals; Henderson, standing aside, quietly trimming a reed, shook the spit out of his sax, engaged in some private Zen rite of ablution. The Soviets caught fire on "Tenor Madness." Oseychuk dragged out all the available pyrotechnics as if this were his last shot, as if he were crowding his entire life into this solo. Henderson, nodding in approval, cut through the plethora of notes left hanging in the air and responded with a simple seven-note folk refrain: "All day, all night, Mary Ann" — the master of understatement and wit. After his solo, Henderson resumed his prayer stance, watching, listening to a superb interlude by Dvoskin, who I think in many ways stole the show with his solid, never showy, musical competence. The Soviets bobbed their heads and dipped their suited shoulders now, Oseychuk loose and agile and comfortable — a fine concert closeout.

Batashev remained on stage after the musicians had left, as if he could not bear to leave the still lingering scent of applause, and, taking advantage of his presence there, I went up and introduced myself. After all my waiting, all these months without a letter from him, he now greeted me as if I were a lifelong friend.

"Beel! Why, yes! I have tried to phone you at your college, this weekend!"

A reception was being held for the musicians backstage, but my wife and I had a long drive home and work waiting in the morning. So I passed up meeting Igor Bril but did chat with Batashev, who was florid and friendly if still a little distracted by the evening's abundance.

"Don't worry about when you come to Moscow 'getting around,'" he assured me. "We will make short arrangements, and next day, just go! Don't worry," he said, backing off toward the curtains as I rejoined my wife and friends. "We go *any*where, *every*where. Don't worry. I know Mafioso!"

We parted, waving. In one night I'd gone from stone-cold silence to a guarantee of safe passage at the hands of the Moscow underworld.

My packet from Dnepropetrovsk and the Bril/Batashev show at Stanford marked a new phase of my dream project. Things began to roll. Bill Smith, editor of *Coda* magazine, accepted an article I'd written on Sergei Kuryokhin, my first on a Soviet jazz figure, and requested a photo of the pianist. I contacted Steve Boulay at the Space Agency in Salt Lake City, the group responsible for Kuryokhin's American tour. (Boulay, David Barrick, and Ted Everts had cofounded East Wind Records, the source of my interest in this music in the first place.) He also knew the approximate dates of the Moscow Jazz Festival: June 27–31. (He turned out to be just a month off, which isn't bad when attempting to gauge things Soviet.) Since his partner at the agency, John Ballard, was about to leave for Moscow to make arrangements for that event, Boulay suggested that I send with him whatever articles I'd published related to jazz and an outline of my proposed journey. "Something good might come of it," Boulay said, prophetically.

I wrote jazz journalist Howard Mandel about his June 1988 trip to the USSR as a guest of the Composers Union (the same organization John Ballard would be contacting in my behalf). Mandel replied that he was uncertain about the date (or possibility) of another Moscow festival, but gave me the name of his key contact, Leningrad critic Alexander Kahn, "who knows everything and everyone jazz-related and new music related in the Soviet Union." Mandel also recommended that I look into "fetes not in Moscow or Leningrad" but in Tallinn and Riga, better because they were "farther from 'official' scrutiny and preserves."

I wrote Kahn, and then Leo Feigin, the man responsible for the New Testament of Soviet jazz books, *Russian Jazz: New Identity*. Feigin, an émigré living in London, was also the producer of thirty some Soviet jazz recordings. I received a quick and encouraging reply from him, mentioning a June recording session with, according to him, "a new fenominal singer from TUVA, Sainkho Namchylak," and the fact that he was "negotiating with Channel Four at the moment to produce a series of eight films of Soviet new music, so I shall be shooting in Moscow."

At the start, and especially during my days of waiting, I felt as if I'd been given a giant jigsaw puzzle, most of the pieces of which were largely monochromatic and some even blank or pure white. Not a single clue about what the completed project should look like had been supplied on the cover, not a hint about what shape or form the end result would take. Now some solid clues, some legitimate pieces — names, if nothing else, of important scholars, critics, musicians, promoters — were rolling in.

Ted Levin, a Massachusetts-based ethnomusicologist, was intrigued by the research I proposed "a propos indigenous influences on the development of Soviet jazz." He knew of no Soviet or American work that touched on classical music influences on jazz, suspecting "that the influence has gone mostly the other way. I know of a number of saxophone concertos written by contemporary Soviet composers (Eshpai is one)." As for folk influences, he wrote, "One can easily trace the outlines of Middle Eastern modes and melody types in the playing of Armenian, Ajerbaijanim, and Uzbek jazz musicians," adding that his own feeling was that "such players have relied more on the most common stereotypical musical imagery of 'oriental music' than on any carefully conceived and crafted transformation of particular folk idioms into jazz. But maybe you'll be able to show that I'm wrong."

Levin said he thought that I'd be able to come up with "some interesting parallels between the current jazz scene and earlier Soviet cultural movements." I had commented, in a letter to him, on the strong connection I saw between Kuryokhin's music and the 1920s "inverted dandyism" of futurist poet Vladimir Mayakovsky, the *Zaum* (beyond meaning) movement in poetry, Vsevolod Meyerhold's theatrical salads incorporating athletes and acrobats, and the absurdist literature of Daniil Kharms. (Kharms once built a machine that did nothing whatsoever and wrote about a play in which actors hiccup on stage and then just walk off, after which a little girl appears, saying her father asked her to tell the audience that the theater is closing because everyone feels sick.) Levin replied, "Kuryokhin's work always evokes in me a sense of relation to the Soviet avant-gardism of the 20s, but knowing Sergei as I do, I doubt that the relation is terribly conscious; rather it might be the result of certain similarities in cultural conditions producing similar artistic reactions. Again, I might be wrong. If you could catch Sergei in a not-too-whimsical or dadaist mood, you might get some interesting information from him. It's worth a shot."

I also heard from Laurel E. Fay, who said she had not done any research on Soviet jazz but mentioned Steve Boulay. "I suspect," she wrote, "he knows as much as anyone in this country about the Soviet jazz scene today." She suggested that, out of some classical avant-garde Soviet composers I had named in my letter (Edison Denisov, Alfred Schnitke, Sofia Gubaidulina), Gubaidulina, in particular, "has connections with Valentina Ponomareva . . . and other improvisatory cross-over artists; but I don't think anyone has begun to study this yet." Key names were now beginning to link up.

Hard on the heels of these contacts came the news that S. Frederick Starr, author of *Red and Hot: The Fate of Jazz in the Soviet Union* and president of Oberlin College, was coming to Monterey to lecture on Soviet-American relations at this key time and also to perform, the next night, with his own jazz ensemble (Starr plays clarinet and sax). My quest was becoming filthy with irony, very Russian with attacks of fatalism — not long before Starr's appearance, I received a large packet of Melodiia reviews written by Alexei Batashev and other Soviet critics, sent to me from Batashev by way of Starr's secretary.

Starr talked before a full house, pointing out that Soviet-American relations, because of the totally unexpected turn of events and attitudes within the USSR, had been stood on their head. The experts had seen none of what happened coming; consequently, as an expert, he was in no position to make any predictions. "Everybody is an expert today," he said. "You are the experts." That certainly made me feel good. I didn't feel quite so pretentious anymore, so uncertain over my somewhat sparse qualifications for the large task I'd assigned myself. "We misjudged the extent to which the system never took," Starr said.

After his speech I introduced myself, saying that I was the person to whom his secretary had sent Batashev's gift packet of articles and reviews.

"Where'd you meet *him?*" he asked.

"At Stanford, with Igor Bril."

"Oh yes," he said. "Well, I've already used that material for the revision of my own book."

Frederick Starr was then engulfed by a sea of well-wishers, and that's all I saw of him. I did heed his admonition (in his letter to me) to bury myself in the language, and I now returned to the tedious job of translating the material Batashev had sent. I also stuffed my head with language tapes five hours a day, setting up lessons with two delightful émigré twins, Olga and Sonya Dragunsky. To this day their grandmother thinks my name is Mr. Slowly, because, having once panicked, buried in an avalanche of Slavic syllables when she answered the phone, I asked her to speak more slowly and she mistook that word (*medlenno*) for my name. After, aware that I was a pathologically shy person, I seriously doubted that, while traveling in the USSR, I would ever be able to carry on a single decent conversation, much less conduct interviews. Yet, determined not to let my handicap deter me, I insisted on speaking Russian one afternoon in a Slavic bookstore in Palo Alto.

"Do you have in Russian any books on jazz?"

The saleswoman took me by the hand and led me to a large section of books on games. "Konechno!" (Of course!) She handed me several books on *shakhmaty* (chess) and stood back, pleased.

"No," I said. "Not chess. Dzhaz!"

"Yes," she said. "Chez."

"No," I insisted. "Not chez, but *dzhaz!*"

"Yes, yes, of course," she said, continuing to smile, amused perhaps by the full extent of my retardation. "These books on chez."

Around March of 1990, I finally heard from Alexander Kahn. In a long letter the Leningrad critic offered to help in any way he could. He suggested that mid-June might not be the best time to get in touch with musicians, for "everybody is using every chance to go and play in the West; there are quite a few offers for the summertime." He added, "Believe it or not, the most representative Soviet jazz event of recent years happened in Zurich last June." He said he was looking forward to meeting me, exactly the way I felt about him.

I had been working to arrange the actual journey, having acquired the phone number of a San Francisco travel agency that specialized in independent treks.

"All of them are Russians?" Sonya Dragunsky asked, when I told her about the firm I had selected.

"Da," I replied, in stunning vernacular.

"Then," she said, "you are in deep trouble."

In spite of this warning I contacted a woman at the agency, who might well qualify as one of the poet Alexander Blok's beautiful ladies ("unattainable, remote, cold, indifferent, and the source of all bliss"). She was patient with my indecision over just where I wished to go. The problem was I wanted to go everywhere. My wife, the practical one in our family, had made the mistake of sending me to the city to set up our itinerary. Map before me, all those options, I went nuts. Quick flight to Alma-Ata and on to Central Asia (I had a CD by a group from there called Boomerang)? To my disappointment, Dnepropetrovsk was off-limits to tourists, on a restricted list. So was Baku (home of Aziza Mustafa-Zadeh, daughter of Vagif, and a fine pianist herself), undergoing its "time of trouble."

I settled for a boat ride from Istanbul to Odessa, then on to Yalta, Tbilisi, Leningrad, Petrozavodsk, Moscow, Tallinn, Vilnius, and home by way of Helsinki. Nastasya Filippovna, my travel agent, seemed puzzled by the system

behind my plans, but the truth was, I didn't have one. She also lacked enthusiasm for my dream of arriving by way of the Black Sea, although she gave me
a list of boats to choose from, all embarking from Turkey. Because of my love
for Russian composers and writers, I preferred the M/V *Tolstoy* or *Dmitri
Shostakovich* but had to settle for the *Bashkiria,* departing June 3. We were set. I
couldn't believe it when I actually saw our reservations filed in the computer.
After almost two years of effort, my dream was coming true. And by now I had
more names of people within the USSR than I could ever personally contact.

  Now's the time.

  I started to get nervous. Although my body was ready to go, I wasn't sure
my head was. Did I know enough about this music I was setting out in search
of? And if not, who in the United States could fill in the empty spaces? I
decided to talk to American musicians who'd performed in the Soviet Union,
and to people who'd produced the recordings that had inspired my interest in
the first place.

# Predecessors

I was acquainted with four musicians who had performed in the Soviet Union: Oregon bassist David Friesen, who had toured with a group put together by Paul Horn in 1983; Larry Ochs of the ROVA Saxophone Quartet, who had made two musical trips, one in 1983, another in 1989; Bob Murphy of the Natural Gas Band, billed as the first American jazz group ever to play in Siberia; and saxophonist Richie Cole, who had returned fairly recently from a concert in Leningrad. Fortunately, these musicians were accessible, living as they did on the West Coast, and eager to share their experiences. I also discovered, close by, two significant record producers who provided Soviet jazz recordings: Ted Everts of East Wind and Herb Belkin of Mobile Fidelity.

My search for the Association of Space Exploration offices took on the drama of a link-up in space itself. Ted Everts had promised to meet me at the association office in San Francisco. The cofounder of the East Wind label had moved on to promoting international cooperation in the use of space. The address I'd been given took me up a narrow alley that housed narrow flats more residential than businesslike, and no one was at home. Browsing in a record store on Polk Street, I asked the owner if he'd ever heard of the Association of Space Exploration. He hadn't. His response included a look that suggested I might be a bit extraterrestrial myself, even for San Francisco.

When eventually I was ushered into the association's flat-cozy quarters, I was left to peruse a copy of the organization's prize-winning book *The Home Planet,* while Everts, preparing to leave on a trip to Holland in an hour or so, got organized. The former record producer looked so much like a red-haired version of Lenin that at first, expecting some sort of theatrical ploy, I found it hard to take him wholly seriously. I'd read about East Wind, the first label to distribute Soviet jazz recordings in the United States. I had seen a photo of Everts at twenty-five, dressed in a lumberjack shirt, a former health food store employee; and Steve Boulay, a twenty-four-year-old mild-looking tax consultant, both standing beside a large poster of Lenin, the inevitable copy of *Pravda* in his fist.

Their recording business was conceived in 1984. After a nine-week postgraduate tour of the Soviet Union, the two former Russian studies majors introduced the music to members of the Grateful Dead, then playing at the hotel where Boulay bartended. Drummer Bill Kreutzmann wanted to know more about Soviet jazz, and Boulay promised that Everts, who had a tape of a festival in Leningrad, would send it. Nothing came of the Dead connection, aside from the notion that there might be a market for the music in the United States, which inspired East Wind records. The company's name came to Everts one stifling day in Cambridge, when a fresh wind, like the sound of a wind instrument, arrived — from Russia? — to cool things off.

Although Boulay and Everts had no business experience, they hit pay dirt with Sovart, a subdivision of the USSR's Ministry of Foreign Trade. "There were extensive hassles," Boulay told journalist John Hubbard. "I beat my head against the wall, but if I beat it long enough the problems resolved themselves." They eventually landed exclusive rights to issue any Soviet jazz recordings requested for the next five years. East Wind thus began peddling a product "once contraband in its native land." Using former high school friends as recording engineers and visual artists, East Wind produced five albums.

Everts eventually dropped out, and Boulay joined entrepreneurs Bruce Granath and John Ballard to form the Space Agency, a Salt Lake City–based organization that organized U.S. tours for the Ganelin Trio, the first jazz group from the USSR to tour here; the Leningrad Dixieland Band; Sergei Kuryokhin; Keshavan Maslak and Mikhail Alperin; and Azerbaijani pianist Aziza Mustafa-Zadeh.

Sitting at his Association of Space Exploration desk, hands neatly folded, Everts described his own early love of jazz as an art form, playing sax in high school, and his early interest in the USSR. He spoke of the music he'd heard in Leningrad as an exchange student, and of driving throughout the Soviet Union in the summer of 1983. He spoke of his desire to bring jazz, "the best art form in the world," to the Russians, before he realized it was already there. That summer Evert's aspirations turned toward bringing the Russians to us: a venture obviously of value to me.

When I asked him how the first thousand records, issued in 1986, had been received, whether the efforts required to establish East Wind had been worth it, he said the results had been predictable. "The recordings were seen as something of a novelty perhaps, but I wasn't particularly elated or let down by the response. The reviews were okay. Some good. Some bad."

They had consulted the ubiquitous Frederick Starr before they chose what albums to produce, Everts said. Starr suggested variety, which showed up in the albums' range: Igor Bril, Arsenal (a fusion group led by saxophonist Alexei Koslov), mainstream guitarist Alexei Kuznetsov, the Ganelin Trio, and Azerbaijani pianist Vagif Mustafa-Zadeh (who was, we agreed, the best, most original musical artist offered on East Wind). Alexei Batashev provided liner notes for four of the five albums released. When I asked about Batashev, Everts said he'd never had any trouble with him. "He's a little arrogant maybe." Everts honored the Soviet critic for being "there from the start," laying the groundwork of Russian jazz as both organizer and writer.

Everts was rushed, preparing for his trip to Holland, so our conversation did not last long.

"Any more records from East Wind?"

"No."

"Any regrets?"

"No. I'm glad we did it. In our way we made a contribution to world understanding among people."

I recalled another statement he'd made to a journalist: "Jazz *is* a universal language. It can break down barriers that each society puts up to understanding the other. The more foot-tapping we can do, the better chance we have of living together." Everts's last musical venture was arranging a Leningrad Autumn Rhythm Festival appearance for "alto-madness" saxophonist Richie Cole, a project he said had received a healthy "domestic nudge" from critic Vladimir Feyertag. (Feyertag's name was turning up for me more and more.) Everts said he was pleased "to have a small part in bringing one of my favorite players to the USSR," and we parted.


Next I contacted David Friesen, a bassist living in Portland, Oregon, on whom I had already written an article for *Down Beat*. Lots of people play jazz. Few, I believe, play it with a deliberate extramusical intention that seems to infuse every note with significance. Enter David Friesen, a man who sees the music and humankind not as ends in themselves but as means to celebrate the gifts of life, mercy, and making music. While Friesen concedes that "all of us have different reasons for playing music, different perspectives," and that "religiosity is not a word or concept I really like," he states frankly that he has "staked all of eternity on a living God," that loving music and being able to play it is "a gift: a gift that takes a lot of hard work; and to put in that hard work there's got to be some purpose."

David Friesen once claimed the bass was the one instrument he did not wish to play ("So large and awkward, and I could never hear the notes clearly"), yet he practiced on it ten hours a day. For him the driving purpose was, and remains, to disclose a divine source—showing beauty that contains "awesome strength and intensity," the triumph of hope and faith in a world that tends to neglect itself through violence and the absence of love. And because he's the sort of person who practices what he preaches, Friesen accepted an invitation from flutist Paul Horn to join him on a three-and-a-half-week, eighteen-concert tour of the Soviet Union in August 1983.

Cultural exchange programs between the United States and the USSR did not exist at this time, so the tour was arranged by the Canadian government, with approval from the Ministry of Culture in the Soviet Union. Horn and his son Robin, who played drums, are Canadian land immigrants. Two Canadian sound people accompanied the group, so the quartet—which also featured the talented John Stowell on guitar—was endorsed as a Canadian jazz group traveling in the USSR, all its members carrying American passports. Such was the cultural state of affairs in those happy Reagan/Brezhnev days.

David Friesen had a personal reason for undertaking this trip. A Christian of Jewish descent, he wanted to visit the town of Smela in the Ukraine, where his grandmother's parents, Gershen and Anna Pekar, had lived; where his great grandfather had once made *maslo* (butter) from a plant called *riji;* and where his mother had been born. David's grandmother's two brothers, Mishka and Yoska, might still be living in Smela or the nearby town of Cherkasi, and David hoped that he would be able to visit them. A Canadian TV documentary failed to materialize, as did the visit itself, yet the musical journey was a huge success. David kept a thorough diary of the trip, and he was willing to share it with me. This became my first chance to get Russia from a visiting American jazz musician's perspective. The group's first concert, in Moscow, was sold out to 2,500 people: "Wonderful reception, and the music will improve as we play more, I am sure. A very long day . . . a very long night!" David wrote. He took a walk with three members of a rock group called Dominac, who complained of difficulty finding "quality instruments" and of the expense of buying such items abroad. The musicians said they loved "the heart" David put in his music. "I would hear this comment many times hence from the Soviets," he wrote in his diary. "They are emotional people and respond to the emotions in one's heart."

Jazz critic and historian Vladimir Feyertag was the Horn group's emcee throughout the trip. David also met Alexei Batashev and was invited to his flat for "food and conversation." Batashev warned that "he is watched constantly by the KGB because of his love for jazz, his connections with Western musicians and because he is a noted physicist in the Soviet Union. . . . On the way back to the hotel we walked past KGB headquarters, perhaps to spite their men who were tailing us." Another jazz critic met with David backstage, touched by his solo playing and his compositions "Seven Cities" and "Ancient

Kings." This man had been born and raised in prison, had been near death on three occasions, and had felt hope when he first heard jazz over Voice of America. "Death was taken from me," the critic said. "He told me that he was sure that in America, and perhaps elsewhere, the art of jazz is taken for granted, but in the Soviet Union every note offers hope, and is lived for!"

In Leningrad, the Horn group played in the Jubilee Sports Palace, "a hockey pavilion" whose skating space was too generous for the quartet and caused sound problems. No matter, David wrote, for this was "the first jazz music to be played for the public by a Free World group in Leningrad in 54 years." A trip to Feyertag's home ended in a discussion of jazz, new music, and other topics that for David became "a little too weighty." Such intellectual activity did not provide the spiritual substance he sought. This he found after one of the concerts, when a girl thrust a piece of paper toward him, shouting, "David, please take this!" Ushers shoved her back abruptly, but David had grabbed the note, which told him "how much the music has touched the heart of a Soviet person."

With a young bass player, Dmitri, he "talked about the bass and nothing more" and was impressed by the specificity of his questions and his earnestness. David felt Soviet musicians were "good learners, no fooling around; they are really interested in developing from a strong foundation." Dmitri said Soviet musicians receive about two hundred rubles a month (about $33) for between eight and thirty-eight state-required concerts, including one month's paid vacation per year. At Dmitri's home, David met Igor Butman, "a young and really brilliant sax player." They listened to one another's music on tape and discussed "the drug and drinking problem" among Soviet youth, a situation "made as quiet as possible," according to Igor, in those days.

A final Leningrad concert drew four thousand people. In Vilnius, on the last leg of the tour, one concert occasioned five encores and new friendships. David met a heart surgeon with "a very large record collection"; drummer Vladimir Tarasov of the Ganelin Trio and his wife, a "famous Russian ballerina"; and a Jew named Leonard Solkolov, who told David he knew he too was Jewish because his "heart was so active in the music, and he was right." While Paul Horn went off to record in "an agnostic church," its main function "to house articles and facts advising children, on mandatory visits, that God does not exist," David visited the home of his new surgeon friend, Jonus.

"To me," the surgeon's wife said to David later, "you are a real person, in all ways and in all circumstances the same. But in the Soviet Union people's personalities change from moment to moment, depending on circumstances."

After the last concert of the tour, according to David, "We were given many gifts by various people from the audience; so many flowers brought to us each night! I wish the people would spend the money on food or something more useful to themselves." They also brought his albums to be signed. "Music that was written in the privacy of my small studio in Portland, Oregon," David wrote, "had found its way to so many people in faraway lands. A nice feeling. I know of no other country at this period in my life whose people have touched me more deeply than those of the Soviet Union."

Petaluma is located on the edge of California's abundant wine country, not exactly where I expected to find a Soviet jazz enclave, but did. Herbert A. Belkin, president of Mobile Fidelity Sound Lab in Petaluma, admits that his motives for distributing Soviet jazz recordings were less high-minded than those of the East Wind founders. His reasons were "personal, and all the wrong ones." The oldest game in the American book suggested itself: opportunity. "The perceived excellence of CDs was running into trouble," and Belkin began searching "desperately for a larger repertoire."

A photograph of Belkin in the Original Master Recording Catalogue shows a smiling, bearded, successful entrepreneur whose original aim had been to produce "the very finest in audio technology . . . small amounts of carefully developed recordings to small numbers of collectors, taking the time necessary to perfect the art." Which is just what the operation did until, apparently, they discovered they could only make "small amounts" of money at it. When Belkin began to shop around for a wider range of appeal, he found it, of all places, in Moscow. The result was Mobile Fidelity's eight-CD "USSR Jazz Showcase Series."

Although Belkin originally committed to master directly from Melodiia classical tapes, while working in the studio with Russians, he formed friendships with young people who introduced him to "hoarded" or "hidden" archives of jazz recordings — "a real revelation," he said. As East Wind had, he invited Frederick Starr to advise on the find and, having selected material, arranged a joint venture with the Soviets in 1988 to produce jazz recordings in the United States.

Belkin and I discussed the difficult destinies of jazz performers in the USSR, and their almost equally demanding option of seeking out the jazz life abroad. "So many stop playing jazz," he said. "It's a tough life." When I mentioned my current attempts to contact émigré tenor saxophonist Igor Butman in Boston, Belkin said, "You know what I'm talking about. Great jazz players in Tallinn or Leningrad become just *good* players in the U.S. It's another sort of tragedy. What's sad is these are people who have really paid their dues, creative people that truly *had to* play. And what's amazing is that they survived it all." He talked about a CD in the USSR Jazz Showcase Series that featured Oleg Lundstrem's orchestra: a "refreshing" case in which an excellent bandleader, now seventy-seven years old, "rehearsed for fifty years to get this recording" and the world attention he deserves.

I brought up the issue I mentioned to Ted Everts, the novelty of producing Soviet jazz recordings.

"It was not a novelty for us," Belkin responded. "We have had the kind of success we would have had if these recordings had come out on CBS. I'm talking in the 25,000-unit range. We have had sufficient success to stay with this market, to stay with this business — a good response. We receive one jazz recording from the USSR every two weeks. New people. People we've never heard before. Incredible people in Vilnius and Tallinn" such as young reed master Petras Vysniauskas, who Belkin thinks can give Sonny Rollins "a run for his money."

Belkin gave me the address of Art and Electronics, a small multitrack recording studio in Moscow that does work for Mobile Fidelity. He talked about "sending a lot of people to the USSR," a growing operation, and discussed what a rich experience the collaboration had been so far for both Mobile Fidelity folks and the Russians.

"If we never make a buck, it's been a high adventure. Dealing with the Russians is going to take some getting used to on the part of Americans. They're coming from a different place. It's like an episode of *Star Trek* at times."

I headed back to San Francisco, always an attractive city for me, even in the rain. That rain lent the city a slightly cloying but compatible port town ambiance as I strolled down by Giradelli Square and up to Aquatic Park and climbed the hill to catch the Van Ness bus, checking my watch. At 5:30 I was to meet with Larry Ochs of the ROVA Saxophone Quartet at a place called Limbo on Ninth and Fulson.

Tall, dignified, his manner as intent as his music, Ochs looked somewhat out of place in the large blue-lit San Francisco restaurant/bar, a musician's hangout. A rock group whose posters I had seen on the street looked very much like their posters, right down to the way they had dispersed themselves around their table, and probably the way they stood on stage. Incongruously, because of a thick wild frazzle of hair, a sort of hirsute halo set on fire, and the demeanor of a fine-looking Woody Allen, Ochs also somehow fit Limbo. He had been rehearsing for two hours and was exhausted, hungry, and articulate all at the same time, like the rich tapestry of ROVA's work itself. I knew that in 1981 the quartet had been voted top combo in an unofficial Soviet critics' poll conducted by the equally unofficial *Chorus* magazine, and that in June 1983 the group (invited by the brave critic Alexander Kahn) had performed in three cities in the USSR: Moscow, Leningrad, and Riga. I was especially interested in what Ochs had to say about the changes that had taken place between that first visit and one he had recently returned from. "The new reality is the main issue now," he said. "Several artists and writers claimed they actually wished things were like they used to be" in the Brezhnev days, because then they had a "totally definable role, knew what they were up against, knew just why they were on the planet." They had a common bond as musicians, whether official or underground.

"You will find lots of confusion now," Ochs said, "an extreme discontinuity, a lot of chains broken, rules, but nothing yet to replace them with."

He joked, perhaps a bit painfully, about seeing a "Joel Grey look-alike" at an *estrada* (variety show) performance, a Miss Sky Bar contest, and so on. "Everybody had a scam for making it in the West, a lot of hustling going on." He spoke of casinos in a hotel in Tallinn, one aberration after another: "You can't imagine how absurd it is until you've been in Russia a few weeks. It's like walking into a Krazy Kat cartoon. Russian disco is everywhere, middle-aged people obviously a completely comfortable clientele. They're supposed to be there now, but they don't really know why."

For Larry Ochs, ROVA's recent USSR tour lacked the close contact with musicians that characterized the first one; in 1983, invited by the Leningrad Contemporary Music Club ("fifty hard-core fans"), they'd had a difficult time raising money. "To our surprise," Ochs said, "no foundations came through until the last minute, in spite of all the press coverage and talk about the importance of cultural exchange." They'd fought not only to go to the Soviet Union, but also to stay there; despite the "official resistance, or at least imposition" they encountered from time to time, it was "the kind of experience you read about in people's travel books: 'the greatest experience in my life.' . . . intense, personal, everyone so warm and open." On the first tour they had performed at the Dostoevsky Museum in Leningrad for a relatively small group of intellectuals, but at the time Ochs had felt that ROVA had "a really significant impact on the direction that a lot of musicians are going to take." From what I would hear later, he was correct.

The more recent tour, fully "arranged, officially Gosconcert," brought much larger audiences (twelve hundred in one hall), but not necessarily people truly "with the music. We did play with drummer Vladimir Tarasov, but we didn't see Chekasin, we didn't see Kuryokhin. As artists communicating with artists, this trip was nothing like the first one at all. A rough place to tour, but it left me with more impressions than I would have elsewhere."

He found Paul McCartney recordings in the stores, but not jazz. "In a friend's apartment, all the recordings had been sent from the West. Even if Melodiia puts out something good, it is immediately snapped up. It vanishes. . . . What you read about what is going on there is not just propaganda. We didn't talk much about politics in '83. People had nothing to say then. They'd learned how to do that, to *not* say anything. In '89 the music was not as important as in '83. Everything's changed. Crime, the government, drugs, the future . . . the new reality, that's the main issue."

Ochs stayed on in Leningrad an extra week after the tour. "I knew that friends had gone out of their way to find food. . . . That place is so *foreign*. It just doesn't *work,* the whole system. It's designed that way, to keep you from getting things done. It's an interesting mirror on this country. We have lots here that doesn't work also, but in a different way. We have *no* information because of so much information input. Returning to New York was like walking back into my own pinball machine."

Leaving Larry Ochs, reentering the rain, I stepped around, or over, grim frayed soaked cardboard boxes on sidewalks, boxes that serve as people's homes. The wind sent several broken black umbrellas caroming down the street. I thought of a piece ROVA plays called "Detente or Detroit": 24:40 minutes' worth of my former hometown with all its false starts and poor finishes, fists, fits, curses, the edgy cacophony of the street scene, the plywood boards that still cover postriot shop windows on Woodward Avenue, vacant lots spotted with debris, bricks and humidity, lazy summer dozing laced with Ivers Galeniek's bass configurations. Vladimir Tarasov's steady accents turn to pocking, scuffling jive, rising to — what? Gathering hopeful fury ending with an astronomic/cosmonaumic lift-off headed for . . . a better world where *detente* is not just a dirty word like *Detroit? Mozhet byt* (Perhaps).


Up on stage, playing soprano saxophone, Bob Murphy of the Natural Gas Jazz Band looks like a large genial bear of a fellow: loose, agile on his horn, ingratiating with the silver-haired crowd that pursues the infinite supply of local Dixieland festivals and ninety-one tours and jazz cruises scheduled annually in the U.S. catering to their social and musical needs. Off stage, Murphy's size does not diminish, but you know you are talking to a basically no-nonsense, dedicated musician and man. I had contacted him because the San Jose–based group he plays with was billed as "the only American jazz band ever to play in Siberia," a tour arranged, as the last ROVA Saxophone Quartet journey had been, by the Space Agency.

"Moscow was a musical garbage pit, the jam sessions there a mega-mess," Murphy said. "Too many musicians of conflicting styles. Too many screeching trumpet players."

He prefers the music associated with David Goloshchekin's Diksi Sving Klub on Zagorodni Prospect in Leningrad, citing the Leningrad Dixieland Jazz Band's twenty-four-year-old pianist, Constantin Dyubenko, as "a very gentle, gifted superstar," and its leader, saxophonist Oleg Kuvaitsov, as "a highly competent player." Commenting on what Larry Ochs had described as "the new reality" in the USSR, Murphy quoted a performer in David Golo-shchekin's band who remarked, "Now we are playing bourgeois music right under their very noses." Musicians are, however, hampered by lack of hardware, especially reeds. Murphy advised me to take along five to ten boxes of them as presents, and the gifts were later greeted as if I had come bearing gold bullion.

Just as Betty had agreed to help turn my dream of a Soviet jazz quest into reality, Murphy's wife had accompanied him to Siberia. She is a doctor affiliated with Physicians for Social Responsibility, and she gave a speech at a patriotic military club in the Siberian town of Barnaul. "Flowers, other speeches, lots of grief being expressed," Bob Murphy said. "Generals down in the front row, kids in khaki clapping and bringing flowers up to her afterward. One couple confided that they had lost their only child in the Afghan war. The woman spoke of other mothers who suffered because of that war, yet now the government was telling them it was all senseless. 'What can I do with my grief?' she asked. The father added, 'We were taught to hate Americans, told that our suffering was all your fault. I don't know what to think anymore!'" Murphy said, "The people had never heard live jazz. The only other Americans they'd ever seen was a whitewater-rafting group. The audience at our concert sent notes: 'How does it feel to be here in Siberia? You must feel like Christopher Columbus!'"


Phil Crumley, cornetist and leader of Natural Gas, is also a dentist whose receptionist, fortunately, regards jazz-related business as every bit as important as periodontal. I say "fortunately" because she put me in touch with a woman close to home, a woman living in Marina, a town adjacent to Monterey; a woman named Anna Markael who has sung with the Natural Gas Band and formerly sang with the trad group Nevskaya Vasmoika in Leningrad. Anna is a handsome woman, floridly but tastefully dressed when I met her, whose English is as yet somewhat limited — but not when she sings: standards such as "You Turned the Tables on Me," and Billie Holiday's (whom she adores) "Don't Explain" and "You've Changed."

"At first," she says, "I didn't even know what songs meant. I was lazy student in school. Only because of my jazz songs I can a little bit speak."

She mourns over the "very poor jazz life in Leningrad," the lack of a permanent place for the music aside from the Diksi Sving Klub. "No room to listen every evening to jazz." She told me a typical Soviet joke: "Today I play jazz . . . tomorrow I sail away from my country." Musicians in the Soviet Union, she claims, "cannot live by jazz music. They must have money from playing other kinds: in restaurants, estrada [variety hall], or rock. Only two groups—the Leningrad Dixieland Jazz Band and David Goloshchekin's band—can have money by music alone."

Anna grew up listening to rock, Joan Baez, and Bob Dylan; then, intrigued by the fusion, she started listening to groups like Chicago and Blood, Sweat, and Tears. The first song she sang in English was "Miss Otis Regrets." On a night boat trip on the Neva, a friend suggested she sing with Goloshchekin's band, which was supplying the music. "I was twenty-six, twenty-seven. I sang 'All of Me,' and David Goloshchekin said, 'Ah, the birth of Ella Fitzgerald!' And *she* was the first jazz singer I loved, before Billie Holiday. I told the pianist with the group, 'I don't know words.' 'It doesn't matter,' he replied, 'it's jazz.' 'I don't know key,' I said. 'It doesn't matter,' he replied, 'it's jazz.' Later, when I performed regularly, this same pianist complained when I wrote out a second voice part for him. 'It's so high,' he said. 'It doesn't matter,' I replied, 'it's jazz.'"

"I like melody," she said. "I like feelings, sad songs . . . what the lyrics suggest." Not very charitable toward fellow Soviet vocalists, Anna did praise two "fine jazz singers" I was not familiar with: Armenia's Datevik Hovhannessian and Larisa Dolina. She also likes Aziza Mustafa-Zadeh, the pianist. As for herself? "Every black woman in America sings better than I do," she said. "I am a computer programmer by training. When I left Soviet Union someone say to me, 'Anna, why not work as a jazz singer in America?' And, incredibly, when I arrive, in just one week, I was singing here with Natural Gas band!"

When I said that I hoped to attend the First Moscow International Jazz festival, she laughed, explaining, "In Soviet Union they call everything 'first.' Even the Leningrad Autumn Jazz Festival, which has been going on for years, they always call that 'first'!"

Of all the American musicians I talked to, Richie Cole was most recently returned from the Soviet Union, his tour set up by Ted Everts. Paradoxically, he was also the most Russian in his madness. Richie has been providing sizzling alto renditions of bop standards such as "Lady Bird" and "Yardbird Suite" for years. Lately he has combined the sublime and near ridiculous, the ingenious and raw, teasing and pleasing his fans with his own sprightly "pop-bop" improvisations on Stevie Wonder's "Overjoyed," "La Bamba," and the theme from *Star Trek*. Richie Cole has a knack for turning whatever he gets his hands on into his own brand of wacky fun—and that was even the case with our phone calls.

Response to first call: "Hey, man, I can't talk just now. My wife's in the hospital. Call me at eleven tomorrow, okay?" Second call: "I can't talk now, man. I gotta go get my daughter." Third call (loud rock music in the background): "Yeah, this is Richie. I'm hearin' a bunch of kids, man. I got all these little girls in the house. Five eight-year-old girls, man. It's a ball, but I want to be fed. Can you call back around two-thirty?" Fourth call (after I ask him if everything's under control now, thinking the "mad Russians" must have met their match with Richie Cole): "Yeah, man. You know how it is. They're all watching cartoons now."

I ask him about an album of Russian songs recorded in Chicago—just Richie and a synthesizer player whose name he can't remember. ("Fred something"). "These were folk songs," he says. "And popular songs. There's one about kids."

"'May There Always Be Sunshine'?" I ask. Then, singing some: "'May there always be Mama. May there always be *me*.'"

"Yeah, man, that's it. That's the one. And the 'Volga Boatmen.' 'The Internationale.' 'Midnight in Moscow.' 'Meadowlands.'"

He took these classic, basic melodies and reworked them harmonically. "Like C major to F♯ minor 7 with a flated fifth, down to D♭. It took us two days. Happy Days Productions. They do jingles and things in Chicago."

The USSR tour was to have lasted three weeks but was cut short by the death of Richie's father, the saxophonist called home. "He was a John Wayne kind of guy," Richie said. "You know, man, World War II. He called me 'Bud' when he talked to me. 'Hey, Bud, don't go to Russia,' he told me. Commies, and all that. He waited until I went to *Russia* to die! The State department called me . . . but the festival was wonderful. I felt like Rocky, man! I was supposed to go to some remote outposts but didn't make it."

In Moscow, he experienced that winter's first snowfall and performed outside Lenin's tomb. I mentioned that some American musicians had reservations about the skill level of Soviet players, their lack of accessibility to the music, but Cole didn't agree. "They knew the songs and arrangements on my records, ones that I even forgot. They know more than Americans know. Guys in their early twenties, who drove thirty miles maybe to play with me."

"People are people," he said, apropos of nothing, but with gusto and good humor. "And politicians are poli-fuckin'-ticians. You know, man. We understand each other. Why, we played eight bars of 'America the Beautiful,' then cut into the 'Internationale.' I look down, and there in the front row these big Red Army guys are *cryin'!*"

He spoke of a Russian alto player. Vladimir Rezitsky perhaps? Vladimir Tolkachev? Vladimir Chekasin? I asked. "I don't know, man; you know those Russian names!" He talked about having been in Finland the previous year, of thinking "bring on the Russians next!" Ted Everts, who arranged the trip, was "primo." Cole had been impressed with Russians, their singing, dancing, fellowship in the Diksi Sving Klub in Leningrad, but he felt the late November weather was "fuckin' cold." "And if you want a burger, man, forget it!"

When I said I was going to nine cities on my own trip, he thought I'd said Atlantic City. Once we straightened that misconception out, Cole said, "Have a good time, man! Tell 'em I'm sorry my father died. I had no control over that. This time I wanna go in summertime. Hey, tell 'em I wanna come back!"

"Jazz music is the music of world peace," he said before we hung up. "It's as simple as that. It's the uniting music of the world. I was in South Africa, making a music video in Soweto. There was this Mau Mau on bass, man, and a Zulu on drums. Traditionally, you know, those cats eat each other!"

Infused with Richie Cole's rich, antic spirit, I was ready for Russia. Yeah, Richie, my man; I'll tell 'em you wanna come back. And as for myself, I'm set to *go!* But fate, as if preparing me for what I would encounter frequently in the USSR, had one last bureaucratic trick to play.

# Homegrown Bureaucracy ...
# And a Citizen
# of Boston

I was reading Greek writer Nikos Kazantzakis's account of his voyage (on *his* first trip to Russia) across the Black Sea from Istanbul to Odessa—the voyage that would soon be mine—when the phone rang.

"Hello, Mr. Minor, how are you?" I recognized the languid, fin-de-siecle voice of Nastasya Filippovna, a voice that sometimes, reeking of telephone torpor as it did, drove me nuts.

"I'm fine," I replied.

"Good," she said. "I'm afraid I have some very bad news for you."

"What, Nastasya Filippovna, is that?"

"The boat you had hoped to sail on ... is full."

Earlier I painted too rosy a picture of the ease with which I had secured reservations through the travel agency. Actually, this operation served as an all too suitable introduction to that bureaucratic morass we would frequently encounter once we were in the Soviet Union—even though, at home, it was laced with just a hint of American goodwill. Betty and I had been on hold for a month, waiting for the new boat schedule, and now that it had come out, there was no space on a boat for us.

"I see," I said to Nastasya. But I didn't, at all. "Ia ne ponimaiu," I added.

"I beg your pardon, Mr. Minor."

"I said, 'I don't understand.' Don't you speak Russian?"

"I am Russian, Mr. Minor. And I'm afraid they have booked a large tour group on your boat," she replied in that infuriatingly lovely monotone. "It is not possible to place you as individual passengers."

She suggested a June 10 departure from Istanbul (a late date) and casually added, "But I'm afraid that ship will be booked up also."

My tutor Sonya's prophetic words came back to haunt me: "All of them are Russians? Then you are in deep trouble."

The problem was that I was becoming somewhat Russian myself, as if I'd set out on some mad troika ride, despairing and resigned, committing daily follies that often "rose to the dignity of crimes," in Alexander Herzen's words, a "monster of eccentricity" turning the "excessively difficult" into the "simply impossible." Over and over, I asked myself that perennial Russian question, "What shall be done?" Yet, unfortunately, I was also still American. Americans love to make plans. Americans love to have their plans work out. Americans like settled dates. They like to pay real money in order to insure that those real dates will be met, that actuality will match up with dream or intent. Americans like to know just where they are going to be, just when and how they are going to arrive there, and they even like, on occasion, to know why they are going someplace, as long as they don't have to get too philosophical about it. They are even willing to make new plans and execute or implement them immediately, should it appear that the first set might not work out. But when all their plans fail, as mine had (or seemed to have at this juncture), Americans, having nothing to fall back on, simply fall apart.

We scrapped Greece, which broke my heart and Betty's. We had been looking forward to some sensual respite before entering the former USSR. A train trip by way of Romania proved as futile as placing two individuals on a boat. We settled for a Boston to London to Helsinki to Leningrad flight.

One afternoon I went up to the office mailroom at the college to see what junk mail had accumulated in my box since my sabbatical started. Junk it was. I began tossing everything out, solicitations from publishers and book reps, meaningless memos, ads for teddy bears sold in the college book store. Just as I was about to chuck what looked like an ad for some insurance company, I noticed that the blue envelope was a mailgram. I tore it open.

> MOSCOW 92/86 11 2118
> USSR COMPOSERS UNION AND ORGANIZING COMMITTEE HAVE
> PLEASURE INVITING YOU AS OUR GUEST TO ATTEND FIRST
> INTERNATIONAL JAZZ FESTIVAL HELD MOSCOW MAY 30–JUNE 5 1990
> STOP HTEL AND SUBSISTENCE COSTS CONCERT TICKETS CULTURAL
> PROGRAMME WILL BE COVERED BY USSR COMPOSERS UNION STOP
> UNFORTUNATELY WE ARE NOT ABLE TO COVER YOUR INTERNATIONAL
> AIR ROUND-TRIP TICKET STOP OUR ADDRESS — 8/10 NEZHDANOVA
> STREET MOSCOW 103009 USSR STOP ORGANIZING COMMITTEE
> YURI SAULSKY ZHANNA BRAGINSKAYA

Yuri Saulsky! I'd seen a picture of the highly respected pianist/composer who'd merited five index citings in Frederick Starr's book: the "energetic and youthful bandleader" trained in Eddie Rosner's orchestra; called upon to assemble the nation's best musicians for the sixth World Youth Festival in 1957; establishing his own orchestra (which included pianist Igor Bril) and achieving, according to Starr, "a lightness and drive far beyond the skills of big bands of the earlier sixties"; the man who proposed establishing a chain of twenty-one jazz academies around the USSR; the musician who was now, according to Starr, "equally respected by the independent-minded avant-gardists, officials of the Union of Soviet Composers, and the various philharmonic societies."

My hands shook, rattling the mailgram. I whooped and hollered and did a wild Cossack dance up and down the hall, amazing my colleagues, who thought I'd lost my mind — which I may have. I was Pushkin's poet who, until his summons from Apollo comes, is "among the most insignificant children of this world," but whose soul, once touched by the divine word, soars like an eagle. My soul had been so touched by a mailgram, and I immediately sent my reply: "Received invitation and accept Stop Have booked May 27–29 in Moscow as part of our trip Stop Will leave May 30 — June 5 open for whatever arrangements you make Stop Please contact me."

Such a sudden shift in plans did not sit too well with Nastasya Filippovna. Our entire itinerary, once again, had to be reconstructed. Yet I never heard again from Saulsky or the Organizing Committee. Steve Boulay, at the Space Agency in Salt Lake City, the man largely responsible for this stroke of good fortune, laughed when I described my frustration.

"They won't respond," he said. "But don't worry. Just go. They'll be there, waiting for you, believe me."

I thought of *The Brothers Karamazov:* "The world stands on absurdities and perhaps nothing would come to pass without them." What consoling words! I cackled madly when someone sent me a newspaper article claiming that the Ukrainian city of Dnepropetrovsk had just been removed from the restricted list. "Everyone wanted to know why it was closed in the first place," the city's one English-speaking guide was quoted as saying, "but we never got an explanation." A few days before we boarded our plane, as I stared at the visa in my hand, I noticed that the city of Vilnius, where we had reservations at the Letuva Hotel, had been removed from our itinerary, struck out, as if the place no longer existed. Lithuania was a trouble spot, I knew, but we had not been informed that we would not be allowed to go there except by way of white-off.

This final absurdity was corrected by a single call to Nastasya Filippovna, who booked us into a hotel in Riga, Latvia. Yet I was far beyond her divinely lethargic voice now — bound to earth only by one last sobering thought: our first Russian stop would be talking to émigré saxophonist Igor Butman, in Boston.

I had found Igor through Mark Hopkins, Boston bureau chief for Voice of America, who had done a special on the young saxophonist. I was eager to talk to this key figure in Soviet jazz life. As it turned out, his insights set me up perfectly for what I would encounter in his homeland.

"Right, Beel. Because it was before rock and roll, so there was jazz orchestras which was not named the jazz orchestras," Igor said. We swung from the straps of a Boston subway, Igor offering me a capsulated history of jazz in the USSR in the 1950s and 1960s, when he'd said the music was at its peak. "They started to go under the name *estrada orchestra*, which means variety music, and there was like a lot of big bands from the World War II. Guys like Germann Lukianov and David Goloshchekin (who played with my teacher Gennadi Goldstein's band), tenor saxophonist Alexei Zubov, could work and not have to be going to restaurants playing some stupid Russian or Gypsy or, you know, Georgian song just to make money on tips. These big bands provided a sort of training ground and musicians were just doing their thing."

"And the general public was interested then?" I asked.

"Right! The general public was really into that, going to dances, like for the time discos, but they were playing actual jazz. Rock and roll didn't yet go through iron curtain, so there was jazz and nothing else."

Igor's English is a lot better than it sounds faithfully transcribed, for this short (despite his big tenor sound that would seem, physically, to put him in the ranks of giants like Ben Webster and Dexter Gordon) sturdy man with nearly cherubic, fresh facial features has a loose, jaunty, American way of talking. I dug his unique syntax as we changed trains and headed toward Berklee College, where Igor was to meet a friend, one who, standing proud and tall on a street corner in new blue jeans, turned out to be fellow saxophonist Alexander Oseychuk, the man I'd heard live with the Igor Bril Quartet at Stanford University some months before. Small world indeed. The next thing I knew we were sitting in a coffee shop together. I attempted to grasp the rapid-fire Russian phrases going by me, but mostly I simply enjoyed being in the company of these real Russian musicians.

That morning, following Igor's instructions, I had started from the Green Line, switched to Blue. "You want Wonderland not Bowdoin" — pure poetry, an impression heightened by two young guitarists playing "Wooden Ships," although my train's arrival drowned out the nice vocal harmony. When I reached my Maverick Station stop and emerged above ground in an area that was no Beacon Hill, a man who wore his liver in his cheeks asked, "How you doin', bud?" When I nodded okay, he said, "Christ, I'm glad somebody's havin' some luck." For good or ill, this was now the world of the bright young ex-Soviet musician I met.

Igor had started off by telling me about an emigration official in the USSR who told him that if he left the country for good, he would "end up playing in the streets." Arriving in Boston, Igor did just that. He took his sax down to Harvard Square and in one afternoon gathered forty dollars in a hat he placed on the sidewalk. Before leaving the USSR he had been offered a gig at the Diksi Sving Klub for the equivalent in rubles of ten dollars a night.

"I wanted to write that emigration guy," he said now, laughing, "and tell him, yes, I did end up playing in the streets, all right — and made thirty dollars more in three hours than I could all night in the best jazz club in Leningrad."

He described the difficulty musicians have acquiring accurate information in the USSR, cut off from what they see as the primary source of the music, the United States. "It goes through so many filters before it comes to us. Let's say someone goes to the States. They talk to musicians and ask, 'How do you do your saxophone? How you play? What kind of chords you playing?' So they come back, and sometimes they don't understand it right. So, you have the wrong embrochure. Or then you just look at pictures. You don't have any video or anything, so you just look at picture of how Cannonball play. I saw his lip was, ah, like this [imitating the position], his lip wasn't inside, it was outside, so I play that way. Then I see Coltrane plays the other way, so I change."

Aside from twice being voted Best Saxophonist in the USSR, Igor was selected, in spring 1987, to open the Siniaia Ptitsa (Bluebird) Club, the first all-jazz nightspot in Moscow (or to reopen it: it had functioned in the 1960s and 1970s, under, as Igor says, "the Komsomol wing; then it was closed when we living happily under Brezhnev"). He also performed with top Soviet artists such as Vladimir Chekasin of the Ganelin Trio and Sergei Kuryokhin, appearing live with the latter at twenty-two in Novosibirsk. Later he attracted the attention of visiting American artists: Grover Washington Jr. in 1986; Pat Metheny, who thought Butman was "better than most European musicians, a real find"; and Dave Brubeck. Just eight days into his permanent move to the States, Igor joined Brubeck onstage at a summer concert series and became, according to one newspaper review, "the highlight of the set." He also played with Gary Burton, who later helped him get a full scholarship at Berklee College.

In Boston I caught him just after a European gig. "I played two concerts in Berlin during the Russian Theater Festival there, and I did some club dates with my friend since I was sixteen, bassist Dimi Kolesnik" — probably the same bassist David Friesen had talked to in Leningrad. Now, Igor having arranged afternoon rehearsal space at Berklee through Sasha Oseychuk, we headed by subway to Igor's East Boston house on Brighton Street, overlooking the bay. There in the downstairs comfort of a kitchen, the young saxophonist prepared me an American-style chicken-and-tomato sandwich.

"Zamelchatno" (Fantastic), I said, commenting on his work, his quick assimilation of native cuisine.

"Zamelchatnogo Amerikanskogo naroda" (Of the wonderful American people), he replied, laughing.

We talked about Igor's early success in another difficult art form: where and how he had first picked up on jazz. "It was the fastest switch ever, I think," he said, "from one music in one day, from 'Deep Purple,' from rock, to jazz." He was playing guitar at the time, learning Richie Blackmore's solos by heart, finding the group's live concert improvisations "really pretty close to jazz . . . probably jazz purists are going to kill me for that, but . . . that's how I felt."

Pure jazz came by way of his father, a pianist who'd been "silenced" during the Stalin era ("Yeah," Igor says, "all that stuff"), and a single "great" record by Louis Armstrong, "Basin Street Blues." ("We had only one.") Igor became interested in the sax, starting with alto, under the influence of Cannonball Adderley, Charlie Parker, and Phil Woods, then switched to tenor. Gennadi Goldstein gave him nearly thirty records ("the best ones"), which a fellow university student encouraged him to sell for their black market value. Igor studied them instead. "Yeah, a treasure, and it came into my hands."

Igor switched from alto because, when he joined Nikolai Levinovsky's group, Allegro, all the charts were written for tenor. It had "a different color of sound," one he liked. "Sometimes it seemed easier to play than alto, because of low register." He said that when he started out, the best Leningrad players were not sax men but trombonists, because "somehow there wasn't . . . well, saxophonists sometime played a lot of bullshit, like they can play fast, but on trombone you can't do that. You can't fool around. They had to find the good notes."

When I mentioned statements he'd made to the press about Soviet musicians being ten to fifteen years behind the times, or that only 3 to 4 percent of the musicians are really top players, he said, "Yeah, I still think so. Like, if you take the best player in the United States and compare him to the best player in the Soviet Union. . . . Compare Sergei Kuryokhin and, let's say, Herbie Hancock. They play totally different, of course, but Sergei . . . what he does, it was done before by Sun Ra. What Chekasin does with his trios was done by Art Ensemble of Chicago. Well, maybe not that close, but it was done before."

He was reluctant to judge individual Soviet saxophone artists I mentioned: Alexander Oseychuk, Anatoli Vapirov, Vladimir Chekasin. "I know Vapirov very well; he's amazing. They're all great. They just play a different kind of music than I do. I was interested in music like Cannonball and Sonny Rollins when I was young. These Russian guys are all technically good, yes. It just didn't go to my heart, and I don't know why. Now Anthony Braxton—he went to my heart. Or Ornette Coleman, who is one of my favorites, one of my favorite music listening now."

"Dusha naraspashku," I said, quoting one of my favorite Russian phrases and one that certainly applies to Coleman—to possess an unbuttoned, or unzipped, soul.

"Yeah," Igor said. "He swings."

I asked him about something I'd heard he and Oseychuk discussing in the coffee shop, what sounded to me like the relative merits of Berklee College and schools in the USSR with regard to training.

"Oh, he said that I should listen to the alumni of the Gnessin Institute in Moscow, where he is teaching. He said it's going to be a surprise; it's going to be something really good, better than anybody at Berklee, but I doubt it."

Because I was about to go there and try to find out, I turned the conversation back to what makes jazz unique in the Soviet Union. Igor mentioned that Nikolai Levinovsky, the former leader of the group Allegro, was criticized in some circles for deliberately using Russian folk themes in his work. "The reaction was, 'Don't play this shit, we hear this shit all the time on the radio.' You know, he plays [he hums "Moscow Nights," jazz style] and people are really tired of this, but some of what he plays was actually different melodies from Seretov, on the Volga. There's a lot of folk villages with a lot of tradition, and he was studying this at the conservatory there, so he was really inspired by that music. Yet he knew his Coltrane well too. . . . But, of course, he could do experiments only with the one band. Chick Corea has his trio, his electric band, his duos with Gary Burton."

"He can move around."

"Da. Da! I don't want to compare them, like their talents. But in Soviet Union you had so much restriction. One of the reasons I decided to live in the United States was just getting away for awhile from that scene in Russia, so they're not saying me that I have to learn this standard or that standard, or I shouldn't play that or I shouldn't play this. You can't perform just anywhere because if you belong to this concert organization you can't go to some other hall. And with Allegro, we play tunes where melody goes on forever, this solo line he has arranged for three horns. Some of them were great, but sometimes it was boring, just to play the notes, the charts. But where are we going? What are we going to do?"

Because of the limited access I'd had to his music up to this time — Igor Butman is not as richly represented on recordings as he deserves to be — I was overjoyed when he invited my wife and me to an afternoon rehearsal session of a group preparing for a club date at the new Bluebird, a New York City club opened by Vartan Tonoian, a twenty-nine-year-old Soviet Armenian impressario nicknamed "Jazznost." Igor was his cordial self, and Betty and I found refuge behind an unused set of drums in a room crammed with instruments, instrument cases, and four other musicians: Wolfgang Muthspiel, his guitar at parade rest; a slender handsome man with dark hair, contradicting any Nordic stereotypes; Andy Azarian at his Yamaha DX-7; drummer Marty Richards flashing a droll smile beneath his frowsy head of hair. The bass player, his back to us, turned out to be California's Larry Grenadier, a youthful sensation I had written about in connection with San Francisco guitarist Bruce Forman.

Given such personnel, the music was bound to be a treat, but the best thing about sitting in on a rehearsal session like this, aside from witnessing the intricate process of developing pieces, is being a part of that loose but warm fellowship that jazz musicians have a knack for, reliant as they are on each other for that joint "sound" or voice they hope to produce, that unified end. Igor is a low-key taskmaster. "You're not playing it the way it's written, Marty," he said.

> *Marty:* I was just playing it "light." You want it more obvious?
> *Igor:* Let's hear it. [*After*]: What do you think? Just tell me the truth.
> *Andy:* I liked it when he did it a little lighter.
> *Igor:* Well, okay. Do what you like there, Marty. But remember, play it
> the way I say, man!
> *Wolfgang* [*Later, on one of* his *tunes, in mocking tone, to Igor*]: Vas ist das?
> *Igor:* Das is music, hopefully.
> *Wolfgang:* It sounds a little square to me. But then I'm just a German
> mo——.
> *Igor:* What! You're German? For years I've been playing with him and he
> always told me he was Austrian!

The verbal lancing was mixed with practical suggestions: "Nobody else play fill there. The soloist should have last two bars for himself to get it just right."

I had come to Boston thinking I would end my interview with Igor on a note of high East-West romance. The saxophonist met his American wife, an exchange student and later "penfriend," at nineteen — but they are no longer together.

"All we do is fight," he said by way of explanation. "Now I have girlfriend. We fight too, but when I get car . . ."

"Welcome to America," I thought, realizing that my day was ending just as it should: with Igor's music, not his love life.

"People started very interested in me at beginning just because I was from Soviet Union," he said, just before we parted. "But afterwards I have to come here and compete with all tenor players, and some of them are amazing. If Pat Metheny listen to them in Russia and they were Russian, he would be killed by them because he didn't expect anybody to play like that in Russia, like I played. But I have to prove that I can be as good here. My dream is to play with people like Herbie Hancock or Freddie Hubbard or Kenny Barron. To play with these guys who make such a great music, to be on the same stage with them!"

"It's going to happen," I said.

"Sure!" Igor replied. "I just want to work harder. I have a lot of support from a lot of people. People are starting to know me in Boston, and even in

New York. I've played with some great players like Walter Davis Jr., and he liked my playing. It's going to happen, yes! If I will keep doing the same I do."

"Konechno" (Of course), I say.

On our last evening in the United States, Betty and I — visiting my sister Emily and her family in Connecticut — went to the Griswold Inn in Essex. We drank John Courage ale to the cacophonous strains of the Banjo Band, a local group offering every pleaser from "Melancholy Baby" to "Side by Side," interspersed with patriotic favorites such as "Yankee Doodle Dandy" and "Grand Old Flag." All these tunes were played at tempos exceeding any normal human capacity for assimilation, although this didn't stop a large red-haired woman from attempting to sing them. When she waxed operatic on "Danny Boy," I wrinkled up my nose. A very drunk woman sitting next to me punched me in the shoulder, shouting, "Well, for Christ's sake, what do ya wanna hear?" I made the mistake of saying "Ain't Misbehavin' " and got it.

We'd spent a great day with my sister, waiting to see if Kate (Katharine Hepburn, who lives in the area) might show up at the James Pharmacy and Soda Fountain, but she didn't. Now at the Griswold I drank tap ale and scanned old posters that adorned the pub walls, "Keep the World Safe for Democracy," or another, "I'd Rather Be Sailing" on cloth tacked to the piano, fortunately muffling its sound, though not enough. The place seemed filled with ruddy wind-glazed Spencer Tracy look-alikes (perhaps Kate would show up after all!), old salts in khaki shirts and suspenders, their sons sporting blue blazers and bright red-white-and-blue nautical ties.

I thought of my new down-east jazz musician friend, citizen Igor Butman of Boston. I toasted him, wishing him the best of luck in his adopted land, knowing that, tomorrow, Betty and I would be high in the sky, heading out for our own fresh world of adventure.

## part two

# Moscow

# A Critic's Apartment
# and the
# Youth Hotel

Many Americans visiting Moscow for the first time probably start out with Red Square, Saint Basil's gingerbread cathedral, and a tour within the Kremlin walls. Betty and I started with a ride in a car with a broken windshield and a hotel — the Molodyozhnyi, which means youth — that resembled a giant youth hostel. I think we were the only people over thirty there, yet the Molodyozhnyi was the only place we could get a room, once we'd switched our itinerary around again to accommodate the First Moscow International Jazz festival. Our Intourist guide, Alexander, or Sasha, met us at Sheremetyevo International Airport holding a conspicuous piece of cardboard that screamed our names; he took us to his car with the shattered windshield. It was parked beside a bright orange splash of sidewalk vomit. Sasha was young also, so my first impression of Moscow (aside from the vomit) was one of *iunost* (which means youth), although the city does not sustain that impression. On the ride to our hotel, tall apartment buildings, immense complexes, loomed everywhere, their dates of construction — 1957, 1962 — belied by their appearance, which is one of decay, some of them resembling relics from bygone eras. Betty — who, up until this time, I had not thought of as an expert on construction materials — said this was due to the use of poor grout, but I didn't ask our driver to verify this. These complexes had been placed in a setting that itself seemed not quite finished yet, as if nature were still putting up a show of resistance, hostile to the intrusion of so much steel and cement, obviously losing the fight but desperately holding its own in the form of ruts and mud, small tracks of waste, bulldozed patches not built on, left to rot.

Alexander had an Intourist-bred passion for facts and stats — "nine million inhabitants in Moscow, a sixty-mile circle surrounding the city, not a solitary single home dwelling" — but that was the only stereotypical thing about him.

He wore a loose sweater and jeans, sported a goatee, and had a face you might find on any U.S. college campus — alert, intelligent, personable — and a brisk yet casual manner. Unlocking his car door while I stepped over the vomit stain, he mentioned a rash of recent car thefts in Moscow, commented on the act of vandalism responsible for the damage to his own automobile, and then offered us a cut-rate excursion to Vladimir and Suzdal (if he reported the trip, his boss would get all the money). Kids played soccer beside each high-rise, the day still bright at nine o'clock at night; birch trees lined the road as we traversed the nineteen miles to the city's heart. Sasha said he was concerned about his son, who had been sick with a fever and congested for four days. For us Moscow was a quite human if not all-too-human place, from the start.

Our flight had been smooth and pleasant, not at all in line with the many Aeroflot jokes I'd heard. Mark and Elizabeth Hopkins (now living in London, these were the friends who'd set me up with Igor Butman) saw us off at Heathrow, which buzzed with planes to Budapest, Stockholm, Paris, Lisbon, Munich, Istanbul, Barcelona, Rome, Athens — and Moscow. Russian travelers carted large cardboard boxes filled with VCRs, stereo equipment, and micro-wave ovens they'd purchased in London. As we got in line, a woman behind us told a new acquaintance, "I speak bad fluent Russian."

When we landed in Moscow, the raucous Georgians who filled the first-class section in front of us applauded, in appreciation of either the pilot or the tenor who had been singing at the top of his voice all the way from London. Even our meal had been interesting, right down to the celery-root salad. Another stereotype was shot at the start. "The food will be awful," former travelers had told us, and even Mark Hopkins had joked about going on an involuntary "Moscow diet." Passport control was manned by baby-faced men in uniform who performed their duties silently and meticulously from behind a glass panel, slyly glancing at us several times to make certain we matched our photographs. I had anticipated customs as a long drawn-out search through the innocuous contents of our luggage; it was a breeze.

As we got closer to the city, Sasha explained some Moscow lore of the road: approaching cars flashed their lights twice to warn others of police cars, the orange-and-blue vehicles of the *militsiya*, lying in wait farther on.

"Why so many police cars on the road?" I asked. "Because it's Sunday? Weekend traffic?" "Maybe," he responded. As the days went by, I would learn more about the gadfly impositions of police: not KGB surveillance as in the old days, but petty, irritating "supervision."

Our room wasn't impressive — an uneven linoleum floor, a broken green plastic toilet seat, a sink wired to pipes protruding from the wall, a tub with plywood siding that eventually fell off. But having seen the rest of the hotel, we didn't expect much. And it didn't matter. I'd like to think we are observant but not fussy travelers. From the start, I enjoyed being surrounded by Soviet teenagers, here playing electronic games in the lobby, all looking and acting very much like their Western counterparts. A row of inhospitable women sat behind the reception desk where Sasha picked up our key. The *dezhurniia* on our floor, the woman with whom you leave the key whenever you exit the hotel, was the sort of stolid Russian figure Americans often see representing Soviet womanhood in magazines and on TV. In our room, the TV didn't work. We did get three stations on the radio, all providing classical music.

The room phone rang. It worked. Someone had the wrong number but persisted in asking, "Ot kuda? Ot kuda?" (Where are you from?). I made the mistake of answering, "California." Later that night I heard drunken youthful male voices in the hall, and around two o'clock a pimply-faced inebriate burst into our room through the door I had neglected to lock, slurring something about exchanging rubles for dollars. Although he seemed bent on establishing a lifelong friendship, he was gracious enough to allow me to escort him out peaceably.

Betty and I still had no idea where we would stay in Moscow once our three-day sojourn at the Molodyozhnyi was up and the festival began. Our first order of business was to go to the House of Composers to find out. This trek took us to an arched entryway on Gorky Street, past a wall plaque honoring the great theater director Meyerhold (who did not survive the Terror). At 10 Nezdanova Street, a giant musical clef containing the words Dom Komposoriterov (House of Composers) stood above an antique wooden door that opened into an even more antique foyer from which we were directed to an even more antique room. Jazz was being planned here?

We sat down on a settee that surely predated everything else. The room was imposing: tall windows, distant ceiling, musty curtains, and lengthy wooden tables at whose end two stately black grand pianos stood conversing in the ancient interior. A matronly female approached carrying a clipboard. Backpack slung over my shoulder, a glaze of subway sweat still clinging to my face, I must have looked like just about anything but an American jazz critic invited to attend the First Moscow International Jazz Festival. She seemed undismayed,

"Mainor?" she asked, scanning first my face, then the clipboard.

"Yes?"

"We are expecting you."

They were? Then why hadn't they contacted me? Why hadn't they let me know before we left the States? Scanning the room, I knew why. Insufficient funds. We went next to a far corner where a Bartleby type sat clacking on a typewriter whose antiquity matched the rest of the decor. He introduced himself as Vladimir Logachev, senior adviser of the USSR Union of Composers, a solemn but amiable man whose physical presence struck me as more diminutive than his title. We followed him through a narrow labyrinth and rode an elevator that went up but not down — not the last one-way elevator we would encounter in the USSR; some refused to go in any direction at all. Finally we arrived at the small, busy office of Zhanna Braginskaya, who with Yuri Saulsky had first contacted me by mailgram. She was a short woman with a bright face slightly clouded at this time by the Herculean organizational task that (it would become increasingly clear over the next few days) she had been saddled with. She graciously welcomed Betty and me, advised us that hotel accommodations for the week of the festival had been taken care of, and said we soon would hear from Irina, who would be our personal guide and interpreter over the next seven days.

Immediate business done, we headed for our first sight of Red Square, the heart of Moscow and the soul of Russia, eager to see everything from GUM department store to the Lobnoe Mesto (Place of Skulls), the circular stone platform where the decrees of tsars and patriarchs had been read for centuries. There other dramas had been enacted, such as the burning of the corpse of the False Dimitry (his ashes fired back toward Poland, from whence he came) and the beheading of two thousand rebellious Streltsy — Peter the Great had supposedly lopped off the first ten heads himself.

Photographs don't really do Red Square justice. The place is so immense you seem to experience the earth's curvature while standing there. As we entered from behind the ornate, chalk-red Historical Museum, the square's spaciousness exploded upon us — a thin line of antsized people crawling up to Lenin's tomb on one side, the extended chambers of GUM on the other, the distant brick splendor of St. Basil's set off by the long run of the Kremlin wall with its magnificent towers and the golden cupolas peeping above. The Congress of Deputies had just been dismissed from its morning duties and they were crossing the square, heading for limousines and lunch. A crowd hailed the members encouragingly, one old crone in a tattered shawl crying out, "Do it, for us!"

The day was hot, bright, and hopeful, so outside of GUM we queued up for our first *morozhenoe* (ice cream) in one of three serpentine lines that curled toward small white carts run by hefty women dispensing small but delicious vanilla cones for twenty kopecks. On the way back to our hotel, we stopped to hear a Dixieland group playing on Gorky Street. Very animated, they had been playing "All of Me" and "Girl from Ipenema" when we first passed the Marx Prospect subway station that morning, and they were doing so again, several hours later.

Since I had first tried to strike up an acquaintance with him, Alexei Batashev, billed as "the foremost jazz critic in the Soviet Union," had proved to be something of an enigma. He was respected. He had written the first book on

Soviet jazz and was a contributing editor for an anthology of writing on Soviet jazz that once had been, according to the *New York Times,* the most popular book in the USSR. His reviews seemed cogent and erudite. Yet people who had been involved in American/Soviet business dealings with him had warned me to be wary. The reviewer was getting mixed reviews himself, and I was curious to know why.

When I phoned, he immediately invited us to his home, and he picked us up at our hotel at 7:30 with remarkable un-Russian punctuality. Here he was an entirely different Batashev than the man I had met in Palo Alto, dressed in jeans, running shoes, a black spandex jacket with large red letters spelling out "KAWAI." He was sturdy and energetic, his face rugged, slightly harried, with nothing of the clown or hustler about him now, on his home turf. I decided that others had judged him hastily. On the way to his house he had to stop for three loaves of bread, which he acquired with a ration coupon. His own bakery that afternoon had run out.

We passed through a tree-lined neighborhood, turned into an alley, and pulled up at a somewhat dingy apartment building. In front of it children played in the dirt. Batashev locked his car carefully, commenting on the rash of recent car thefts. We climbed five flights in what I would come to recognize as a typical Moscow apartment dwelling; its dark corridors and dank smell reminded me of flats in the Brooklyn slum-clearance zone where I had lived. We halted in front of an impressive thickly padded black door, number thirteen; when it opened, we were greeted by Batashev's wife, Larisa, dressed in jeans and a t-shirt that read "Quinnipiac College," and their son, Ivan. On a small table stood cakes, cookies, crackers, cheese, salami, and, once it had been sliced, the recently purchased bread. All this was joined by the ubiquitous Russian tea.

"Russians do not like an empty tea," Larisa said, urging us to eat. My wife and I glanced at each other, silently agreeing to go light on the bread, since it was likely to be their ration for some time. Alexei had been rummaging through an extensive file of video tapes he wished to show me of the TV program he hosts and of a world and folklore festival held in Abakan, not far from the Mongolian border. The latter featured some Soviet groups I was familiar with (former Leningrad alto saxophonist Anatoli Vapirov, now living in Bulgaria; Tri-O, with singer Sainkho Namchylak; the groups Arkhangelsk and Boomerang, the latter from Alma Ata) and some that were unfamiliar (the Khakasski ensemble, Gorni Altai, and an Abakan big band under the direction of Alexander Kutz).

The comfortable apartment could have belonged to a jazz enthusiast in the States: many jazz festival posters on the wall, photos of Batashev playing sax, a map of his extensive trek across the United States via rental car, a generous row of Melodiia records (Batashev himself has produced more than sixty), stereo equipment, a VCR, a computer for writing, a black upright piano. Batashev treated me to a portion of his own jazz show in which he drew an interesting analogy between Central Asian folk melodies played on a Jew's harp and Dizzy Gillespie's scat. He then showed me an excellent documentary he produced that should be shown in the United States. Titled "Autumn Leaves," it contains interviews with survivors of the "hard days": trumpeter Wilhelm von Dragel, who spent twenty-five years in the camps, and other musicians who at one time were forbidden to utter the word *jazz* itself. Batashev grew up in the camp at Magadan. The first sound he recalls hearing was that of Duke Ellington's orchestra on an illegal VOA broadcast.

Frederick Starr writes of the trials of these musicians. One was Eddie Rosner, son of a Polish-Jewish shoemaker and the leading jazz musician in the USSR from 1939 to 1946. When Louis Armstrong gave him a photo signed "to the white Louis Armstrong," Rosner reciprocated with his own photo dedicated to "the black Eddie Rosner." He gave a command performance for "the Boss" — Stalin — in 1941 at the Black Sea resort at Sochi yet ended up in the camps himself in 1946, having complied with an emigration officer's request for a "handsome bribe" in the hopes of reaching Poland. Rosner arrived to serve his sentence in Kolyama equipped with a new cornet, and he was permitted to form "one of the best swing bands ever to perform in the Soviet Union," assembled from convict musicians from camps on the peninsula, a group with "plenty of time to rehearse."

Batashev and I discussed Starr's book, which he feels is "not very scientific," showing me a host of exclamation marks he'd inscribed beside passages containing factual errors. Trained as a physicist, he values an objective approach to the music, with a solid historical basis, a study of the "scientific facts." He objects to Starr's having begun with a framework of opinion or philosophy (Soviet jazz as "freedom from restraint," for example) and finds the book "social history . . . a good story."

I knew that I was in trouble. If Batashev objected to Starr's scholarly slant on Soviet jazz (in spite of the book's obvious ideological framework), what would he think of my own more lyrical approach, my strong interest in the personalities of artists, my desire to achieve a synthesis that would include cultural history as well as analysis of the music, my belief that surrounding color was as important as chords? We had an interesting disagreement over approaches to jazz criticism, the music to Batashev being "just music." He went so far as to claim there is really nothing for a critic to say about players such as Art Tatum or Oscar Peterson beyond commentary on harmonic structure, the nature of arpeggios, tempo, and substitution chords employed. He acknowledged the existence of other types of jazz — sounds to work to, chat to, background or ambience; work in which the primary concern might be extra-musical, even philosophical — but he wasn't much interested in them.

While he was expounding these ideas, his wife was listening to Boris Yeltsin and the Congress of Deputies on a radio in the kitchen. She came bounding into the room with reports of these proceedings that were deciding the fate of the Soviet Union. When a vote declaring confidence in the present government came up, we watched on TV: 145 *da*, 44 *net*. Batashev resumed his argument. Even though I knew I was losing the verbal contest (he is an insistent, focused man), I kept thinking, "No way! Especially in *this* country, where it seems, no matter how *pure* your intentions, everything sooner or later gets mixed up with politics." I also knew that, in the past, Batashev himself had not had an easy time and had been made to suffer for his love of this music.

Later I worked up the nerve to play some portions of the tape of my article on Sergei Kuryokhin, which Leo Feigin had translated into Russian and broadcast on the BBC. Larisa frowned, I think, and Alexei squinched up his face in protest: Too subjective, too extraneous, I could hear him thinking. I tried to explain my interest in the 1920s Russian avant-gardists and my curiosity over the extent of their influence on current practices.

"Theater is there, yes, in Kuryokhin," Alexei conceded. "I know, I know. And what you say about him is true enough, but . . ." Alexei said he did not regard Kuryokhin as "high art" and added that Leo Feigin did not really "produce" records so much as he "let them out."

It was a good evening, talking shop so far from home with a man obviously committed to jazz, and I was digging it. In the meantime, Larisa was telling Betty that she had stood in line for an hour for a sack of flour that day. She spoke of the tension, frustration, and anger people felt over price hikes and hoarding; people from Gorky, seventy-five kilometers away, had invaded Moscow's stores so that now it was necessary to prove one's residency in the city. She spoke of being rationed to six kilos of sugar a month (they use lots, in tea), of excitement over Yeltsin and the possibility of change. But Larisa also expressed fears over the threat of civil war between those who have and those who do not. If the times were exciting, they were also uncertain and frightening.

Their son will start school when he turns seven. Already, he wants to play saxophone. I couldn't help thinking of the history of that dreaded decadent instrument in the USSR, a decree having been issued in 1949 demanding that every saxophonist in Moscow bring it, and his I.D. card, to the State Variety Agency office, where the despicable sax was confiscated; one player, Yuri Rubanov, emerging as a bassoonist (even though, according to this account by Frederick Starr, "he had never so much as held a bassoon"), another, Thomas Gervarkin, as an oboist.

"I hate to think of what things will be like a month from now, a year from now," Batashev said, when the conversation came back to the present uncertain times. He defined a pessimist as someone who thinks things are not going to get better, an optimist as someone who thinks they can get no worse. "Change will take generations," he said. "I live in a very special country. But it's my country. It's where I live."

The night grew late. Batashev, concerned that hailing a cab on the empty streets would make us easy foreign marks, offered to drive us back to the hotel.

"This isn't California, Beel," he said. "This isn't Monterey."

He told us that, while on his own U.S. trek, he'd been given a traffic ticket in Monterey, our hometown.

"The police don't let you get away with anything there," Betty said, a bit naively given the history of the state we were visiting.

No wonder most Americans come across as pathetically innocent. (My Russian tutor in San Francisco told me, "You are children, Mister Minor, *children!*") We get away with anything and everything. This realization would haunt me throughout our stay in the USSR. Another realization that rankled was that we entertain several notions as truth, simultaneously. Most of the Russians I would meet had, like Batashev, narrowed their truths down to one, and they presented it as an absolute: the right way to play jazz, to write about it, to live. I would encounter a wide range of opinion on many topics in the Soviet Union, but each person would present his or her opinion as if it were infallible, even in this time of great uncertainty, or perhaps because of it. I grew self-conscious over my ironic laughter, a response that stems from my sense of ambivalence, of funning or playfulness — an American luxury. Not that the Russians can't, or don't, laugh. They have a rich sense of humor and laugh often — but not at the truth.

On the way to the hotel Batashev talked about the Composers' Union, which was obviously slighting him ("kicked out" was the phrase I'd heard back in the States). He claimed he did not understand what they had against him ("Zhanna can't stand the sight of me," he said), that he was deliberately being kept in the dark about the festival schedule of events; yet he had started the first jazz club in Moscow, organized the first festival here. "Now they think they can do it themselves," he said, proudly and somewhat bitterly, yet, as time would show, somewhat prophetically, in the light of the difficulties the inexperienced festival staff would encounter.

Between appointments Betty and I quickly mastered the Moscow subway, descending past young gypsy mothers begging on entrance stairs, rocking their babies; past the many kiosks hawking everything from Gorbachev dolls to once dissident literature. My favorite subway station was Revolutsii Ploshchad, with its statues of heroes, as if Rodin had taken a day off from his customary nudes, lowered his standards somewhat, and shaped these menacing yet well-meaning (if you happened to be on the winning side at the time) figures, all in bronze pairs: kneeling Young Pioneers with gun straps slung round their necks, the crew of the cruiser *Aurora*, a frontier guard with his ever faithful dog. I can still hear that priestly voice on the subway intoning, "Ostorozhno, pozhaluista, dver zakryvaetsia; sleduiushchiia stantsiia . . . Izmailovskaya Park" (Be careful, please, the door is closing; next station . . . Izmailovskaya Park).

We tried to pack as much sightseeing as possible into the three days preceding the jazz festival. I wanted to get as Russian as I could, to see just how much all this stuff might have to do with the music: how much of the culture in general it was absorbing—and in so doing we absorbed quite a bit of the culture ourselves. We went on one of the few packaged tours I had arranged back in the States—through the Kremlin. Our personal guide, Ira, remarked that, accustomed to leading large groups, she had never seen the armory displays up so close: everything from the intricate miniaturist artistry of Fabergé, the blue-and-gold crowns given to Pushkin and his flighty young wife, Natasha, by Nicolas I, to Ivan the Terrible's ivory throne. We traced the evolution of Catherine the Great's waistline from a slender coronation gown to one that disclosed days (and nights) of caloric accretion.

We also took delightful treks with a young man we'd met as a student at the Monterey Institute of International Studies, now working for 350 rubles a month for a Moscow TV station. Igor met us outside the Bolshoi Theater and took us on the sort of tour only someone born in, bred in, and in love with a place can bring off: a jaunt on foot that included the ring of parks around Moscow, the long green-leaved boulevards; Pushkin Square (where a pigeon perched on the poet's head) adjacent to McDonald's and a line of customers several blocks long waiting to receive the sacramental Big Mac; Gogol's home and a monument that includes delightful relief carvings of the characters in *Dead Souls;* the house in which another of my literary heroes, Alexander Herzen, had lived at the time of his arrest in 1834; the Arbat cobblestone mall, Moscow's Greenwich Village or North Beach, where artists and artisans sell their wares beside the walls of buildings; Detski Mir (Children's World), a department store, where Igor unwittingly unveiled a tea cozy doll he had purchased somewhere else for our granddaughter and a flock of *babushki* descended upon us, thinking he'd found it there; KGB headquarters next door— and, beneath the statue (which has since been toppled) of Felix Dzerzhinsky, founder of the Cheka, the infamous Lubianka Prison; the Metropole Hotel, with Mikhail Vrubel's intriguing exterior mural; the Moscow Art Theater, with its logo for Chekhov's *Sea Gull;* plus all the visual riches of the Pushkin Museum.

We had saturated ourselves with Moscow, hoping to provide a wider context for its jazz, and it was time to leave the Molodyozhnyi. The sliver of a new moon sliced our window that last night. In the morning, at 7:30, people already stood in line outside the *frukti-oboshchi* (fruits and vegetables) store across the street, and a man walked behind a horse and plow in a field nearby.

We had been told by the festival committee that a guide and translator, Irina, would meet us in the hotel lobby at noon. Between then and her arrival three hours late, many Central Asians arrived, their luggage wrapped and sealed in brown paper, the women wearing brilliantly colored saris or long maroon skirts and dark blue jackets, turquoise slippers, bright green bandanas spotted with sickly red roses. Their cheekbones were prominent and high. They had pitch-dark plummeting eyes, gold earrings, and gold-capped teeth — a mark of beauty and status, we would learn. Betty and I had been sitting at one end of a couch, waiting, and three of these women came and sat at the other end. I got up to check the entrance for signs of Irina and when I turned around, I saw that another Central Asian woman had slipped into my place. This was one of those all-time great "photographs I should have taken but didn't" — or couldn't, out of respect — for there sat Betty, small and gray of hair, dressed in a plain poplin coat, flanked by the blazing Asiatic splendor of these women in garish silk, each of them smiling to beat the band, revealing a solid row of gold-capped teeth.

When she finally arrived, Irina was a flurry of apology and purpose, asking us to call her Irene. She was a professor of American literature at Moscow University, smart, salty, curt — a no-nonsense woman who did not waste a second getting us into a car. Our driver, a sullen student named Sergei, and Irina discussed the miserable roads of Moscow, she verifying the use of the word *potholes* in English, my wife commenting that winter is rough on roads anywhere.

"Yes," Irene said, as we passed a *vino* shop, the first I had seen in the city. A long line had assembled outside at 3:15. "But they could fix them in spring. Yet they won't."

We mentioned the difficulty we'd been having with meals at the hotel: refused service, inexplicably, on the very first night, pleading with a waiter named Misha who seemed sympathetic enough but couldn't serve us because we were not listed as part of any *groupa*. "Tolka moia zheniia i ia," I said (Just my wife and me), and we learned that a couple traveling alone constituted an incomprehensible unit in the once collectivized Soviet Union. Explaining that I was in the city as a guest journalist attending the First Moscow International Jazz Festival (I even showed my mailgram) only made matters worse, for it suggested group affiliation for which I lacked the proper identification or — sacred in the former USSR — "papers." On another evening a woman with a sense of humor had actually smiled when I said, "U nas ne mesto!" (For us there is no place), but her superior, a man who bore an uncanny resemblance to Nikita Khrushchev, grew irate when I added, "Groupa, groupa, vsegda groupa!" (Group, group; it's always which group!); he uttered harsh words directed at *perestroika* before he expelled us from his restaurant.

Irina listened and smiled, saying they—meaning the Soviet Union in general, I supposed, or the powers that be within it—should have waited before inviting foreign guests, should wait until the country is prepared to service them.

"But don't worry about them," she said, her smile mischievous. "It's their mess."

# First Concerts,
## Our Dinner with Irene,
### and a Man Who Loves the Blues

On the third day of the First Moscow International Jazz Festival I told Irene — my guide, interpreter, and by then familiar sidekick — that I wanted to get backstage to see Vladimir Feyertag, festival program master (or master of ceremonies) for the event. I knew he was perhaps too busy for an interview, but I wished to arrange a meeting for that time at the end of our trip when we would be in Leningrad, where he lives. Scrappy, accommodating Irene nodded. "Let's go," she said. However, security guards posted at a door would not let us pass, claiming we lacked the proper credentials. I showed them my complimentary ticket (as guest of the USSR Composers Union). *Net.* I showed them my National Writers Union press card. *Net.* Something was missing. What was it? They couldn't say, but, whatever it was, we didn't have it. They were determined not to let us by. Just then a ruckus started outside, a man shouting, "Ochen zhal! Ochen zhal!" (For shame! For shame!). He began shoving people around, and the guards leapt into action. As they did so Irene grabbed my arm and we went racing up a flight of stairs, and backstage.

I felt as if I had suddenly been thrust into a KGB/CIA chase scene and, conditioned by films to anticipate gunfire, began to think of ways to preserve my own life once the shooting began. I could thrust Irene (a fairly substantial woman) in front of me as cover, but that wouldn't speak very well for our newly formed friendship, nor international goodwill. On the previous day I had interviewed Russian pianist Igor Bril and he'd told me that he would be making a sound check in the afternoon for his concert that evening. When I heard tinkling onstage I rushed out there, only to discover an innocuous man tuning the Steinway. By this time we had been apprehended by a second set of security guards. We were taken first to a *mladshii administrator* (junior administrator) of the Variety Theater, then to the *starshii administrator* (senior administrator). Each said we lacked the proper credentials to get backstage, but neither could tell us what they were.

The senior administrator advised that we find the festival's Group of Managing Staff, and, when we arrived finally in a room so distant it seemed to be in another building, Irene had some choice words for these people, their festival, and the half-hour process we had just been put through. "Sadites! Sadites!" (Sit down! Sit down!), she barked at a young man who was already seated. I assumed this word meant "chill out," a state Irene was by no means approximating, having completely lost her own *spokoistvie* (cool). I was escorted to an unsmiling young woman who informed me that I lacked the appropriate blue card, an entire foot-high stack of which stood on the table before her. Nobody, apparently—not even the performing musicians themselves—had yet been issued a card to get backstage, for, unable to find mine, the young woman gave me the blue card of pianist Mulgrew Miller, appearing with the Benny Golson Quartet.

Official now, I miraculously ran into Igor Bril and Anatoli Vapirov discussing that evening's upcoming performance. They took us to Feyertag's office, where I rushed in shouting, "Ia velikii chernyi pianist iz Ameriki!" (I am the great black pianist from America!)—a contention that surprised Feyertag, although he granted me his business card and phone number, and we set a date for an interview in Leningrad. (Later, Betty would use the Mulgrew Miller blue card to make phone calls backstage.)

This incident is characteristic of the weeklong First Moscow International Jazz Festival, an event fraught with mirth, mismanagement, grandeur, chaos, testy wills, human warmth, overt joy, and—most important—much fine music. In short, the event was very broad, very Russian. Irene's earlier comment that the nation was not yet ready for wholesale tourism proved true of the committee that had planned this jazz event, although it had come up with a stellar lineup of American musicians: Sun Ra, Freddie Hubbard, Chico Freeman, the Leaders, Branford Marsalis, Benny Golson, and Buster Williams among them.

The festival kicked off at 3:30 P.M. on May 31 with the Oleg Lundstrem Orchestra, its leader an appropriate patriarchal figure, the band itself having accumulated an interesting history. (Frederick Starr calls it "bizarre.") In *Red and Hot,* Starr tells how some jazz musicians, exiled from major cities to the provinces during the late Stalin years, actually discovered "a period of great productivity." But Lundstrem did things in reverse. Born in the remote Siberian town of Chita and raised in China (the family emigrated to Harbin after the civil war), he formed his first band in 1934 at the age of eighteen and took it to Shanghai in 1936. When Mao took Shanghai in 1948, the group moved on to Moscow (where the word *jazz* had been banned) and so impressed the manager of the Metropole's restaurant that he hired them. The inevitable scandal broke out, and the entire orchestra was banished to the Volga Tatar town of Zolenedolsk but settled in Kazan, where they became known as the Shanghaitsy. Novelist Vassily Aksyonov, then a student in the city, recalls visitors from Moscow and Leningrad listening with "stunned amazement" to arrangements that would have led to "instant arrest" in any major Soviet city.

Here was Oleg Lundstrem at the age of seventy-seven, safe and esteemed and a Moskvich (native of Moscow) once more, opening a festival at which the word *jazz* was no longer an obscenity, a festival presenting the largest array of American artists ever assembled on one of the city's stages. It must have been a thrill for Lundstrem, whose music owes a considerable debt to Stan Kenton and Woody Herman, and he rose to the occasion with dignity and style. Little is Russian about his music, even Tolstoy's agonizing question "Pochemu?" (Why? — the title of one of the group's pieces) rendered swinging but harmless through tight section work and solid seasoned riffs. The band features some fine sidemen, such as Yuri Parfenov, a distinguished-looking white-haired trumpeter who used to play with the Alma-Ata group Boomerang. Parfenov offered his own composition "Dervish," which does contain the Central Asian love of movement and decoration, a handsome theme repeated over steady Eastern percussion and drone bass.

"I Remember Clifford" disclosed another fine player, a pianist who is one of the most respected jazz musicians in the USSR, Mikhail Okun. Unfortunately, his inventive phrasing and intelligent runs got somewhat buried in bigband volume, and I would have preferred to hear Okun with a smaller group, such as a trio. The Lundstrem orchestra closed with large Kenton splashes of sound on "In Retro," and a vamp opening, growing concert-Gershwinesque version of "Saint Louis Blues."

Singer Lynn Carey, the first American to perform, knocked the crowd dead — attentive, appreciative, respectfully still — with "Let the Good Times Roll"; the Ray Charles cry, "Go out and spend some cash," provided a touch of painful irony, considering the Moscow economy. It was an appropriate and energetic East-meets-West opening, and the crowd brought Carey back for more. (I don't want to focus on the American performers except to show their effect on Soviet audiences unaccustomed to a long-established, uninterrupted jazz tradition. The music, as Frederick Starr has thoroughly illustrated, has been around since "the waning years of Nicholas II's reign," when the Sumskoi Hussar Regiment issued a hit record of "Alexander's Ragtime Band" and the tsar's own Volhynia Life Guards "delighted the public" with its version of "At a Georgia Camp Meeting" and some two-steps and cakewalks; not to mention Rasputin's timely demise, on the night of December 29, 1916, to the lively strains of Prince Felix Yusupov's gramophone recording of "Yankee Doodle Dandy." I say "uninterrupted" because that's the rub as far as jazz in the USSR has gone: the music, on occasion, has been seriously disrupted by the political climate.)

On the night of May 31, 1990, the audience at the First Moscow International Jazz Festival brought a healthy curiosity and respect—if not always a lot of discrimination—to the concert. They were gratefully enthusiastic. I was eager to see the response to pianist/composer/arranger Sun Ra's innovative and offbeat offering, next on the bill. I had been informed that Sun Ra had already demanded that his hotel accommodations be changed—not an easy thing to do in Moscow—because the first hotel was not in proper or propitious alignment with the astronomical bodies by which he ran his life.

However, his Russian audience ate up the raucous costuming, ritualistic gestures, flamboyant parading, and cosmic light show that accompanied his playing. The piece was a suite written for the festival, dedicated to cosmonaut Yuri Gagarin, whose destiny also has been favored by space. Sun Ra himself, decked out in a dazzling gold robe that clearly marked him off as high priest or pope, sat in a trance at the piano, his sidemen (constellations?) undergoing an extended warm-up the Russians responded to with cheers and applause long before the set itself commenced. Feyertag, introducing the leader, alluded to his celestial origins (which include a stint with the all-too-human Fletcher Henderson band), and the percussive assault began: two drummers, plus a flock of congas and a giant monolith that required its practitioner to mount a chair in order to draw sound out by way of wooden hooks. The music was relentless, what Mike Hennessey in a *Jazz Forum* review appropriately called "commotional," and the Soviet audience loved it, right down to a final cosmic parade about the stage, the leader swirling round and round like some slightly geriatric dervish—the set, closing with a rock and stomp hand-clapping rideout (those two drummers *can* provide wonderful swing).

Thus ended day one of the First Moscow International Jazz festival. We left the Moscow Variety Theater and walked past the House on the Embankment next door, that infamous gray constructivist-style building on Serafimovich Street, just across the Moskva River from the Kremlin. Designed as a residence for military, state, and political leaders, its eleven stories housed a laundry, canteen, outpatient clinic, gym, nursery school, post office, movie theater, hardware store—all the comforts of home until its privileged residents started disappearing in the night, replaced by others who disappeared as well.

The building earned the reputation of being "not a house of the government but a house of preliminary detainment." Svetlana Stalin lives there now.


Once we had plunged into the festival, I was grateful we'd done as much sightseeing as we'd managed, and as much eating. Special festival programs began at noon. The concerts themselves began at 3:30 and ran well past midnight, with jam sessions following at a medical institute.

Irene was great at scouting out food. Before the concert on that first day she took us to the Stork, a restaurant with Victorian decor, right down to the heavy crimson curtains. There we had a true Russian meal, although when Betty's salad arrived, Irene, a bit of a cynic, said, "How touching; one tomato." When I gently attempted to attract the attention of a waiter, she said, "Under socialism, you must wave your hand a lot." In spite of my wife's solitary tomato, the meal was good, and throughout Irene treated us to gossip related to the festival's organizational committee.

"It's Zhanna, Zhanna, Zhanna," she said, commiserating with the small, busy woman we had met on our first full day in Moscow, whom Batashev had referred to as "just a stenographer." She was apparently saddled with a nearly impossible task that involved everything right down to composing the program notes.

"These people don't know how to organize anything," Irene said. "They must come from a village. Probably never been in a city before."

Irene herself, we learned, had been born into the intelligentsia (a genuine class, still, in the "classless" USSR) and had taken ballet and piano lessons as a child. At eighteen, she had defied her parents and danced with Eddie Rosner's band, with his musical review. As part of a chorus line that made up an undulating staff of music, she said, "I was an eighth note." She spoke of Yuri Saulsky's arrangement of "St. Louis Blues" (he was our other Composers Union host, whom we had yet to meet), how he would tell her, "My darling, we have no music; we are only *playing*, improvising," and of singer/poet — "not serious singing, but jazz singing, fun" — Yuri Tseitlin, "who was madly in love with me."

We pressed her for the details of her time with Rosner's band. She had been dancing with a folk group and heard that Rosner was holding rehearsals, she said. He needed "one more girl," so she auditioned "for the fun of doing this," got the job, rehearsed for three days, and left with the band and chorus line for Lvov. Rosner was "crazy about girls," she said, "a very nice man but very hard to live with." She had a friend, a "young, beautiful girl who had been following his every move for months." He promised this girl to marry her on a particular morning but got sidetracked and went off and married someone else. "What a Guy" was the title of one of his most popular songs. Tseitlin had written a song about cowboys, for which the band wore special ten-gallon hats and also supplied the clattering of horse hooves. Reminiscing with us in the restaurant, and with a mouthful of *pelmeni,* Irene began to sing:

> Why such passion, why such passion,
> And for what purpose, when you are able to coax her,
> Will you steal this pretty girl away?

"We Russians feel the rhythm of jazz," she added. "I think I can safely say this music belongs here."

On that second day Irene located another good restaurant, in the Composers Union building where all noon programs took place, but I didn't get time to eat. I was suddenly ushered into a hall by an uncompromisingly earnest woman whose festival function seemed to be forcing as many foreign journalists as she could to attend these concerts, which presented a problem for me (aside from hunger) because they took place during time I wished to use for interviews. Over the next few days I was given fliers on and listened to artists not scheduled for headliner slots at the Moscow Variety Theater: pianist David Gazanov; a band called Super Balls (which included a fine trombonist, Vadim Akhmetgareev, who'd played with Oleg Lundstrem's orchestra); and Oleg Kireev's ensemble, Orlan, a group that combined small jungle chirpings, strident fusion, and an eerily precise duplication of the Beatles' "Norwegian Wood" and "Lady Madonna" and had been represented on the tape sent to me from Dnepropetrovsk. On that second day I also got to hear Igor Bril's twin sons, talented young tenor and alto saxophonists.

Evgeny Yachinikov, chair of the Gnessin Institute, gave a brief talk about jazz education in the USSR, describing the progression from music school to college to institute, a three-stage program that includes a special jazz faculty at the college level, inaugurated just fifteen years ago.

"We set much hope in these students," Yachinikov said. Yuri Saulsky, speaking before Yachinikov and recalling his student days playing French horn, said that "the best musicians in the world are playing in the hall, and we hope these young musicians here will be good enough to perform there also some day." Alexander Sukryi then directed a student group through three pieces: "Things Are Getting Better," a riff tune that featured Bril's son Dmitri on alto; a Sukryi original, "In the Kingdom"; and "Karila" (Carillons), whose march tempo start converted to Latin swing. Bril's son Alexander provided handsome tenor sax work on the last two pieces. The third tune also included an unfortunate drum solo (not the last I would hear in the Soviet Union, I'm afraid), this one aping all the anatomical exertions of Gene Krupa, but little of his skill. A young violinist, Radion Ivanoff (who looked as if he'd never taken a drink in his life), then offered a slow, brooding, gypsy-style "Days of Wine and Roses"; and a talented institute saxophonist, Olga Konkova, in low heels and a prim blue dress, proffered "Lover."

At intermission on the first night I had noticed a short, intense bald man talking to friends and well-wishers. This was pianist Igor Bril. I told him how much I had enjoyed the music he'd provided at Stanford. By now I prefaced my attempts to speak Russian with "Ezvinite mne, pazhalusta; ia govoru kak malchik, kak rebenok" (Excuse me, please; I speak like a child, like a baby), a sentence that had the unfortunate effect of leading people to believe I spoke Russian fairly well. Bril smiled graciously when I asked if he would grant me an interview the next day, saying, "Konechno" (Of course).

"I am interested in your sons," I said when he, Irene, and I took seats for the interview in one of the House of Composers practice rooms.

"Ia tozhe" (I am also), he said.

He told me that the two boys had taken an interest in jazz at an early age, put it aside, taken up saxophone, and, once Bril saw their zeal was genuine, allowed him "to push them." They are in their second year at the college. Bril elaborated on Yachinikov's explanation of the course sequence for me, which consists of not just instrumental instruction but a study of classical as well as jazz music (Soviet, European, American) history, and also work in the fundamentals of harmony and composition.

The pianist is a soft-spoken, modest man with a wry, slightly sad smile that makes it impossible not to like him. He feels that composing is the best way to learn to improvise, and he said he gave his sons his own book, *Basics of Jazz Improvisation*, to study. When I mentioned the exercises Igor Butman had said made up one technique employed at Berklee College in Boston — composing over a given set of mainstream harmonies — Bril said that, as a teacher, he uses this method also.

Liner notes on Bril's recordings ordinarily mention his polystylistic approach to jazz. Listening to his East Wind recording at home, I had been struck by an agile, atmospheric, nearly saccharine spaciousness; a fashionable obsession with "time"; a predilection for Windham Hill; but also, like many other Soviet performers of the period, a penchant for the Spanish tinge as embodied in Portuguese bossa nova. When I brought this matter up he offered me his wistful smile and said, "I knew you would ask me about this." He said that when he plays for a concert audience he offers as many standard forms as he can, seeing himself as "more like a missionary," hoping the audience will "understand" him. For example, he always includes a set piece called "Voyage in Blues."

Yet Bril also has his own music, compositions he regards as standing apart from the main jazz scene, special ambience pieces preoccupied with texture and tone, as indicated by their titles: "Silvery Clouds," "Before the Sun Sets," "Dance of the Seagulls." He feels that sound should never become too concrete; that it should suggest rather than assert; that music should afford the same variety and luxury of color schemes as painting does; and that, like painting, music should be intimately connected with nature. However, in a concert he sees his function as educational, instructing audiences, especially in the USSR, as to history, the full range of jazz.

I asked him if he felt there were forms available to Soviet musicians not accessible to Americans — the issue of national musics. "There was a time when people here took folklore or art as the basis for music, and that was good for the formal rhythm."

Bril regards Azerbaijani pianist Vagif Mustafa-Zadeh, as "a rare case," interesting because he could combine jazz with mugam, a native melismatic mode — here, saying that these patterns, based on diminished chords, were difficult to describe in words, he stepped over to a grand piano nearby and played them for me. Yet he feels another approach was required, because Russian folklore in particular is very difficult to combine with jazz, producing a special form of music with an uneven measure, one constantly changing. The time for nationalistic adaptions and adoptions has passed, Bril feels.

"I will explain why. We now understand that the birthplace of jazz is the United States, and we have decided that we would like to speak the same language as you, musically, and this was the starting point of moving more in your direction."

"A universal language?"

He nodded.

I asked him about a statement he'd made earlier on just how much he loved the blues. Why?

"I started with the blues. And boogie-woogie. I found a special book on the blues, with good lyrics. I thought I might be able to understand the soul of bluesmen better through these 'poems.' But my problem was . . . I am not a black man."

He talked about first hearing Willis Conover's VOA broadcasts, of first hearing trumpeter Clifford Brown, regarding those days as "a kind of school, very interesting, but a difficult school. I had nobody who would tell me, who could explain, what this was all about. I had to analyze the music all by myself.

Prior to this I had only played academic piano. I was always on the verge, trying to find *my own* music. A very difficult time."

"Yes," I said. "But with great results."

"Maybe," he replied, offering his shy, wry smile again.

"What was it like playing with Bobby Hutcherson and Joe Henderson?"

"Fantastic. In the first place, we had no rehearsals, no chance to. Both of them arrived just ten minutes before the beginning of the concert. That's all. We just sat there waiting for them, and then we started playing. But we were ready for this meeting, because we were familiar with the genius of these two men, and we had played some compositions by Joe Henderson ourselves. That's why, when someone suggested we play with these two, I agreed. Hutcherson was very attentive, just listening to us, saying, 'Oh yeah, oh yeah.' I can recall that meeting even now."

I asked about the recording he'd made with Mobile Fidelity, *The Igor Bril Quartet: At the Village Gate*. Had the too sympathetic, mutually exclusive role of piano and Alexei Kuznetsov's guitar accompaniment presented problems? (Many American jazz guitarists sit out and let the pianist "comp" behind a horn player.) He said, "That was difficult for me. But this was not my group really. This lineup — an 'All-Star Soviet Jazz Band' — was the condition of our trip."

I decided not to mention that I had once thought the quartet, on this recording, seemed overly busy, nervous, too eager to please its American audience on terms they'd let that audience set; that the result had struck me more as rehashed ground than Russian originality. I liked Bril. He is a genuine classicist whose subtle originality as a performer is matched by his gentlemanly behavior.

We closed out on the future of Soviet jazz. "I have no idea," he said honestly — a conclusion I would hear frequently as our trip progressed. "Everything will depend on who wants this jazz. Our friends from the U.S. help us a lot, from the point of view of moral support. They have opened themselves to us."

"Dusha naraspashku?" (Unzipped soul?), I asked, dragging out what was now my favorite Russian idiomatic expression.

He laughed, nodding.

"I will be happy to continue this dialogue," he said, "if it is at all possible." Fortunately, I would see Bril frequently over the next few days and came to regard him as a friend.

The second night of the festival, in the concert hall by the House on the Embankment, master of ceremonies Vladimir Feyertag was forced to kill time awaiting American trumpeter Freddie Hubbard's group, making a joke about it being "cool and normal" for jazz musicians to be late in America, although Soviet audiences don't cotton to that and this one grew all the more impatient after Feyertag's observation. The Hubbard group, apparently, was plagued by another Moscow exercise in futility, hailing a cab, a task that my wife and I gave up on after our first attempt. (Irene, on one occasion, displayed the elaborate and prolonged bargaining process necessary for success. "There is the city of 'Yes' and the city of 'No,'" she said, quoting Yevtushenko's poem to me, "and this is the place of 'No.'" Yet once the driver had been secured, he proved a nice enough man, Tchaikovsky's *Romeo and Juliet* playing on a radio he'd strapped between the front and back doors of his vehicle. In the cab Irene told me a joke: "What is a muzh?" (husband). "I don't know," I said, being one. I felt that, angered by her bargaining bout with the driver, she was ready for a round of male bashing, which she was. "A handbag without handles," she said, a statement that, given its slim content, occasioned far too much laughter from my wife. "It's too heavy to carry," Irene offered by way of explanation, "but you'd be sorry to throw it away.")

Freddie Hubbard, when he finally arrived, was in no mood to joke. Hubbard's group, in suits that made them look like Wall Street brokers compared to Sun Ra's crew, turned in a handsome job on Cedar Walton's "Bolivia" and did some serious hard-driving business on a Hubbard original, "Red Clay" ("favorite of all the stuff I've written"), pleasing the crowd but possibly also offending them—certainly the many fine dedicated Soviet musicians present—when Hubbard said afterward, "That's American jazz. You guys got the classical music; we got the jazz." There was no lack of American ego that week in Moscow, but Hubbard's group did play well.

I'd seen a lot of stomp and show so far, including James Blood Ulmer decked out in a crimson skullcap, high-heeled white boots, and long black-and-white robe, singing "Would You Like to Go to America?" over and over again, until he got the crowd clapping in unison—a thing, apparently, they love to do. But I think, musically, the richest portion of the evening aside from Hubbard and a fine performance by pianist Benny Green was provided by two excellent Soviet duos: reedsman Petras Vysniauskas with drummer Arkadi Gottesman, and French horn player Arkadi Shilkloper with pianist Mikhail Alperin.

Vysniauskas was a pupil of saxophonist Vladimir Chekasin, but he's well on his own now, some people saying he has surpassed his mentor. He has found his own unique voice and a more self-consciously serious manner. On a piece that runs 37:45 (on Leo Records's *Document*), "In Memoriam," with keyboardist Kestutis Lusas, he performs exploratory surgery on, evaluates, and exhumes all the resources of both alto and soprano sax. *Virtuoso* is a much abused term and, as such, an endangered species, but if someone finds a new word that means the same thing, Vysniauskas certainly deserves it; his sax

work is deft and intelligent and employs handsome intervals and superb texture, timbre, tone. He may call too much attention to himself at times, his
technique untransformed into anything but itself, and he has a sentimental
streak; but it's a delight, after an extended middle section of church organ
cosmic wavering, to hear Vysniauskas step back into "In Memoriam" again.

At the First Moscow International Jazz Festival, he and drummer Gottesman, a brave duo in the wake of the highly disparate big bands of Lundstrem
and Sun Ra, stood out by virtue of the very restrictions placed upon them: this
first (but not last) example of fine couples I would hear, created from necessity — that notorious mother of invention — the vast distances in the USSR
separating top players. These distances and a dearth of suitable *partnery* (partners) forces top players like Vysniauskas and Gottesman to seek each other
out and team up, the situation fostering considerable — naked as they are in
pairs — rapport. Gottesman played drums that ranged in size from thimble to
tympani, obtaining intricate melodious shading, steady pats, or riffling flicks
beneath Vysniauskas's joyous soprano or Pan-proud or skittish twin flutes.

Arkadi Shilkloper is a thirty-four-year-old Moscovite educated at the
Gnessin Institute, an accomplished classical musician who performed for the
Bolshoi Theater Orchestra for seven years, the Moscow Philharmonic for four.
His pyrotechnics on French horn, jaghorn, or flugel seem to defy the potential
of human breath. Even as a soloist he sounds like an orchestra, but he has
teamed up with Alperin, a pianist who grew up on Moldavian folk music
(memories of playing at weddings, he claims, "just grew stronger" when he
moved to Moscow) and who believes that current European jazz can embrace
all the music in the world. A typical Shilkloper/Alperin performance such as
"Song" (featured on their ECM recording *Wave of Sorrow*) initiates a melancholy theme, a soft, clearly stated melody on piano, setting up call and response, with Shilkloper contributing his own handsome folk tune, held notes
on horn laced with rapid piano configurations, precise, classical, then turning
liquid, the pattern reversed, a return to solemn themes — all quite seamless and
impressive.

Other pieces, such as my favorite, "Short Story" (with its nearly infinite
variety), introduce prancing piano figures, the French horn dancing above
them; a trilling "call" above a heavily accentuated bass note, the horn stating
one of those fine memorable melodies again, simple, basic, this converted to
stride, a stroll, deft, droll, Garnerisms turning barrelhouse with flugelhorn
topping and the sudden cry, "Heh! Ya you ya ya, Ho!" then more stride and a
last quick but lingering "Ho!" It's fun, exploratory stuff, a mix of crazy clusters
and structured sprightliness; chutzpa scat vocalizations, music that contains,
Alperin admits, "the Jewish element," sorrow expressed in a manner "that does
not necessarily convey sorrow . . . the need to laugh between the tears."

# The Belle of Baku and the Bear of Bulgaria

The second day of the festival had started, for me, with a great deal of confusion. I had been herded into the small Dom Komposoriterov auditorium by that zealous woman I mentioned before. My wife, meanwhile, had found Aziza Mustafa-Zadeh. I might have done so on my own, given the chance, because you truly couldn't miss her. The twenty-one-year-old Azerbaijani pianist, daughter of Vagif Mustafa-Zadeh, was dressed in a manner that would put a toucan to shame, make it feel dull or ordinary. She wore a sea-green woolen shawl with tassels thrown over one shoulder and a brilliantly patterned outfit in strawberry, orange, blue, fuchsia, and rose. Her pitch-black hair, pulled tight at the side of her head, dropped like the shawl, and just as long. Her wondrous eyes and eyebrows recall an Azerbaijani folk song, "Dark Eyebrows," that her mother, Elza, sings. Aziza also has a wondrous nose. The French painter Degas once said that every beautiful woman possesses a touch of ugliness, without which, "no salvation." Aziza is striking, beautiful—and constantly accompanied by her mother, another colorful (literally, in dress also) creature.

My wife had introduced me to Aziza, along with her mother and an Englishwoman, Veronica Crauford from Henstridge, Somerset. (Because Irene did not show up the next day, Veronica would serve as my interpreter. As I would discover when I reviewed the tapes, she possessed a voice so soft it resembled disappearing ink, threatening to vanish upon contact.) Veronica in turn introduced me to Anatoli Vapirov, the former Leningrad saxophonist now living in Bulgaria, with whom I set up an interview for the next day. Leo Feigin came on the scene and introduced me to Alex Kahn, the Leningrad critic, and Tatiana Didenko. The cast of characters got as thick as all those

Bolkonskayas and Bezukhovs, Drubetskayas and Novosetsevs one gets hit with in the first chapter of *War and Peace*.

Tatiana said that she hoped I would make a special effort to attend the presentations at noon the third day because they would consist of "new music," work she felt was unique in the development of jazz in the USSR. "We think this music is more important than anything you will hear in the concert hall at night," she and Leo had affirmed.

And here we all were on the third day, yet these performances conflicted with my scheduled interviews. I ended up pleasing almost nobody, missing the "new music" activities Leo and Tatiana had wanted me to hear, which included German clarinetist Hans Kumpf and Moscow trumpeter Andrei Solovyov, both of whom I'd also just met, further complicating the cast of characters. On top of all this, another peculiar situation was shaping up: Soviet musicians were beginning to mistake me for a manager or agent, no matter how much I protested that "Ia tolko pisatel" (I am only a writer), and I was being besieged by mysterious creatures who slipped out of the walls, woodwork, ceilings, floors, handing me fliers, cards, and even demo tapes. The morning after I'd heard a twenty-one-year-old pianist play his own compositions, I was assailed by this "amazing prodigy" (as Irene caustically referred to him) and his mother, the latter asking what she should do to ensure her son's musical future. When they mentioned Berklee College, I thought of Alexander Oseychuk, recently returned from there, and advised them to get in touch with him. The young man persuaded me to write, on the spot, a blurb about his performance on the previous day. Other musicians would attempt to arrange late-night meetings so that I could hear "the only really serious music being made in the Soviet Union"; in the case of one earnest supplicant whose group I learned was quite good, they would then fail to show up.

By comparison, Aziza Mustafa-Zadeh was a joy of brightly colored actuality. I still love listening to the tape I made while interviewing her, because she has a lovely speaking voice, and she sang for me as well: "Beautiful Love," in English, a language that, I believe, she does not know. Early in the interview, when I complained that U.S. critics frequently mentioned "folks songs" and "Azerbaijani modes" with regard to her father's music but never explained what these roots consisted of, she explained that it's much easier to explicate through music than with words, because music "speaks for itself." Here was the opportunity — the same handsome grand piano upon which Bril had played sat in the room — to ask her to play for me, which she did, handsomely.

The patterns are called mugam, generically, but there are many of them, melismatic in nature — not just melodies or scales because they have emotional or poetic significance as well, like Indian raga. Aziza plays a mixture of them, not just one at a time, but the first she played, alone, contained the first five notes of "'Round Midnight," exactly. Her mother, who began barking commands the instant her daughter began to play, named some of these handsome, delicate, haunting figures for me. Aziza plays them with great respect: *bayati shiraz* ("the most famous one and they call it 'the bride'"), *shu* and *sauga chargia* ("many names"). Each player develops harmonies from these melodic foundations. When I asked Aziza if there were rhythmic patterns also, specific Azerbaijani rhythmic patterns that might not be accessible to Americans, she said it was difficult to say, "because I don't think of particular rhythms when I play." Her mother added, "It just comes out."

"Dusha naraspashku?" I used that buzz phrase with which, by now, I could always get a healthy dose of nodding and a laugh, translated as "unbuttoned" or "unzipped soul". Aziza and Elza blandly stared at me.

Elza said, "There were rhythms only Vagif [Aziza's father] could play. No one else could play them."

"And the same is true of you?" I asked Aziza.

"They come from inside," she said. "Each musician plays his own, just as each person is different."

"You sing also, and your mother sings. Can you give me some idea of the content of these songs, the lyrics?"

"Eto narodni" (They are folk songs), Elza answered. "The words are about love."

"Konechno" (Of course), I said. "Can you give me an example?"

Elza chanted, nicely, "'Beautiful black eyesbrows, and eyes' . . . I can't remember. Such a long time ago . . ."

Aziza said, "There's 'Sadu'" (In the Garden).

"Ah, that's the one I have on record," I said, "with Vagif, and you, Elza."

Elza mentioned Vagif's last album, *Vagif Mustafa-Zadeh in Kiev*, but said she had never heard it.

"Ochen zhal" (That's a pity), I said. (Later in our trip, I would find this album, appropriately enough in Kiev.)

I mentioned a reference I'd read somewhere to "Moslem jazz" and attempted somewhat clumsily to name Central Asian instruments I'd heard about. The two women instantly asserted that, whereas the Moslem republics are very close to one another, Azerbaijan is unique, its music "totally different" from that of the others — from any other music in fact. "Its melody, rhythm, even its beauty is different. Everything!" They did concede that it has been compared to Indian raga, that mugam is like "starting a dialogue with Indian music."

I asked Aziza about her connection to mainstream American jazz — what she and other musicians I talked to in the USSR call "classical tradition": Monk, Charlie Parker, Bill Evans. She said she had been influenced by these three, especially Evans, and by Keith Jarrett, and she likes Herbie Hancock, Chick Corea, McCoy Tyner, and Marcus Roberts, the latter a favorite among all the younger pianists I talked to. Coached by her mother, she quickly included her father. I asked if she could play something mainstream, preferably the blues, to see what she might do with that. While she was reluctant at first, she relented when I said I had never heard her play before, which was true.

After flipping through a fake book she asked, "Does it have to be blues?" I said, "Anything that's classic jazz," and her mother suggested, "Whatever you wish." She played, and sang, "Beautiful Love," beautifully. Her rendition included calculated "negroid" slurs, a smooth scat with wide range and lovely high notes, then a fleet and feisty mostly single-note solo with fine attendant voicings underneath, building to block chords, back to the words and a poignant Lady Day ending.

She then played one of her own compositions, "Chargah." I was sitting on a windowsill, not more than a couple of feet behind and to the right of her, fascinated by not only the music but the hands that dispensed it, in and of themselves: long, seemingly slender fingers, infinitely agile like those of many pianists, but also thick, strong, percussively powerful — muscular and graceful at the same time: both aspects, the lightness and the strength, employed in the overall voice of her music, just as they were in her appearance.

This piece held the variety, and the attendant wild dynamics, of a suite: dazzling right-hand forays accompanied by slashing left-hand chords, a romantic melody emerging, lyricism laced with arpeggios; then passages with an obvious mugam base that fit handsomely, just as quickly converted to a strut and stagger dance played off heavily accentuated bass configurations that first suggested boogie-woogie and then became it; these patterns turning, at the end, into a soaring concert lushness — some dense, rich percussive antics reminiscent of Tyner and of her father's severe rhythmic drive, a sweeping, dramatic closeout. The music was like much that I would hear from pianists over the next few weeks — a host of disparate genres exploited by superb technical facility combined with genuine passion, the legacy of nineteenth- and early twentieth-century Russian music. Aziza mixed these with a power and melodicism unique to the Azerbaijani soul, clearly having emerged from the tutelage she had mentioned — even that of her mother, so close by her side — disclosing handsomely felt invention amazing for someone her age, just twenty-one.

After she played, when I asked about the nature of Soviet jazz, she (and her mother) said that such a thing did not exist, that jazz was born in America (Bril's starting point, but this time with a twist). *Azerbaijani jazz* — Elza asserted that such a term appeared in the encyclopedia — its own music, however, shares more with improvised black American music than any other. Having heard the force, the power, the soul with which Aziza played, I was not about to argue. (I was fortunate to obtain this tape, for she would not perform at the festival and a CD promised by Mobile Fidelity for over two years now is not likely to appear in the States.) Aziza or her mother (I forget which) complained that the work of more "traditional" pianists, such as Leonid Chizhik, who would perform that night, lacked "invention." "It's like a . . . a . . . what kind of machine?"

"Xerox?" I suggested.

"Yes," they chorused. "Such performers do every phrase the same. They need a more original approach. They need to look more inside their souls."

This was not my first encounter with the internecine wars that occur on the USSR jazz music scene, and it served as intimation of more to come. One complaint Aziza shared with just about every musician I was to talk to in the Soviet Union was the lack of adequate *partnery* (partners) or rhythm sections capable of solid interaction, like the best of Bill Evans's trios, for example — musicians always listening to one another, responding in kind. She and her mother told me they were waiting for a phone call with regard to her forthcoming U.S. tour (a tour that, unfortunately, would not take place), and I promised that, should she come to California, I would walk to wherever she was if I had to, just to hear her play.

"Prekrasnyo" (Beautiful), Elza said gently.

Aziza's ebony eyes lit up when I gave her Keith Jarrett's latest solo cassette, *Dark Intervals.* "I hope you do come to California," I said.

"Ia tozhe" (I also), she replied.


I couldn't reconcile Anatoli Vapirov's physical appearance with the music I'd heard, prior to the First Moscow International Jazz Festival, performed with Sergei Kuryokhin: broodingly solemn, introspective, dramatic, slightly fragmented, brittle even in its wild dark assertion. Vapirov in the flesh turned out to be warm-blooded, open, even jolly, the most overtly friendly Soviet musician I'd met. He wore jeans (right down to the denim jacket), sported a shaggy beard, and was the sort of Russian "big bear," Veronica Crauford told me, you want to hug. That wasn't exactly my response, but I understood the analogy. And Vapirov *did* hug me, after our interview, a typical Russian response that took me back to my Clement Street, San Francisco, "Russian Town" days: that unaffected display of deep feeling (*umilenie*) I had so admired then.

To start the interview, I mentioned Leo Feigin's description of Anatoli as a "lone wolf." "Eto pravda?" (Is this true?)

"Da, eto pravda," he replied, laughing loudly. "Eto pravda. Lonely volf."

"Pochemu?" (Why)

"I don't know why. It was very difficult to find *partnery* if you lived in another town, a small town, or another country. And it's still the same."

Here again was the perennial complaint, fully justified in Vapirov's case; before he moved to Bulgaria, he had lived in a provincial Russian town following his musical genesis in Leningrad. When I mentioned the lack of depth, the absence of adequate sidemen and especially rhythm sections, that Soviet musicians were complaining of, he agreed.

"Da, da. Eto pravda. I have known drummer Vladimir Tarasov for about twenty-five years, but I just got around to playing with him last year. We are now cooperating quite closely. I managed to contact him — Tarasov lives in Lithuania — from Bulgaria. God said to me, 'Go to Bulgaria! Only when you have done that will you play with Tarasov.' Fate is really inexplicable."

Vapirov is an interviewer's dream come true. You nudge him, then sit back and enjoy the highly individual results. When did he first discover jazz?

"I can't remember — either when I started to listen or play. Such a long time ago. I was about eleven or twelve maybe. Living in a small town where there was absolutely no jazz on the radio at all. Only Soviet music. In the Ukrainian town of Berdyansk. Azovskoye More [the Sea of Azov]. I took to the saxophone. Charlie Parker? Oh, no, no! That came way after. There was only Soviet radio there. It was totally the other way around for me. No Willis Conover. No Voice of America. And I never wanted to play like Charlie Parker."

"Nikogda? [Never?] A true lone wolf!"

"Yes! At fourteen I heard Paul Desmond. You see, my life has not been standard."

"It's better that way perhaps?"

He seemed to take for granted it was. He feels he may be the first Soviet jazz saxophonist to have graduated from a master class at the conservatory, followed by Alexander Oseychuk. "I also taught at the Leningrad Conservatory. For five years. Classical saxophone, not jazz. My students played jazz, and I taught them, but after. But first, classical." I asked him about a statement made by critic Efim Barban that mentioned him in connection with "a superb balance between improvisation and composition" and "a level of ideas . . . qualitatively equivalent to that of the work of European composers of the post-Webern era." I asked about work I'd seen cited, work written for the theater and ballet.

Long pause. "I haven't taken the customary path toward art. I don't write music specifically for theater and ballet. Do you know my 'MacBeth Suite for Ten Pieces'? It contains scenes for instrumentalists, but also for dramatic art, actors. Are you . . . are you *familiar* with my history?"

I was familiar with his "MacBeth," which I owned (on Leo Records): I considered it one of the finest pieces to have emerged in the Russian "new music" — a rich suite that kicks off with a thick tympani roll and wild alto scrawl, a "Rite of Spring" rhythm so brief it's just a tease, followed by rippling, tocking chimes and some somber, mood-establishing string work. Throughout this suite, Vapirov provides those lush symphonic melodies he seems to have an endless supply of. Yet you can also find him at the far sane edge of pitch, threatening to cross over, as he sometimes does, into cacophony. Sax trills turn to soaring rapid runs. High squeaks and squalls subside to a low, dark mood with a sad, singing cello counterpart. The second side of this album may seem tame compared to the first, but appropriately so. More skittish, it retains the A-minor mood, with A serving as Vapirov's punctuated root note, handsome sax intervals laced with quick triplets, Alexander Mikhaylov's massive tympani washes sustained, and the mood of destiny fulfilled, played out by way of an agonizing, percussion-assisted blaze at the end and a plaintive melodic close.

I was not as well acquainted with Vapirov's own destiny, his history, as I was with the music, but I knew bits and pieces of it. Leo Feigin had written, "In 1981 saxophonist Anatoli Vapirov was sentenced to two years in prison." Leo Records released his album *Sentenced to Silence,* the release "especially painful," according to Leo Feigin; "What would be his fate?" According to the MCPS (Mechanical Copyright Protection Society) law, Leo Records was required to pay royalties to the Soviet authorities. "In short, Leo Records was supposed to pay for suppressing human rights," Feigin said. "That was totally absurd."

" 'MacBeth' came to me in prison," Vapirov now said. "All of the music I have composed has been for myself. I needed something to surround myself with. Music! I rarely play solo, so if I was to surround myself with musicians also, I had to write something for them: string quartets, string orchestras. But I hate to write in false ways, 'made to order.' I don't like to be thought of as a 'professional composer' in that sense. Of course I can do it, but I don't like it."

He mentioned that, up until now and his work with his "first absolutely equal partner," Tarasov, he has performed with his pupils, for example, Sergei Kuryokhin. These young people were learning from and drawing energy from him, and he enjoyed it, up to a point. I asked if Kuryokhin was not an "equal partner," and, while he never answered the question directly, he did say he hasn't played with the younger Leningrad pianist since 1987; that Kuryokhin, at twenty, knew where he was going, yet it's "only from *not* knowing what you can do, *not* knowing just what you are capable of, that you can get the right interaction between two musicians. When you know someone's limits, and what they can do, you can repeat a certain kind of music but not necessarily make it new."

In Bulgaria, Vapirov is at present unemployed. He had been directing a state big band, but finances were cut 50 percent when the cultural revolution started. He joked about Adam being tossed out of paradise. I asked him about another Efim Barban statement, that free jazz in the USSR could never be a mass movement, for there were not more than forty people playing it.

"Konechno" (Of course), Vapirov responded, adding that he found that figure too charitable. "Even that number is too much. It's one thing to play new jazz, or free jazz, and another to have talent, to create art. Many travel down the road of free jazz because they can't or don't know how to express themselves and they think that's the easy way. But I absolutely believe you cannot play new jazz unless you know how to play the traditional musical culture. After you have command of all types, you can decide where your true talents lie. You have to truly learn instruments, *all* of them, and only when you reach a certain level of professionalism should you decide what you want to play. Some people pick up a saxophone and blow any note and think that sounds good, think it's 'new jazz.'" Here he offered a very accurate, and funny, flatulent imitation of someone doing just this. "Kuryokhin did that. Picked up a saxophone and was playing with sounds. But that's just small intellect. It's not really connected with music, it's . . ."

"Like what children do."

"Da. Da. Yet the public likes this!'"

Vapirov's own preference — free jazz or mainstream — depends on "who I am playing with. Whatever they like playing best I like playing." He mentioned Tarasov again, how natural it was to play *svobodnuiu musyku* ("free music") with him, and then he spoke of Benny Golson, the much respected mainstream tenor saxophonist and composer who would be performing that evening. Anatoli said he wouldn't feel right playing with him. It wouldn't be natural. So his favorite form is free jazz. He loves playing mainstream but feels he "doesn't do it quite right." Yet if he's got his own style of free jazz, that will be similar to, or run parallel to, someone else's "mainstream."

Asked about his major extended compositions (what one critic has called his "epic approach") and his use of myths, Vapirov said that, when musically depicting such types of Okhnu, an historical Siberian (Khakaszi) shaman, he doesn't just go through the motions of telling the story or myth but tries to let people actually *hear* the character.

"But how do you transform myths into something just musical?"

"Dear God! It just . . . arrives! I can't explain it. As in my 'MacBeth,' the names are secondary, the story is secondary. The *music* is first. Other people might just 'quote' folklore, but that's on the surface. That's just elements of one culture taken into another. It all depends on talent. Sometimes it works. Sometimes it doesn't. I'm not trying to criticize these people, but that's just not my way. When I look at folklore I'm looking for something deeper, something I can identify with at any given time, something inside of me identifies with it, with the . . . the . . ."

"Dukh?" (Spirit).

"Da. Da. Da. There are people in Bulgaria who use specific rhythms [and here he both sang and tapped out some of those driving sprightly ⁵⁄₄ up to ¹³⁄₄ dance patterns for me] but I am more interested in melodies. Because melody is right at the heart of Slavic culture and it unites a number of different countries. Not technically, no. No special scales. Nothing like mugam, as in the Azerbaijani folk-oriented music of Vagif and Aziza Mustafa-Zadeh. I look for what links Bulgarian and Russian culture. The old Bulgarian state was originally Russia, on the Volga. That was a long, long time ago, so I had to look very, very deep. *Too* deep."

When I asked him about more recent historical gleanings — from, say, the revolutionary Russian avant-garde work of the 1920s — he said that such matters were best left to critics. Contemporary performers had taken elements, obviously, from many different musical styles or sources — jazz, avant-garde, classical — but such borrowings were not, he thought, "conscious." Even though various avant-garde artists have interpreted his works visually, he does not feel that, in his music, he needs the help of the other arts.

"I never see a *picture* in front me," Vapirov said. "My music comes from strictly musical ideas."

As far as a comparison of current American and Soviet jazz goes, Vapirov says too much of his exposure to American music has been confined to pieces like "Stardust." It is difficult for him to compare because, he feels, he is "not all that well versed in American music." He has listened to a lot of the Marsalis brothers, Branford (performing at the festival) and Wynton, but finds much of current American jazz — he mentioned Berklee College in this context — "like a conveyor belt, and that's too bad." The music lacks what he calls "inner person." It all sounds the same to him. He feels the same way about the products of the Gnessin Institute in the USSR, although some Soviet musicians have their own musical identity, he says.

"It's mass education. Out of a hundred of them, 99 percent will make good jazz audiences someday, but only one should actually go out and play. Yet a hundred want to, and they do."

"Kak pisately" (Like writers), I say.

"Da, da. It's an irreversible process."

A lone wolf, Vapirov, truly — a master performer and excellent composer whose "MacBeth," "Thracian Duos" (with Kuryokhin), "De Profundis," and "Lines of Destiny" (dedicated to Alban Berg) are rich, solemn pieces. This side of the composer/performer is offset by humorous sketches — "Benny

Goodman Is Just around the Corner" and "Duke Ellington in Bedroom Garb" — that show his wit and range of tone and invention. Apart from Vagif Mustafa-Zadeh, Vapirov was the most comprehensive, intense, and moving of all the artists I had encountered so far. I thanked him for the privilege of having met such a genuinely original person. "And the future?" I asked.

"Skrytiye pokazhet [Only what is concealed can tell]. Postmortem."


The afternoon and evening performances of the festival's third day included the music of two fine American groups: Buster Williams's quintet, Something Else, reduced to four by, one account had it, "last-minute visa problems." (The story circulating claimed that pianist Roberto di Gioia had not been met at the Moscow train station because the welcoming committee, assuming he would be a black man, failed to recognize him once he'd disembarked.) In spite of this loss, Williams's *quartet,* with Ralph Moore on tenor sax, gave an exhibition of solid musicianship, unencumbered by gimmicks or costumes, disclosing just that sort of genuine interaction Soviet artists need, given their concern over the lack of adequate *partnery.*

Benny Golson's group, featuring the man whose backstage blue card I now proudly toted (how had *he* gotten in?), pianist Mulgrew Miller, just whetted my appetite, giving the crowd another lesson in musical excellence by way of Golson's own fine compositions "Blues March" and "Along Came Betty." Miller offered tasteful topping or middle-range comping behind superb sax work, combined with the fine interactive drumming of Tony Reedus, everything from soft cymbal washes to press roll assaults, reading his leader just right — showing the Soviets, I hoped, what a truly attentive, more than just eavesdropping, drummer can do. They were interrupted by Rufus Harley, a musician I was unfamiliar with, who came onstage in a red tam and kilt to present the people of Moscow with a *kolokoi klobodnyi* (liberty bell), a goodwill gesture from the mayor of Philadelphia. Then he gave the good people of Moscow a second gift: a heavy dose of himself by way of bagpipes and duck-call soprano saxophone work atop backing tapes, playing a medley that included everything from "Got Rest Ye, Merry Gentlemen" to "Stormy Weather."

This third evening turned out to be a grand night for corn or kitsch. Leonid Chizhik, whom I had until then regarded as one of the world's fine "taste and touch" pianists, must have received the wrong sort of backstage advice from Rufus Harley. Equipped with a Roland synthesizer, and Estonian singer Sergei Manukian, Chizhik somehow managed to evoke the gaudy ambience of a Las Vegas skating arena, right down to its hollow muddle of overly amplified sound. Chikhik did little to soften the impression by way of his own seal-sleek and shining silver-gray suit, conjuring up, in my mind, the ghost of Leonid Utesov, a Soviet musician who, according to Frederick Starr, was always "on the verge of becoming a purveyor of kitsch, a kind of Soviet Lawrence Welk," a man who lent some dubious legitimacy to *Teatralizovan-nykh estradnykh predstblenii* (Theatrical review presentations) or *Tea-dzhaza* (Theater-jazz).

The comparison is not wholly fair to Chizhik, an excellent pianist and composer, a world-class musician, for there's an unpleasant side to Utesov: a showman of proverbial wealth ("after Stalin, probably the best-known person in the Soviet Union during the 40s"), but a musician and band leader who, starting out as a circus clown in the twenties, had written—assisted by "Stalin's sinister aide" Lazar Kagonovich—a "widely distributed brochure" called "How to Organize Railway Ensembles of Song and Dance and Jazz Orchestras"; conceived of American music in strictly "visual and theatrical terms"; denounced Duke Ellington on political grounds and then in 1954 (Stalin one year safely, or not so safely, dead) wrote an article defending Ellington; called for the "rehabilitation of the saxophone"; and confessed, at the age of seventy, that Soviet musicians had been "forced to pull our left ear with our own right hand and our right ear with our left hand; we work as, in ancient times, Comrade Aesop worked."

The disease seemed to be catching. Although the Alma-Ata group Boomerang played well, it seemed to succumb to the virus in the air. Percussionist Farkhad Ibrahimov, sitting on the floor, switched from tabla to a large hand drum, then pranced about the stage, à la Mick Jagger, and paraded out into the crowd, the drum flipped overhead and rolled back across his shoulders. Ibrahimov never missed a beat of his fiery attack or wild dancing, even using his thighs as a springboard for the drum, which by now had assumed an acrobatic life of its own. The stunt got the audience clapping in unison. A second Ibrahimov brother, Takhir, lay down a surging, boiling, slowly fermenting background, yet Farkhad seemed to get more sound from his hand drums than Takhir did from an entire kit. The former, returning to the stage, first kissed the tenor man on the cheek, then blew kisses to the audience. "He's cute," my wife said, and I had to admit *it* was—exactly my word for this sort of artistry—and I also had to admit I preferred to remember both Boomerang and Chizhik as I first heard them, on record.

The pianist has been compared to Keith Jarrett in his Köln solo concert days, yet aside from a fondness for a prolonged sit (or in the case of Jarrett, sit, stand, kneel, squat) at a grand piano, the two have little in common. Chizhik rarely performs in excess of the actual sound being produced, his romanticism anything but febrile, his stance less matadorial. What is uniquely Russian about him is a knack for converting superb technical facility (Sergei Kuryokhin's "Russian disease") to pure feeling—a trait he shares with the Leningrad-Kirov ballet, and maybe with Soviet ice dance and hockey. Chizhik also swings, providing rich diversity: subtle rhythmic variation, tasty sublayers to the continuous surface and charged bop runs on "Möbius Strip" (from his Mobile Fidelity *Leonid Chizhik in Concert* album), straight-to-the-heart melodic invention on a number listed as "Composition on the Theme 'Embraceable You,'" a bouncy playfulness amidst formal ragtime proprieties on "Spontaneous Improvisation," and a spare sensitive rendering of "Creole Love Call."

The most Eastern sound I had heard from Soviet artists was that of the Boomerang Soviet Jazz Ensemble (represented as just Boomerang on Mobile Fidelity also), a group from Alma-Ata in Kazakhstan that represented fusion at its best: seamless assimilation of disparate sources. It is also bizarre in the homonymic sense of evoking the sound, sights, and smells of the oriental marketplace: Aport apples (Alma-Ata means "father of apples"), a garden city with temperature swings of -28° in winter to 104° in summer, steppe and semidesert spaciousness, copper and gold, snowcapped mountains with China just four hundred kilometers away—and a language in which *zhok* means "no." All this is reflected in the music: twittering chimes, fine Turkish cymbal work, precise tabla percussion, smooth midriff undulations, and a seraglio ambience mixed with morning calls to prayer. A lurching modal insistence undergirds it all, and above soars the soprano sax work of Viktor Nikolaev, the wavering snake-charming pitch of this instrument having found a context in which it is truly at home. Again, the tunes—"Minaret," "Dervish"—all tell stories, the expert trumpet skills of Yuri Parfenov evoking *Sketches of Spain*. And finally the universal glue that binds this host of moods, less self-consciously flashy on record than in concert, the fine percussion of the brothers Ibrahimov, Takhir and Farkhad.

# Two
# Bad
# Boys

The Composers Union had assigned Betty and me just about the most inconvenient location conceivable for getting to and from concerts: the Ishmailovo Hotel all the way across town. It took us a long time to realize that all of the foreign journalists had been housed there, and what a shame, for we could have formed a *groupa* and actually procured meals. A much lauded shuttle bus never seemed to materialize, and Betty and I had to leave the evening concerts early to make sure we got down to the Biblioteka Lenina station in time to catch the last train. Consequently, we got some sleep, whereas some of my colleagues attended all-night jam sessions at various sites around Moscow and got back to the hotel as best they could, or not at all.

Always fresh in the morning it seemed, when Betty and I arrived at the Dom Komposoriterov coffee shop, was London émigré record producer Leo Feigin, even though I suspect he never missed a single after-hours session. He was customarily surrounded by an entourage that included interesting people such as Polish *Jazz Forum* editor Pawel Brodowski and a writer from Latvia named Anthony Marhel. Occasionally, I got Leo alone, and we continued the conversation we had begun in London, where I'd stopped off to see him just before flying to Moscow. Although we now discussed First Moscow International Jazz Festival concerts, oddly enough we spent more time talking about Soviet musicians who were not present, such as the Ganelin Trio, or what was left of it. Slava Ganelin had left for Israel in 1987 and "doesn't even wish to remember the Soviet Union."

"He realizes how lucky he is to be out," Feigin said. "Ganelin is an orchestra now, a one-man orchestra, playing all those parts, those permutations, bringing it all back together at the end. He doesn't need *them* (reedsman

Vladimir Chekasin and drummer Vladimir Tarasov), those two idiots — and I'm calling them that lovingly. He was just keeping them at the music, keeping Chekasin in line, as if he were in kindergarten."

Feigin described his current project: a series of eight thirty-minute films produced by Associates Film Productions in London in conjunction with Leo Records, to be shown on Channel Four television. The series will present some background on Feigin himself, chronicling the history and background of Russian new music and his involvement in it, then feature the work of Sergei Kuryokhin and his group Pop Mechanics, Slava Ganelin, Anatoli Vapirov, Valentina Ponomareva, Petras Vysniauskas, Aziza Mustafa-Zadeh, and the Volgograd avant-garde group Orkestrion.

"Will we ever get to see it in the States?"

He shrugged his large shoulders and looked at me as if I were a fool. His opinion of the American response to his projects is not high.

"What makes this Russian art distinct from all the rest?"

"Sheer madness," Feigin said. "Compare Mussorgsky and Wagner. Mussorgsky is totally mad. All Russian art is sheer madness, because of the lack of borders, boundaries, to the Russian soul. Because of Russian extremism, excess."

He spoke of the major breakthrough he feels Sergei Kuryokhin had made, his main contribution: presenting, for the first time on stage, by way of his "extended family group" Pop Mechanics, a psychiatrist discussing the "psychic disorders" of musicians, and also such heretofore taboo topics as first love, masturbation, homosexuality, transvestitism, Marilyn Monroe — "things that had never been talked about in public before." Feigin thinks that reality is something far removed from a Soviet musician's understanding, and he spoke of Kuryokhin's interest in "books, books, and books." When I asked whether contemporary musicians might have been consciously influenced by their Russian forebears, especially avant-garde artists and writers of the 1920s, he answered, "Some of them."

"Your sight is being trained by the ambience in which you live, obviously," he said. "The influence of something like futurism is not obvious on the surface, but somehow *underneath*. Of course it was there all the time. The intelligentsia has always been there." I found it hard to believe that I was sitting in Moscow chatting so amicably with a man whose single-handed devotion (and, according to critic Alexander Kahn, "heroic but desperate solitude") had brought most of the existing Soviet jazz and new music recordings to the Western world.

Just two days before, in London, I had dreaded meeting him. Like a number of American jazz writers, I'd been both put off and fascinated by his book *Russian Jazz: New Identity,* especially his own final essay, "Notes of a Record Producer." In this piece, Feigin had stated that the attitude of the

Soviet authorities to jazz in their country is in many ways similar to the Western establishment's attitude to Leo Records, "with a few honorable exceptions." That attitude, according to Feigin, was largely one of neglect or derision. In typical Soviet fashion, he went on to separate, or purge, the bad guys from the good, the disloyal from the loyal, the unfaithful from the faithful.

New Russian music, Feigin wrote, was not just new Russian music. It was a religious faith, a credo, a "new aesthetic," a "great musical revolution." He excoriated writers for their ignorance about the Soviet Union and the history of Russian culture and art, their failure to discern the "Russian spirit" in the music of Soviet improvisers — a situation I'd been trying to correct. Feigin made a good point: what was different about new music in the Soviet Union was that its exponents had "managed to raise themselves above any political or dissident movements." True art is always "above politics," he said, but — inevitable Russian paradox — this statement came on the heels of accusations that people had failed to grasp the music's social and political significance.

After lengthy diatribes against everything and everyone from the record distribution system ("full of crooks") to the very public whose support he sought, his essay ended on a positive note: "Russia is truly a country of jazz miracles," genuine jazz resurfacing "in the midst of the most cruel spiritual oppression." The essay was an amazing, exasperating, contradictory performance. And its author was the man — cranky, combative — whom I had arranged to interview the morning after I arrived in London.

Betty and I stayed in East Finchley with our friend Mark Hopkins, then working as VOA bureau chief in London, and his delightful English wife, Elizabeth. I'd warmed up for Leo Feigin by "meditating" in their long narrow backyard, in the shadow of two large clay-spigot chimneys, drinking Earl Grey tea, listening to JAZZ FM 102.20 London: Gene Harris and Stanley Turrentine doing "Since I Fell for You," then Stan Getz on "Here's That Rainy Day." We'd had a beautiful warm dry day in London, although my attempts to track down a gallery exhibition, "Soviet Artists' Images of Women," had been in vain. I sipped tea amidst the sounds of squawking magpie and twittering thrush, close by a potting shed over which hospitable English clouds passed. Elizabeth was telling us about her locksmith, who "travels all the time."

"He went to Egypt last year," she said in her lovely accent, "because he'd, as he put it, 'already done the holy bit' in Israel."

Next day I waited in the lobby of the BBC, where Feigin works in the Russian-language broadcasting division. It was a bit like sitting in the foyer of the United Nations building. Tall black guards were stationed to ensure that all employees and visitors carried an appropriate pass, and the range of languages ran from Cypriot Greek to Swahili to Chinese. Two Pakistanis waited on a couch with me. I counted more turbans, shawls, sarongs, saris, and sandals than I'd seen in my lifetime. Among them arrived smartly dressed young Brits in crisp suits along with tired old Churchills, complete with the cigar.

I'd already reported my presence to the receptionist at the front desk and now I was recalling that, in a recent *Coda* article, I had seriously questioned the messianic claims made for Russian new music, saying I wasn't sure they were either "merited or necessary." Anticipating Feigin's response, should he have seen the article, I was sure he would tear me to shreds immediately — verbally and perhaps physically as well. Whose side would the tall African guards step in on, his or mine?

"Mai-nor! Beel Mai-nor!"

The voice boomed across the lobby. It issued from an immense man with a white well-trimmed goatee, a face that spelled no compromise, and shoulders like a Volga boatman's. He wore khaki trousers and a light-gray shirt. His sloping forehead was made prominent by his baldness. His eyes glistened; he had huge fierce ears. His gestures were extravagant.

"Beel Mai-nor!" the voice thundered again.

As I rose from the couch, he crossed the lobby with giant Mayakovsky strides and, ignoring my outstretched hand, slapped a BBC pass (VISITOR BBC 02986) on the left shoulder of my sport coat. "You will need this!"

"I have just finished making your tape," Feigin said as we entered the elevator.

"My *what?*"

"Tape!" he said. "I have translated your *Coda* article on Kuryokhin. It is the best thing ever written by an American on Russian jazz."

Feigin next introduced me to a young woman who he said had done the sound work on my tape. I still couldn't believe I was hearing correctly. Then he and I sat down to lunch in the BBC cafeteria. This fierce, bitter, messianic record producer turned out to be one of the most cordial, quick-witted, re-silient (at times), entertaining, funny, and a bit mad correspondents I had encountered so far in my quest for Russian jazz. And this wasn't just because he had liked my article — although, of course, that helped. I liked him immensely, immediately, and the first views he presented — his appraisal of the current state of the music — struck me as surprisingly sensible, not at all inflated or infuriated like those in his book.

"The euphoria is over," he said. "We have lost our audience. The underground audience. The underground is over. The music is overground now — and now they understand that it's all about *music*."

He admitted he was painfully aware of the paradox Larry Ochs had presented to me: the "new reality," in which *glasnost* (or fresh freedom in the arts) was juxtaposed with economic calamity. "You need all this freedom *after* dinner," Leo Feigin said, "not before." He went on to discuss the disadvantages, to the musicians themselves, of having to spend "twenty-four hours a day hunting for food."

"As far as the Moscow festival goes," he said, "money will present a permanent crisis." He went on to describe a "fantastic, two-in-the-morning boozing party" he had attended with organizer/composer/musician Yuri Saulsky as "one of the best moments of my trip," referring to a recent excursion that had offered him his first opportunity, since his "exile," to explain "firsthand" to someone in an official position just what he had been trying to do with Leo Records.

"I'm a very poor man," Feigin had told Saulsky. "But I'm obsessed. An émigré, a layman. What I do is entirely by choice. I don't represent *anybody*."

Feigin told me he'd "beat the KGB twice, in '85, in '86, and that's not easy." Then he offered a *shutka* (joke) related to Russia's new democratic political future: "There are no more cannibals in the world; we have eaten the last one!"

His BBC office is small and crowded. One large poster advertises Chekasin alone, another the Ganelin Trio; a sign shows Stalin and reads "Eshche opasei!" (Fearsome still!). When we entered, Feigin kissed his blond, sturdy, stoic secretary, then turned to me. "Seventeen years we've been together," he said. "Tak [So], this lady never really reciprocated."

Feigin laughed—a mad cackle—when I said I wanted to hear about his life.

"I just did a program on *you*," he roared, "and now you want to do *me*? Ah, now, Kuryokhin would love it!"

His story is classic: love of jazz, the X-ray plates, VOA broadcasts, "lots of trouble," constant observation by the KGB, a lexicographer by trade but "sacked from every job I used to get," five "pretty bad years," the decision to leave permanently in 1973. "I never look back," he said, then switched to self-mockery. "The most ridiculous thing? To produce noncommercial recordings in this commercial world. But I have no alternative. Oh, what I could do! If only I could get my distributors to pay me!"

He opened a desk drawer and showed me fan mail for the jazz show he beams into the Soviet Union, the one on which his translation of my article on Sergei Kuryokhin would be broadcast for the next three nights: letters of gratitude from Smolensk, Dnepropetrovsk, Lutsk, Donetsk, Gorky, Irkutsk—"the whole of the Soviet Union."

When Leo Feigin asked and I told him that this was my first trip to the Soviet Union, he looked concerned, as if I were a mere baby set adrift in a leaky boat upon a very rough sea. He was right, I was, but luckily for me at the time, I didn't know that.

That evening Betty and I spent our final moments in the English-speaking world with Mark and Elizabeth, spent our last night chatting and sipping wine. Feigin had promised to drop off some records so that I could send them home rather than cart them all over the USSR. When the bell rang, Elizabeth danced to and opened the front door on the massive Feigin, reaching forward to shake hands.

"*Don't* shake hands with Russian with razor blade!" Feigin roared, disclosing that implement cupped in his fist for slicing twine for the record cartons. The contrast was perfect: West meets East — the demurely buoyant English lady with her accent, and the mad Russian standing there with the frail and meager but dangerous blade in hand. We packed up the records for Mark to mail to me; then we retired, for Betty and I had to catch a plane for Moscow first thing in the morning.

And who was one of the first people I'd run into at the First Moscow International Jazz Festival? Leo Feigin, *konechno* (of course). Now we sat at a table in the House of Composers, sipping coffee and yakking away like old friends. Or at least Feigin was yakking away. My job is mostly to listen and ask a lot of questions. When I mentioned the possible influence of this historic meeting of Russian and Western musicians on a Moscow concert stage, he said, "I have great hopes that some kind of synthesis will take place. The 1990s will bring a synthesis of East and West. It's already happening, but this will be on a larger scale. The Soviets will get rid of their inferiority complex. They will be able to play with Westerners on equal ground."

He mentioned the skill of a musician such as Lithuania's Petras Vysniauskas, and he cited the recent demand for appearances by the amazing Sainkho Namchylak, the *hoomi* or *golovoi pinia* (throat singer) from Tuva ("she could ruin this building with her voice"), who, unfortunately, did not appear at the festival. Yet all of this, he added, will depend upon the future political situation.

What, amid all the turmoil, will happen to these musicians? And the music?

"I don't know," he replied. "Nobody wants to record for Melodiia anymore. Soviet musicians are beginning to understand that the only way to sell records is through live concerts, that you can't sell records unless you perform. It's a huge country, but somewhere a lot is happening. There are more than twenty regular big festivals a year . . . yet they have a totally distorted view of the West. They are great technicians, well trained, classically . . . but they lack depth. They need congenial musicians to work with, allies."

Feigin spoke of John Zorn and other Westerners who had performed with Russian musicians. "First of all, it was a lot of crap. Then the tension, the drama started, and it happened. Do you know why? All because of the Soviet musicians. They didn't know—they had no idea—just how good they are! They will never know!"


I've never been to Volgograd, and I'm not sure I want to go, anymore than I want to do time in Akron, Flint, Pittsburg, or Detroit, where I grew up. Sergei Karsaev was born, lives, and suffers there. I met him in Moscow at the festival, a darkly handsome man of medium height, late thirties I would guess, a somewhat ragged cross between Bruce Springsteen and James Dean, with a touch of Mickey Rourke thrown in for good measure. "We live in the dirtiest industrial area of Volgograd. This is a huge ghetto with a very mixed population," Karsaev has written. "Naturally there is absolutely no cultural life at all. It is a very reactionary city. Stalingrad!" (Tsarytsin until 1925; Stalingrad until 1961; now Volgograd). I've been told that more old men, women, and children died of starvation during the seige of Stalingrad than the number of American soldiers killed in World War II.

Karsaev has commented on the dualism of his situation, living among "filth and stink" but surrounded by gray monuments in his "land of heroes." He has, he confesses, a pathological attachment to it all. He is in love with it. Musically, this love is celebrated in pieces such as "1987," in which Karsaev recites the following poem, enveloped in the gray sounds of found instruments—metal buckets, gongs, bells, kitchen utensils, drinking glasses, iron blocks, and pipes mixed with the persistent laughter of Yelena Chashchina, a stunning blond suspended in a cage above the poet's arch-serious, soft delivery:

> We are crossing now to a realm of magical biblical finesse,
> of souls in harmony, stepchildren of light.
> At the edge of rule in endemic summer
> we speak as equals with its prodigal leaves.
>
> Fortunately, we did not build this disintegrating fate, were not its
>      masters;
> just blind arrows headed for transparent targets.
> Only the delight of idle, haphazard gun play
> can dissolve the blood's sad sensual shadows.
>
> Pictograms found in forgetful hands,
> we so easily recline in any direction,
> and in this thin dream of irradiation
> everyone seems a fellow traveler, a cordial shepherd, friend.

The group Karsaev works with — Chashchina ("voice," not "vocals"), Ravil Azizov (clarinet, trombone, piano, bass, xylorimba, guitar, percussion, "voice" also), and Oleg Lubimov on Argentinian flute on "1987" — is called Orkestrion. It specializes in urban effects, committed to the cultural deformity that is Volgograd, alias Stalingrad, alias Tsarytsin. The group is also committed to an ardent and arduous pursuit of fresh, original intonational properties: oinking, gurgling, glicking, clacking, and munching produced by every conceivable instrument. This is not easy-listening music. Orkestrion, like Karsaev's poems, deliberately courts disparity or stark contrast, the earnest and mundane set side by side.

The pieces (on Leo Records's *Document*), with titles such as "Abyss," work through startling juxtaposition of intensive poetry and a host of aleatoric sounds: in "Tsaritsyn," snatches of conversation turn into a Tower of Babel (Russian, Spanish, English, Italian), a feeling that, no matter what happens or evolves, the raw moment of inception is everything. "Abyss" begins with an intrusion, the traffic of the external world, "blossom heaps of garbage," then fades to sanctity, serenity, safety — *zvezdy bez golosa* (stars without voice), a play off the poet Lermontov's "star talking to star"? When Karsaev chants, "Zdes zyblius tolko ia" (I alone sway here), the abyss itself sways with him, turns empty, anguished. Cold urban noise again crowds out the momentary privilege of meditation. The sound properties of Karsaev's poems add to the texture and rapport of the music — "v zabrene / v zaikane / zamochinikh skrazhin" (into forgetfulness / into the stuttering of keyholes).

Leo Feigin had given me Karsaev's name in London, but Veronica Crauford, the English translator, arranged our meeting at the Variety Theater. Orkestrion had not been invited to perform at the jazz festival in Moscow, but the poet was in town checking out the not exclusively mainstream music. (A rural avant-garde group, Arkhangelsk, good at evoking *its* bitter northern ambiance, did perform on the main stage at the State Variety Theater.) Sergei Karsaev possesses an intensity, a raw earnestness, likely to make many Americans — with our sometimes touristy, wishy-washy, smiling curiosity and graciousness — ill at ease. From the start, he means business (*delo,* in Russian: and not just commerce, but "affairs, matter, point, fact, deed, thing, case, action" rolled up into one: *v samom dele,* reality, indeed). He was deadly earnest with me, sitting on a couch in the Variety Theater foyer, condensing his elaborate philosophy to twenty or so intermission moments.

He told me that Orkestrion offers its audiences "not a song, but emotion, improvising on emotion, declamation with music that might, or might not, correspond to what he is declaiming himself" — deliberate dissonance, contrast. The text, he said, might be sentimental, the music itself totally nihilistic. He said he wants to create the ambivalence that, he feels, he has in his lifetime been surrounded by, submerged within. "Everything should be there. Happy and sad. Nothing is separate from the music. We do nothing consciously. We don't repeat anything. After all, we grew up in a situation in which, well, you just never *knew* . . . yet I never overlook the syntactic meaning. The sense should be interesting, always. And the sound as well. But then again, we use everyday speech of people as music, independent of meaning."

"A singer/poet such as Bulat Okudzhava cannot tear your soul apart as this young man does," a Russian woman for whom I later would play Karsaev's music in Monterey told me. She felt the distortions in spelling and grammar (using nouns for verbs, as just one example) reflected distortions in feeling, that the music and poetry together represented "the soul's desperation." She said that such disillusionment, a sense of impotence and fatalism, made her feel deep sorrow and shame herself. "I wanted to shake him back to life," she told me. "I have been watching the Congress of Deputies in the Kremlin, on TV. A bunch of old men shouting, arguing, talking, always talking but doing, accomplishing, nothing, *nothing!* — just crying, always, on each other's shoulders. It's so Russian! And this poet of yours is so *young!*"

What I heard in the music was wild, wry, dark, highly rebellious humor that reminded me of the Russian absurd comedy authors I liked, the Oberiu group of Daniil Kharms and Alexander Vvedensky. Even more, I heard echoes of the visual artists of the 1920s Soviet avant-garde, people I felt had lived, thought, and worked close to the spirit of the Russian new music — its predecessors. The theories of Varvara Stepanova in particular (wife of the equally adventurous, experimental Alexander Rodchenko), whose work had ranged from graphic poetry to textile and clothing design, intrigued me. Stepanova had experimented with "audacious optaphonic synthesis," or pure sounds arranged in syncopated patterns, displaying that unique Russian facility for synthesis of sensation. (Even Alexander Herzen, in the nineteenth century, had spoken of "hearing an odor, of smell on a level with sound.")

Stepanova had not just seen sound, she also devised a slogan, "temporary and transit," that matches the formal concepts of the new music performers. She had a notion of tectonic form as the principle of endless change, of simultaneous disintegration and evolution, an action composed of diverse elements. Not just the revelation of a set idea according to synthetic principle, but "organic form," ceaseless, shifting, transmuted. What she described, as expressed between 1917 and 1926, could easily constitute a manifesto for the new music I heard in the USSR, so great are the similarities.

Orkestrion has other historical precedents, strictly musical. The first Russian to use the word *jazz* in a Soviet magazine, Valentin Parnakh (whom Frederick Starr, in *Red and Hot,* describes as "Russian Futurist poet, Dadaist, Surrealist, editor and dancer but non-musician"), loved the visual, theatrical aspects of jazz—bass drum lighted from within, that sort of thing. He organized, in 1922, the "First Eccentric Orchestra of the Russia Soviet Federated Socialistic Republic," which played syncopated rhythms provided by drums, banjo, and xylophone, accompanied by dissonant sax work. This group performed alongside a genuine "noise orchestra" organized by composer N. N. Foregger, which featured, according to Starr, "artistic performances on bottles, sheet metal, sirens, whistles and machines of various sorts." ("That such an arsenal might produce the music of the future became an article of faith among a handful of Russia's left-wing avant-gardists," adds Starr.) In 1923, pianist Leonid Vargakhovsky's First Experimental Synthetic Chamber Ensemble contained nineteen players performing on "no fewer than 124 noise-makers," baroque classics rendered on "slide whistle and kazoos."

Orkestrion can be linked—although by way of a large jump of some sixty-seven years—to this tradition. In genuine comedy (not frivolous or "situation") the desirable state of nonsense is achieved, according to Max Eastman, when we anticipate "approaching sense," yet that sense fails to arrive. The result, if the form is "well managed," is a pattern that "abruptly fails of closure," frustrating but fun. The greatest nonsense artists, from Aristophanes to the Marx Brothers, create an unbelievable world, invite us to enter it, and then *keep* us there (that's the important point), amazed, dazzled, dazed, dismayed, apprehensive.

Karsaev claims that, while he now knows about previous avant-garde movements in the USSR (musical, visual, literary), he did not when he got started, because so much of this information had been withheld and is only now trickling out. Whatever Orkestrion may share with avant-garde artists of the past is strictly accidental, he claims. The group's work, and Karsaev's, has been modeled on the life, and mostly the sounds, they found surrounding them firsthand in Volgograd. He has been influenced, he admits, by "academic music," especially the avant-garde work of Luciano Berio, Karlheinz Stockhausen, and John Cage, and he enjoys combining traditional instruments with "anything that makes a noise."

Although he participated in a "Orkestrion-trio Performance & Jazz & Poesie au der UdSSR" which took place in Salzburg, Austria, and has hopes that Leo Feigin might bring the group to London, Karsaev is not at all pleased with his situation as a poet in the town of Volgograd. "Official circles do not wish to print me," he said, "and the means of getting published, in spite of perestroika, still reside in their hands, so I find myself shut out of literary life. In order to let my work appear at all before an audience, I organized a festival in Volgograd called 'Unidentified Traffic,' a gathering of poets, musicians, film makers, painters—their work shown in direct confrontation with official Soviet art. This festival has been held in Volgograd for five years now, but each time we've presented it, we've had to fight for it, to struggle. Full awareness, and recognition, in this country has been repressed, forbidden, for so long that any change will be long in coming."

He gave me a dictionary he'd compiled of thieves' jargon, prison slang, and words the younger generation finds hip. Some crisp phonetically interesting substitutions for standard phrases were *bombit* ("to be sexually active"; also, "to rob somebody"), *chernukha* ("to see everything as black; nothing is good; everything is shit"), *deshevka* ("more crap"), *fuflo* ("phoney, good-for-nothing, rubbish, trash"), *ne v kipish* for *bez shuma, spokoino* ("without noise, peaceful"), *skhavat* ("to believe, or buy into, all this crap"), and *zona* for *mectozakliucheniia* ("place of imprisonment"). I wasn't surprised by how negative these expressions were. The same feeling is present in nearly all of Sergei Karsaev's poems:

> Not to read, nor write — but to contemplate, contemplate
> the cleansing light beyond the factory buildings;
> no one to love, nothing to desire or wish for.

This poem and others depict stark images of sliding, melting glass, "drops of singing metal," "the steppe senselessly flowing on," August turning from side to side "like sluggish water," an old man "chewing on his colorless lips," his house dying "amidst the compost heaps."

> We all share limited time, without remission.
> Even this corroding fruit is cast down
> by one who will judge, will teach us a lesson.

Another poem, "1990" (with the epigraph "My God! My God! Why have you forsaken me?"), states the same grim feelings:

> My thoughts aslant, like ants, creep aimlessly . . .
> > my heart splashes
> in sulfurous and hunchbacked streams
> to the sly music of a Judas on piano.

I received a letter from Karsaev after I returned to California.

Greetings, Mr. Minor!
   This is very disturbing, very strange, that I am writing to you. Why? This is the first letter I have ever written to an American artist, a poet. Your book *Poet Santa Cruz* was given to me by Nikolai Dmitriev, the editor of *Dzhaz* magazine.
   Just now I am glancing out the window in Volgograd. Beyond my mind a bird is singing in a brilliantly colored elm tree. Somewhere

further in the distance the sour nasal tone of a motor is distorting the air and street urchins are fighting in the garbage pits. The factories fill the air with ugly sound, yet in the distance grasshoppers and gophers make their own chatter of more pleasant noise. The steppe is roaring, and I think to myself:

Five years ago I could not even imagine that I would ever be able to break loose from the confines of Orkestrion and Volgograd. Even in a letter. And all the more a letter to California, in the USA. I have seen photographs of the California landscape and the towns and cities. Mentally, they appeared to me like photographs of the moon, *its* fields and craters. So now, writing to you, I still have the feeling that I am writing a letter to the moon. . . .

In our Soviet press they write that in the USA no one is interested in poetry, but I do not believe this. Some sort of small circle of both experts and fans must exist in *any* country. Otherwise, humanity has failed completely and we, truly, have descended to the rank of wild animals. But then I think, this American I have met has read the poet Osip Mandelstam, who, at this time in Russia, only a very few people know about. And this fact, to me, confirms the indestructability of the poetic word. With hope of an answer. . . .

Sergei Karsaev

London record producer Leo
Feigin (Ralf Emmerich)

Igor Butman, of Boston
(Karen Klitgaard)

*The Ganelin Trio with Steve Boulay, 1987.* Left to right: *Vladimir Tarasov, Boulay, Vyacheslav Ganelin, Vladimir Chekasin (courtesy of Steve Boulay)*

*Leningrad critic Alexander Kahn — beard, hands on waist — with American composer John Cage (Anatoli Syagin)*

*"The Bear from Bulgaria,"
Anatoli Vapirov (Niklaus
Strauss)*

*Leningrad pianist Sergei
Kuryokhin (Andrei Ussov)*

David Friesen, performing on "Oregon
Bass," 1983 tour of the Soviet Union
(courtesy of David Friesen)

"The Belle of Baku," Aziza Mustafa-
Zadeh (Konstantin Kokhreidze)

*The ROVA Saxophone Quartet.* Left to right: *Jon Raskin, Steve Adams, Bruce Ackley, Larry Ochs (Matthew Goldberg)*

*Jazz group Arkhangelsk (Bert Noglik)*

*Irina Novikova — ninth from far right — as dancer with Eddie Rosner's review (courtesy of Irina Novikova)*

*Paquito D'Rivera, Germann
Lukianov, Dizzy Gillespie;
concert in Moscow, spring
1990 (courtesy of Germann
Lukianov)*

*Eddie Rosner's Orchestra, the
leader — with trumpet — out
front (courtesy of Irina
Novikova)*

*Arkadi Shilkloper (Hans Kumpf)*

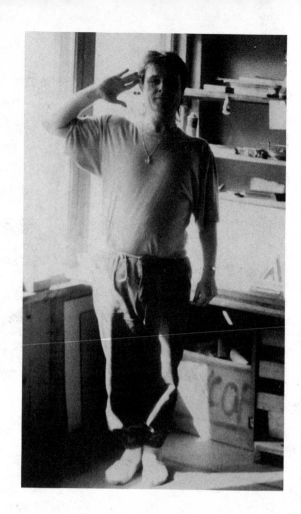

*Yuri Kuznetsov, saluting in studio of his friend Vasya (photo by author)*

*Interior of Germann Lukianov's apartment in Moscow (photo by author)*

*Petras Vysniauskas (Raimondas Urbakavičius)*

*Luda Stepchenko serving Ukrainian meal, in Odessa.* Left to right: *Vasya Stepchenko; Luda; Yuri Kuznetsov's wife, Lena; Yuri;* and *Olya (photo by author)*

Sainko Namchylak, "throat singer" from Tuva (Alexander Zabrin)

Yelena Chashchina, of Orkestrion, laughing in her "cage" (Leonid Toprover)

*Sergei Karsaev (with bull horn), Ravil Azizov, and Orkestrion's instruments (S. Bolotin)*

*Richie Cole with,* left to right,
*Boris Kuzlov, Andrei Ryabov,*
*Andrei Kondakov (courtesy of*
*Andrei Kondakov)*

*David Azarian, Armenian pianist now living in Boston (Herb Snitzer)*

*The Jazznost Quartet. Left to right: Louis Scherr, Sergei Gurbeloshvili, Viktor Dvoskin, Tony Martucci (Sandra Rodger)*

*Georgian bassist Tamaz*
*Kurashvili performing with*
*American pianist Sun Ra*
*(Konstantin Kokhreidze)*

*Poster advertising*
*Starptautiskais Jazz Festival*
*in Riga (artist, R. Liepins;*
*courtesy of Anthony Marhel*
*and Leonid Nidbalsky)*

*Pianist Mikhail Okun*
*(Konstantin Kokhreidze)*

# "Man,
# He Is
# the Best!"

Looking for apartment sixty-seven, we entered the wrong end of a building on Kazakov Street and — after the lift went dead on the second floor — found ourselves ascending a grim flight of stairs that also died. We stood on one of those abandoned warehouse landings where (complete with bolted giant rusting metal doors) film murders — and maybe real ones for all I know — are likely to take place in America. But this wasn't America. This was Moscow where, if at first you don't succeed (and chances are you won't), you go back down and try again. A sort of grim fatalism sets in. Perhaps the *next turn* will be the right one.

And it was, in spite of the lumber stacked in the hall, along with other assorted constructional debris. Irene (my interpreter grown invaluable sidekick), Betty, and I arrived at yet another of those thickly padded doors that, once opened, free you from the external world, disclosing a private magical kingdom within, in this case, the apartment of Germann Lukianov — composer, arranger, master instrumentalist (trumpet, flugelhorn, and piano), and, as I would discover, poet.

I had first heard Lukianov on record, as I had so many other Soviet artists: the Mobile Fidelity CD that featured his group, Kadans (the Moscow Chamber Jazz Ensemble), just about the most polished, precise, original mainstream group I'd come across. I'd spotted Lukianov sitting on a couch after one of the festival concerts, made my pitch for an interview, and received instead this invitation to his *dom*, or home.

Following the customary effusive Russian greetings, we were ushered past a cubbyhole kitchen and closet bathroom into a dining room that, though small, did not seem that way. The ceiling was high, and light fell on a large glass case that housed books, photos, ceramic plates, handsomely adorned

cups, and other Russian art objects—varnished wood toys, animal stick figures. The room resembled an intimate museum of Lukianov's life. Rows of
hand-decorated cutting boards, old clocks, and a hand-carved wooden frame
hung on one wall. The glow from a pale-fringed umbrella lamp merged with
the day's light as we were directed to a table covered with a checkered cloth on
which tomatoes, onions, cucumbers, and cognac had been arranged.

This is the interior world of Germann Lukianov and—somewhat formal,
somber, elevated—it matched our host: a handsome man with fine soft features, a strict mouth, if professorial (wearing horn-rimmed glasses), professorial emeritus with dignity of pride not age. He was dressed in a striped
shirt and maroon tie; not casual at-home clothes by any means for, as we soon
found out, he was anticipating a film director I had also been introduced to the
previous evening, and a camera crew, who were to film a documentary on
Lukianov in his home, a documentary in which—apparently—we had a small
part.

"Have you ever been a film star before?" Irene asked, leaning over to me.

"No," I replied—which wasn't entirely true, for I had once been included
in about five seconds' worth (my wife claims about half a second) of a dreadful
film my cousin Max Gail, the former Wojo of the *Barney Miller* TV show, made
with Lindsay Wagner, myself cheering in a crowd scene. But, here in Moscow,
I didn't want to fulfill any stereotypes about every American's having appeared
in at least one Hollywood production at some time or other in his or her life.

I couldn't help thinking that—American stereotypes aside and in spite of
the hard life many jazz musicians lead—an artist of Lukianov's stature would
probably be living on a farm in upstate New York, or in a stately refurbished
Victorian in San Francisco—but I was learning that it's futile to attempt this
sort of comparison, that Moscow has its own laws of survival. We were introduced to Lukianov's wife, Inna, an appropriate counterpart, somewhat somber, elevated herself, possessing that hint of sensuality combined with substan-
tiality, durability laced with grace (someone you want by your side when the
bombs fall or you are overwhelmed with the need for a good sturdy embrace)
that seems characteristic of many Russian women—and her sister. We also met
a large German shepherd, a dog about whom Lukianov has written a poem,
brief—as all, or most all, of his are:

> For eight years
> in my house a dog has lived
> daily
> granting me
> small lessons in kindness.

Two others he read to me seem even more like haiku: "Here comes Spring
again / that lonely attempt / to try on joy"; and "Such tenderness in the soul of

Spring / It wants / to pet insects" — the word *stroke* or *pet* a play on *glasit* (say or announce), as in *glasnost*.

We had *glasnost* galore that afternoon, in the term's literal sense of "publicity" perhaps. Once we had been seated at the table as satellites, it was clear that all subsequent events would be orchestrated by Lukianov, who remained proud, eager, and slightly imperious in an eccentric manner that I liked. He informed us that we must eat and drink right away, for the director would be arriving at any minute. Consequently, the interview I had also come for was packed in amongst considerable activity, such as chomping on food. Lukianov answered questions urbanely while he ate ravenously, encouraging me to do the same ("Eat! Eat!"). He launched into an autobiographical monologue that included the poetry of his stepfather, Vladimir Burich, a man who at times worked in a style similar to his own:

> Just as my face grew accustomed
> to being shaved,
> it was time to die.

Or this poem about Louis Armstrong:

> Black archangel
> who prophesized the decline of the harp
>
> Prometheus
> chained to a trumpet.

Lukianov told me that his mother, a playwright, had just returned from Paris. When she had first discovered that her son was taking up jazz, she had protested that it was "not a serious thing for a man to do," even though she was a conservatory graduate and had once played in a dance orchestra herself "just for the experience." Apparently at this point I was falling behind in my masticatory chores for Lukianov — relating the moment to "free verse," a form, like jazz, not previously "accepted" in the Soviet Union, "but now everything is changing so fast" — said, "*You* too must do everything fast here," advice I noticed Irene was taking to heart, snatching first the tomato, then the piece of fine black bread I had been contemplating for some time. "Any more questions?" he asked, his posture erect, haughty in a charming way. "They live like nineteenth-century Russian aristocrats," another foreign visitor would say that afternoon.

Munching fast, glancing at my notes, I asked Lukianov about his studies with Aram Khachaturian and about his refusal to leave Moscow in 1960 to accept an assigned, and distant, musical post. Although he did not choose to talk about this, the decision apparently cost him his degree from the conservatory. He told me he "took to jazz" at the age of twelve, a "secret love affair," having first heard the music on a gramophone at ten. Even though the music was illegal, he "couldn't help listening." Lacking records, he listened by telephone at night; a friend placed the receiver near the radio while an enthralled Lukianov caught Voice of America broadcasts at the other end. Launched into his life now, yet recalling events nearly as if reading from a script, he told me (once we discovered that we were both born in 1936) that because his mother loved Pushkin, when his own birth was delayed, she named him in honor of that rapscallion who, in Pushkin's "Queen of Spades," shows up late for a midnight assignation with his lover. "Germann hasn't shown," the doctor told Lukianov's mother shortly after midnight on the evening he finally did arrive, and the name stuck.

He went to a large glass case and removed a picture of himself standing on stage with Dizzy Gillespie. I felt his pride by the way he handed it to me. "An old man," Lukianov said, "but interested in everything; he keeps his eyes open." Later, he would read two more of his own poems related to age: "Old men sitting in the public garden / discussing art as friend to friend / awaiting, patiently, their deaths"; and "The village elder, so impoverished / he has not a thing to wear / but his governmental decorations." The photograph depicts Lukianov showing Gillespie a trumpet mouthpiece he fashioned himself (certainly an act of necessity, given the dearth of Soviet musical supplies) and Gillespie apparently amazed by the artistry.

Lukianov then expressed surprise that, for as long as Russians have been interested in the American contribution, and its development "We now have Americans interested in Russian jazz." I told him I was interested not only in jazz in the USSR but in its literature as well, and that I taught it. I mentioned the connection I had been exploring between the work of young avant-garde pianist Sergei Kuryokhin and the 1920s absurdist writing of someone like Daniil Kharms. Although Lukianov said that Kuryokhin was not his "cup of tea," and I could not pin him down on any direct connection between that time and present music, we discovered that we both love Kharms.

"Ahhhh!" he said. "You have his complete works?" Not all of this author, still, is available in the Soviet Union. He seemed disappointed when I said I did not, as if he hoped that somewhere, somehow, someone did.

The doorbell rang, and the first of the Tele-Film people arrived. "Now we have many new organizations or agencies," Lukianov said. I exploited the ensuing surge of hospitality and confusion to take (with Lukianov's permission) some snapshots of their handsome apartment before the documentary took over. Lukianov's small study has a black baby grand piano in one corner, many scores and charts on its rack, and his flugelhorn nearby, along with a metronome and innumerable (handmade, I assumed) mouthpieces. The room is inviting, muted by subdued light, a pastel soft and somber Vuillard flavor, a decidedly nineteenth-century ambience: a writing desk littered with poems and correspondence, a chair with delicate arms, a baroque wrought-iron-framed mirror, a luxuriant couch and scalloped lamp, heavy crimson drapes, and a tall stolid grandfather's clock—all this was watched by a wall on which a stunning gold icon, a chalk-white desk mask of Pushkin, and a dark metal crucifix stood.

Another wall held several paintings by the once forbidden artist Anatoli Zverev, who believed in a "short and concentrated act of volition, the brush . . . allowed to follow the path prompted by the artist's innermost powers of perception," according to *Soviet Art in Exile*—like Lukianov's music, a dangerous approach at one time in the USSR. I thought of the sharp distinction Russians make between interior freedom, or life, and whatever may lie without. This apartment was a sanctuary of various arts; installed inside, I could barely recall the tawdry hallway, with its residue of lumber and construction materials, we had passed through on our way to reach it.

When I returned to the dining room more guests had arrived: an artist with dark Georgian features and Pawel Brodowski, editor of *Jazz Forum* magazine in Poland. Lukianov remained cool in spite of the domestic bustle and official busyness. Nothing seemed to deter him for, no matter where he sat or stood, he remained the center of attention, his scenario of remembrances, once I touched on a particular date—"You know more about me than I know about myself!" he exclaimed—continuing to roll, and just about the time the cameras started.

In 1978, Alex Filokovsky, the deputy minister of culture, decided to organize groups for special tours, and Lukianov's Kadans was one. Up to that time, according to Lukianov, anyone who played jazz had strictly amateur status. With the right to play regular concerts, the word *jazzman* appeared, and "new professionalism" along with it, he said. I mentioned the First Moscow International Jazz Festival, and Lukianov commented that not until seventy years after the revolution had this sort of "special cultural" event been arranged. He reflected on how difficult it had been for jazz to arrive at official status "in this country, even now," yet called the process "irreversible," especially in light of "our new situation."

"Now that jazz has become official, Soviet musical circles do have a new dimension of freedom, a new level. We have had so-called international festivals before—in Tallinn as early as 1967, for example—and it was a mark of Estonia's independence that they could hold such an event without official approval, but as a result, many of the city's leaders were sacked, and such a festival never occurred there again. An important event was the first international festival held in Georgia last year, an event at which many Americans— Freddie Hubbard, Jimmy Smith, Sun Ra—appeared for the first time. A very powerful festival—but that was Georgia. Everybody was still watching Moscow. And now, finally, Moscow has gone ahead with this labor of love, and we are starting a new life."

"Jazz is the sort of art that is doomed to suffer a lot," he continued. "Not only here but in the United States as well. I think musicians who play jazz have to pay a price for the freedom they have in their improvisations, for that form of self-expression. They *must* pay for it."

"That's why we have the blues," I said.

"Well, the blues come from blacks because they suffered in chains," Lukianov responded, "in slavery, and later in segregation. Whites could never have introduced the blues. But the blues is like a contagious disease. Now whites share the same destiny. It's no secret that jazz musicians have more personal problems in life, and challenges, than, say, a classical pianist. The situation is the same here."

When I mentioned pianist Igor Bril's notion of a universal musical language as opposed to national musics, Lukianov frowned. "That's a very difficult issue. The language of jazz *is* an international language, no doubt, because of its universal influence, or effect, on people. Yet at the same time there is no denying the existence of national elements, a unique way of life or a mentality. We *begin* with a different musical language. These languages *do* differ from one country to another. That's why I've always been optimistic about the development of jazz in this country, because in spite of all the differences, such as the great distance that separates the Soviet Union from the center of jazz . . . you know, we have a joke about how you can calculate a nation's distance from that center. You take any three clubs in New York and you will have a triangle; the center of that triangle is the center of jazz and the further a country is from that the more difficult it is for its musicians to play jazz . . . but this is not just a joke. How difficult to imagine, for instance, that Portugal or Spain will produce a great hockey player. But it is not at all difficult to imagine these countries producing a fine guitarist. Because that fits."

He never really finished his thought on the "optimism" he felt about the development of jazz in the USSR, but Irene now said, "Scratch every other American and you will find a Russian."

I asked Lukianov what aspects of jazz in the Soviet Union were unique to that culture.

"Everything!" he said.

Camera rolling intermittently—distracting me but not Lukianov; just how much of this was intended to be documentary and how much not, I wondered, but perhaps that was the whole point—Lukianov described the task he had set himself as a young man: of finding, as a beginner, his own jazz "voice." I made the mistake of saying that I had read about his coming to the United States soon, and all hell broke loose, for Lukianov had had no word of any such plan or possibility. The mistake—unpardonable in the eyes of a

Soviet musician, so large is their desire to play with world-class musicians —
was mine. Lukianov sprang from his seat waving his arms, pacing the floor in
consternation, shouting to Irene who conveyed the question to me. "Where,
where, *where* did you read that?" I had read it on the liner notes of Lukianov's
American, Mobile Fidelity, CD, where the Soviet bassist Viktor Dvoskin had
been quoted as saying — but only in reference to the recording — "Man, he is
the best! America, get ready for something fantastic." There was little I could
do to repair the damage. When things settled down, he smiled wistfully and
said, "Let's wish the best for the Germann Lukianov who *is* going," adding that
he would like to visit America but only to play, not as a tourist.

"If I was as smart as Sergei Kuryokhin," he said, "I would have visited the
U.S. many times already."

He gave me an anthology, *Vremya IKC* (literally, "Time X"), that contains
twelve of his poems and signed it, "In the hope that you will come to stay, for
good, in Russia." He added a generous hand-typed sheath of thirty, which, he
said, were "different from what you will find in the book," and a small collection by his stepfather, Burich.

"I think you must open a museum when you get back," Irene said.

All of Lukianov's thoughts had been delivered to me — and the tape recorder I had running, my own minidocumentary — amidst more arrivals, the
most significant of which was the director himself, although his camera oper-
ator had gone to work long before. I noticed that Lukianov, not a large
man really, was becoming so. This was *his* day, and he was growing a shade
pompous perhaps, pontifical with it, but in a somewhat whimsical, charming
way — shades of Daniil Kharms? — that did not bother me, although I could
see that, across the table, in Irene's eyes, a more negative response was taking
place. The others, as Lukianov held court, became audience. When he read
two short poems — moving poems in their quiet way — about life in the Soviet
Union, Irene's eyes softened, and she said, "So many innocent people per-
ished, and they started with fingerprints."

> How well I know
> this time
> of half-life
> in my country.
>
> My native land, I am yours
> from the tip of my hair
> down to my fingerprints.

"When Stalin died in 1953," Irene said after the reading, "he was buried
with Lenin. Then he was put in the Kremlin Wall and now we want him taken
out, for that wall is a special place of honor." An excited discussion, in rapid

Russian, followed—everyone, including Pawel Brodowski, joined in, but I could not follow much of it. My own feelings got spun up with what was going on around and outside them, and they in turn became meshed with images I imagined being recorded on camera, until that solid Russian distinction between inner and outer no longer seemed to exist and I, looking over Lukianov's shoulder as he read, found myself treading water in a world of small strange—haiku in Moscow!—poetry.

Germann Lukianov is the only Russian poet I've ever heard actually read. Most say or recite their work direct from the *serdtse,* the heart. Lukianov's wife had pointed to another of Zverov's paintings, saying, "Do you recognize me when you look at this portrait?" To which I replied, "Of course, because of the beauty there!" You can get away with this sort of thing in Russian, a language much geared to aesthetic compliments, as the poem Lukianov was reading testifies:

> Beautiful woman
> It's as if you were aging gracefully
> in my very own hands.

I never did satisfy my curiosity about his musical compositional techniques, whether his "Ivanushka the Fool" was based directly on the Russian fairy tale, conceived as a story in itself, or merely "C major, only music," as Alexei Batashev had insisted. Before Lukianov set about the filmed reading of more poems, we nevertheless managed to discuss everything from the Ganelin Trio ("I don't like them," he said, "they lack the most important element in music: fantasy, mystery. Their sort of freedom is a very good thing in free verse or poetry, but brings only chaos in music"); freedom in the arts in general (Pawel Brodowski said that "free artists should be free to do anything," a contention Lukianov did not agree with); and what I felt had been pianist Leonid Chizhik's unpleasant, skating-rink-loud, disjointed, tacky, performance the previous night at the festival.

"Perhaps he was trying to find a new conception," Lukianov said, "a conception he felt people at the festival would like. Every musician is supposed to have his own conception. Yet if you do, it's hard for you to play with anyone else." Lukianov told me that Chizhik, accused once of being "too eclectic," had merely smiled and replied, "It's called 'poly-stylistic.'"

When I responded to this, employing the term *jazz,* both Lukianov and Irene laughed at the way I used that most American of words.

Irene said, "Americans are great experts on jazz, but you have a very strange way of pronouncing it."

"It should be *dzhaz,* not *jac!*" said Lukianov.

Of the American groups that had performed at the festival so far, Lukia-

nov liked Buster Williams's quartet best — their carefully worked-out pieces —
in spite of the absence of the group's piano player. One possibility, someone
said, was that his body might one day be found floating in the Moskva River.

On this cheery note the formal documentary began. Lukianov squared his
shoulders, adjusted his tie, smoothed his hair, and while the camera went to
work again, read — in a soft, sonorous, but appropriately crisp when necessary
tone — more poems, those about jazz having the most immediate interest to
me:

> Not lightly, the piano perks up at night
> an old man with numb legs folded
> slunk, every strained nerve
> aware of age
>
> At dawn only, the piano finally falls
> asleep, and dreams
> of a large black whale
> aswim in a sea of eyes and ears.
>
>       Jazz
> The sounds compressed
> honed small
> searching for their place
> in time —
> pagan idolators who worship clocks
>
> The scream of the swan
> repeated, intensified
> through the bell of a sax
> a philosopher's dance
> the lame would learn by rote
>
> This piano, black elephant
> standing on three legs
> just as it was trained to do
> by the force of ten fingers —
> a clown's giveaway laughter
>
> The artist's copyright
> released to the air
> infinitesimal thoughts resounding
> through a microphone
> mute
> song sung for the mute only.

After the meal and the documentary had been consumed, consummated, along with a good share of fine Moldavian cognac, we drove to the Variety Theater in Lukianov's spotless, sporty, Jeep-sized red car. Ready to perform on stage at the festival that evening, he talked about jazz as "a powerful means of expression," of its "difficult means of acquiring harmony." He mentioned the original compositions he intended to play that evening, saying that I could judge for myself — since I had asked him this question earlier but not received an answer — whether or not Soviet jazz was equal to jazz in the United States. He mentioned a critic who had said that jazz in the USSR was "fifteen years behind that of the rest of the world," and he cited the many "flaws" he felt he'd encountered in the playing of American musicians at the nightly jam sessions after the concerts — how surprised he had been to find these weaknesses; how poorly, at times, he felt these people played. He spoke of drummers who receive undeserved applause from a Soviet audience just because they are black and from the United States. "Where are the masters? Are these really the best musicians the U.S. has to offer?"

"Americans smile a lot, are very polite," he continued, "and by comparison, we Russians don't have good manners. But many of the American musicians I have encountered at the festival are like people who must elbow their way through a crowd."

He spoke in particular of Valery Ponomarev, an émigré who had "made it" in the United States with Art Blakey's Jazz Messengers. He was regarded in some circles as the festival's returning hero; British critic Mike Hennessey later wrote, "Some moments to remember . . . Valery Ponomarev, after 17 years in voluntary exile in the United States, was reunited with his family in the Moscow apartment of his mother, Ludmilla." But many of the Soviet musicians I talked to viewed him as — freely translated — "a conceited demigod."

Lukianov thought Ponomarev now "more American than Russian" by virtue of his willingness to push musicians off the stage. One night, according to several reliable sources, Ponomarev and highly respected pianist Mikhail Okun nearly got into a brawl when Okun told Ponomarev during one of the jam sessions that he was playing off the wrong chord. Ponomarev exploded. "I didn't come back after all these years to have *you* tell me what to play!" — Okun retaliating with, "Then get out of here!" Lukianov has concluded that, in the arts in America, one does not really become known "through talent so much as elbowing" — an observation that I have often found hard to refute.

"Critics are fools," he said. This was another position that I, too often, and occasionally passing for one, find difficult to deny. "And that is why we see musicians who are not really the best being called the best."

We parked in front of the Variety Theater, the spiffy little car and its occupants attracting considerable attention. Lukianov headed indoors for a sound check and warm-up as we remained behind, thanking his wife for the afternoon meal. She was attracting some attention on her own, striking in her shimmering silver lamé open-collar blouse, black hair pulled back and offset by large silver pendant earrings.

I'm not sure Kadans was at its best that night — at least not at the start. Lukianov's compositions are intricate and demanding: precise, low key, nearly logical at their core, as in his recording of "Three Blues," a suite more cool than blue perhaps, featuring appropriate ghost-note economy by way of Lukianov's trumpet on "Miles Davis"; trombonist Vadim Akhmetgareev, not a saxophonist, paying homage on "John Coltrane"; the entire group providing apt — clean and consigned — Afro-Cuban carnival flare on "Dizzy Gillespie." Over the years this group, like Art Blakey's Jazz Messengers, has fostered and featured some of the best performers: trombonist Vadim Akhmetgareev, alto saxophonist Yuri Yuperkov, tenor saxophonist Nikolai Panov, Mikhail Okun on piano. It has provided some of the more distinguished and imaginative mainstream jazz to emerge in the USSR, reminiscent of the better groups in the United States — that of Benny Golson, for example, an instrumentalist/composer with whom Lukianov invites favorable comparison. Lukianov's "Ivanushka the Fool" is a masterpiece, recreating an old Russian fairy tale about a man who feeds dumplings to his own shadow. The opening percussive tocking evokes the sounds of spoons in a sack slung over Ivanushka's shoulder — the plaintive horn work and lurch and stomp polyphony perfect, plus the mischievous drumming. Critic Vladimir Feyertag would later tell me that he feels Lukianov "could be a brilliant improviser, but he stifles his abilities with a rigid structural approach, falling victim to his own dogmas." Still, there's little denying the strength, charm, and swing of these original compositions.

As leader of Kadans that night, Lukianov was very much the Lukianov of the afternoon: formal, exacting, sophisticated, playing headmaster to what seemed a young, too young — somewhat stiff, businesslike — group. They lined up behind music racks that created an unfortunate schoolroom atmosphere, playing from charts: the drummer working too obviously to keep up with the rest of the band; Professor Germann's own fine flugelhorn work spare, tasteful, muted, like his poems. Some Salsa–West Coast sprightliness ran flat — the players seemed to be nearly reading their solos — until Lukianov's "Carmen" sequence took off with his handsome trumpet statements on Bizet's handsome themes and some thoughtful polyphony. Then Lukianov switched to piano and inspired the group with his genuine fire and rhythmic drive. A man sitting next to my wife began to snap his fingers in time. The drummer and alto sax man shed whatever confining text they'd been clinging to, and the audience responded immediately with one of those odd but apt Russian compliments, *"Molodets! Molodets!"* (Well done! but literally, Fine fellow! Good boy!). The group came alive, Lukianov swaying his patrician head in time, smiling, the soul of Kadans truly unzipped now (*dusha nara-spashku*), a fitting close to my day with Germann Lukianov.

# The
# Last
# Supper

On the night of June 3, Chico Freeman's group, Brainstorm, represented the United States handsomely. Freeman himself was quite popular with the Soviet audience, someone calling out, "Home boy!" and Freeman crying back, "Yeah!" He also won people over with his music, looping swirls of sound, a capella, on "No Greater Love," then taking it to a fine swing tempo that got the crowd clapping in unison. A tune with a hot Jamaican jump to it and Freeman chanting, "Take a trip, take a trip" seemed to take people just where they wished to go—reality brought home at the end by, "Exotic places . . . Moscow, Moscow, Moscow." (He endeared himself to the audience forever on the next night, playing with The Leaders, by tossing t-shirts to the crowd.)

Moscow had started to feel like home to me, and I found myself merging not only with the fine musical offerings but with the crowd that strolled the foyer at intermission time. A Soviet jazz crowd seems far less casual, more sober, and more sophisticated in appearance than its American counterpart. Alexander Zabrin had an exhibit of handsome photographs at the far end of a lounge just outside the concert hall. Its other walls were filled with paintings whose styles ranged from 1920s surrealism to 1950s abstract expressionism, all contemporary, as far as I could tell, and well executed if not exactly groundbreaking. Portions of the jazz crowd studied these paintings with great interest; others seemed to simply cruise by them. The men were dressed fairly casually, the women stylish with a vengeance. There's something about the face of a male Russian intellectual that sets him apart from his countrymen, although I'm not positive I could verify this by a street test. Among the women I saw Greek *kores* with giant circular earrings and oversized nearly transparent sweaters; tall, balletic types with handsomely arched backs and endless necks; women in elegant blue-black dresses that cost about ninety-five rubles — a goodly portion of the average monthly salary. One young woman sported a black jersey that read "THE END."

The music continued to provide the same variety and surprise. That afternoon, back in the Dom Komposoriterov hall, I heard a pianist who should have appeared on the main stage. This was Igor Nazaruk, whom I'd heard backing guitarist Alexei Kuznetsov on his East Wind album. Nazaruk now played "Love for Sale," subtle plinking converted to imaginative chord sequences, followed by lovely impressionist passages — this skillful use of dynamics a trademark of the best Soviet pianists. Nazaruk has it all: an amazing rapid-fire right hand, a stunning left that he employs often, not as an afterthought but as a mate, his light dancing treble held aloft by strong, steady chords. Like the work of Mikhail Okun, this union creates the impression of commanding intelligence and taste, technique employed in the service of jazz expression. Nazaruk rubbed his accomplished hands together at the end, deservedly pleased.

The pianist compares improvisation to "flight"; not "cheap romanticism" but "a minute of natural flight for which people risked their lives, a natural flight over the Olympus of the eighty-eight gods." French critic Francis Fremier, hearing Nazaruk play, once said, "If I didn't know this was the twentieth century, I would think Liszt was playing!" The pianist himself says, "Haven't we all come to the conclusion after a thousand years of musical history, that the height of it all is revelation: the eternal, invaluable human prayers to one's neighbors?" Nazaruk cites as peers Michelangelo, jazz guitarist John McLaughlin, pianist Chick Corea, and Soviet composer Alfred Schnitke. At last I had found at least one pianist with acknowledged roots in the recent Russian classical avant-garde, and also one who could match his penchant for high-flown rhetoric with fully realized musical effects.

On the other hand, I was disappointed in a performance by the avant-garde group Arkhangelsk on the main stage at the State Variety Theater. Leo Feigin claims Western critics misjudge this group because they have no conception of what it's like to play in a cold and ungodly place night after night for drunken sailors who dance with one another — but I once played keyboards with a rock group called the Salty Dogs in Jaynesville, Wisconsin, where — I'd be willing to bet — even the weather conditions just might not be all that dissimilar. The night I saw Arkhangelsk they sat in a circle on the stage floor and chanted. I was hard pressed to decide whether this was because that's who they are, or whether they were scared to go up against the likes of Chico Freeman on real instruments.

Once again, as in the case with Boomerang and Leonid Chizhik, I found myself preferring a recorded experience to an actual one. Arkhangelsk's "Above the Sun, below the Moon" (39:55 on Leo Records's *Document: New Music from Russia*) draws you into their world almost against your will by means of little sounds, a capella alto sax fragments, rattling, and scratching until you cannot extricate yourself, nor do you care to. The means of evoking this bitter northern ambiance are conventional to new music: a solitary note fading in and out of a continuous discomforting surface, repetition devoid of increment, flute sounds interwoven with arctic wails, parsimonious conga pats, lackadaisical arco bass, cymbal washes, the silence of cold space, rich classical piano, a congress of small sounds building to cacophony—all brilliantly put together. You wouldn't want to live there, but you have, through the music.

I fell in love with the delightful Irina Vorontsova the instant I laid eyes on her. Her face is round above Tatar cheekbones (an ancestry of which she is proud), framed by long hair, with unzipped dark eyes beneath handsomely arched eyebrows, a small pug nose, and a generous mouth. My meeting her came about by chance. I had shown Irene a booklet of photographs my son Stephen took of my woodblock prints and paintings of Russian poems, the text included in each work. Irene was interested in my having chosen poems by Anna Akhmatova and Osip Mandelstam, for she had a friend who'd set their work to music, he an excellent composer, his wife a famous singer. She arranged for us to meet them.

Neither Irina Vorontsova nor her husband, Igor Egikov, speaks English, so we relied mostly on Irina's cheerful disposition and devastating smile to convey the meaning of her brilliant chatter as we set out, packed into their small car, on a grand excursion to a Moscow we would otherwise never have known. Our first stop was the Moscow Monastery of St. Daniel, a large complex designated only by an open green field and small black cross on my Baedeker's map of Moscow. It is the city's oldest monastery, built in 1282 by the Orthodox prince St. Danelil, son of Alexander Nevsky, and now the spiritual and administrative center of the Russian Orthodox Church.

"I am a Christian," Irina said to me, smiling, as we entered a chapel where she lit a candle.

Portions of the monastery were closed—nothing ever seems completely open in Moscow—but we paid our respects to what was available, then left to their business the thirty monks and novices who now inhabit the site. Outside, Igor replaced the windshield wipers he had removed for safekeeping, even in the parking lot of a Moscow monastery. We drove in a light drizzle to the fifteenth-century Novospasky Monastery (New Monastery of the Transfiguration of the Savior) not far away, on Krutitsy Hill just above the curl of the Moscow River leading out of town—a splendid gray stone church with green trim that rises to a spire instead of to the customary Orthodox onion dome. In spite of the drizzle, we strolled the monastery grounds, Irina singing Bulat Okudzhava songs at my request, and sauntered down paths strewn with leaves, which she handed me, from fragrant lime trees. Igor was cheerfully reticent. A pupil of Aram Khachaturian, as Germann Lukianov had been, he specializes in writing music for his wife. According to a review in the *Boston Globe* when the couple performed in this country, he is interested "in finding a new direction for music, a third stream, that would reconcile serious classical music with popular idioms." The *Globe* referred to "the vibrant Vorontsova, a world class cabaret singer," as a woman who talks with her eyes. She does, so I listened.

Outside the monastery we sat in the car and drank fine Georgian wine they had given us as a gift along with a large poster announcing "Dvoe i Pecnia" ("Two in Song," the name of an album they also gave me), an evening of *pecni, romansy, ballady* (songs, romances, ballads) and poems by Anna Akhmatova, Bulat Okudzhava, Marina Tsvetaeva set to music. We had insisted on sharing the wine there and then, Igor acquiring a glass, our loving cup, from one of those vile *gazirovannaia voda* vending machines (mineral water dispensed in cups that everyone shares, a highly suspicious rinsing device also provided). We chatted and joked, exchanging pictures of respective families, discussed art and music and life and all things under the sun as best we could with what we had by way of mutual language. Then it was time for our return to the Variety Theater for the jazz festival's final concert.

Before we reached the theater I learned that the couple was close friends with poet/songwriter Bulat Okudzhava, and that, were Betty and I not leaving Moscow in the morning, they would have been happy to have arranged a meeting with him. I kicked myself for not having met Igor and Irina sooner (Okudzhava is one of my musical heroes), but, saying goodbye, I felt fortunate for having spent as much time with them as we did.


Irene accompanied me to a press conference on the festival's last day. I wanted to make sure I got a word-by-word translation of what I knew was going to be an interesting proceeding. Irene had grown invaluable as both an interpreter and a friend who provided humor and insight into this strange new world into which I had plunged. Her frank opinions and honesty had become a source of delight to me. Her views ranged from a conviction that Lenin should be removed from his fancy mausoleum and stuck in the ground (where his wife, Krupskaya, wanted him in the first place, she said) to describing as "tacky" the brides I'd found so charming, who stroll around Moscow in full wedding dress with their entourages. "It just shows they're low class, from working-class families."

Yet, for all her intelligentsia airs, Irene was down-to-earth. When one of the musicians we were to interview showed up two hours late, she shocked me by berating me afterward. "Let me tell you something, Mr. American," she hissed. "And *remember* this: one does not ever waste two hours of a Moscow woman's time, *ever*—do you understand?" I understood. And I also understood that—in spite of the prestige her job at the University of Moscow might provide, and her husband's being a distinguished scientist who lectured in the West—Irene was not exempt from standing in line for a single chicken, that "waste" that takes up so much of a Moscow woman's time.

"If you print this book of yours when you get back," she said to me one day, "I'll probably end up in prison." But that didn't stop her from immediately offering another outrageous opinion on affairs of state. I forget just what it was, but I recall that we were driving to the State Variety Theater past graffiti scrawled on a wall: "Ilya and Olya = LOVE." These two citizens, probably very young, had managed, for the precious moments it took them to write this, to outwit or forestall the ever present *byt* (daily round, everyday existence) that circumscribes their lives—just as Irene seemed to do every day.

So here I was, seated with my sidekick, awaiting a press conference I knew would be enlightening. The room was packed. Leo Feigin sat directly behind me, Andrei Solovyev in front. A fine musician/critic, Solovyev had introduced himself the night before. He was someone both Feigin and Larry Ochs had recommended I meet, a member of the musical group Roof. Festival committee chair Yuri Saulsky, whom I still had not officially met, stood at a table up front.

"Not everyone is here but . . . my dear friends," he said, "the festival is coming to a close. I would like to summarize what we have done. The festival has taken place, and it was successful. Whatever drawbacks occurred were mostly technical. But the festival itself has produced much beautiful music. You cannot deny this."

He went on to say that, in spite of "great difficulties" encountered from the start, the music itself remained the single most important thing. Then he began to itemize the difficulties as if *they* were. Not many people in the audience needed to be reminded. He cited everything from lack of sponsors and shaky finances (nearly causing the festival "to collapse before it even started") to quarrels among musical factions (more mainstream performers invited than new music or avant-garde). Saulsky said that it had been important to hold the event in Moscow, even at this difficult time in the city's history; whereas Soviet musicians had performed in many places throughout the nation (Novosibirsk, Donetsk, Krasnodar, Petrozavodsk), Moscovites had *never* heard a large body of "standard jazz music" that included so many foreign musicians before—so the committee had decided to hold a truly "*First* Moscow International Jazz Festival."

Critic Tatiana Didenko had a number of questions. Why were guests made to stay in a hotel so far from the concert hall? Why did so few people attend the noonday productions at the Composers Union hall? Although she praised the concerts themselves, saying she found "the spirit of the music beautiful; I enjoyed it all," Didenko then dropped a bomb: "Why, at a time when people are suffering so much in Moscow, why did we try to put on a major festival here in the first place?"

The room buzzed. Moscow was hurting, obviously. You could see the evidence everywhere, and not just in the long queues of people waiting to buy everything from soap to cosmetics and from cheese to shoes.

Saulsky replied that it would not be "correct" to stop all cultural activities just because external circumstances were rough. He appealed to the need for *silyi dukh* (strong spirit) under duress. "Yes, there is a shortage of everything here," he admitted, "but we *had* to organize this festival, in spite of all difficulties. I am very pleased that young people were able to come and hear this music. I am very pleased that many of them offered to help, and did, even though they claimed they were not really all that fond of jazz music. We *needed* this festival!"

The dialogue grew spirited and spilled over into the audience. Someone offered a plea that, since the whole world was watching Moscow, the festival had an obligation to rise above this "historic moment," to "overcome." "The labor will be difficult," another person said, "but the baby will be born."

Leo Feigin then stood up and made what I thought was the most sincerely inspired oration of the day. Speaking "as a foreigner," he said, "as someone who has not been here for seventeen years," in some ways his visit had wrought a "devastating effect" on him. He'd seen empty shops; crowds of people standing in line at embassies, waiting for visas "to get out"; faces without smiles, a situation that was "sad, dramatic, depressing . . . yet suddenly, when I came to the festival, I saw people who were different from these others — people in high spirits, happy, talking openly with one another, discussing the music, whatever music. I think this festival was absolutely necessary now, even in light of the difficulties Yuri Saulsky has outlined. It must continue, for people will tell other people about it; the word will get out; it will help people survive. The audience here is what was of primary importance. Whatever was arranged should have been arranged for *their* sake, for the sake of their musical development. The major consumer here was the audience, and I, for one, am proud to have been a part of that audience."

Feigin commented on everything from the comfort of the seats in the auditorium to the theater itself, the sound, the lighting, right down to the sandwiches offered in the lobby, which he said he ate even though he is a vegetarian. The audience, he added, also loved all this and was not aware of the behind-the-scenes difficulties that Saulsky had spoken of. Feigin's speech had a salutary effect on the somewhat addled aggregate of journalists, promoters, presenters, and critics assembled in the room. It made everyone feel better about themselves and the enterprise, until Germann Lukianov spoke up, having prepared a poem for the occasion, he said. The poem seemed to be largely a list of rather trivial complaints, but it also disclosed an important issue: the preference given to American performers at the festival. Did they truly represent the "international" scene? The response was divided. Some people cheered, "Molodets! Khorosho!" But saxophonist Alex Kozlov was not pleased. "Germann reminds me of a very naughty little boy whose parents sacrifice their own meals in order to bring him caviar," he said. "And still he complains about not having enough."

Other factions began to air their complaints. So here it was at last, *glasnost* in action — spontaneous outcries against the Jazz Federation, of which people such as Saulsky, Igor Bril, and Lukianov were a part, even cries over the "lost identity" of the Russian Federation itself and a need to restore one. One man complained that Freddie Hubbard's set had been ruined because "the acoustics were terrible," and when told, not too kindly, that he was speaking beside the point and should sit down and shut up, he responded angrily, "I will not! I am not a machine!"

"No fighting, please!" someone else called out.

"We're acting just like the Supreme Soviet deputies on TV!" offered another.

Levelheaded and obviously respected, Vladimir Feyertag quieted things down with a frank admission that no Soviet committee would have been "strong enough" just now; that someone with a sound knowledge of the Western market, a Western consultant, was needed. He talked frankly about mismanagement, of foreign musicians stranded or lost at the airport. "We have been hungry too long," Feyertag admonished. "We wanted everything at once, but we invited too many top, expensive musicians. Germann may complain about his bass player paying for a taxi, but in the West, he would have had to pay far more just to stand near some of these musicians and listen to them play."

The director of the successful Tbilisi Jazz Festival turned our attention to Zhanna's solitary efforts, comparing her to "Jeanne d'Arc." This added a touch of class Irene liked. "You can always count on a Georgian to relieve the tension with humor," she said.

"Don't worry," the Georgian director said, "festivals will be held, because we have something rolling here. We have people independent of the federations, yet we need structure, a group that will take full responsibility for truly organizing this festival, perhaps a jazz festival board of directors that gets paid, that meets every day, so that people can truly get to know one another and not just come together on the eve of a festival." Then, echoing Feyertag's admonition, he said, "We need to send people to the West to study just how festivals are arranged. We must learn how to socialize, not just with musicians, but with ourselves. Freedom is a very important thing, a necessity, but when you are free you must also be responsible."

Saulsky congratulated the group on an "interesting discussion" and said it was time to wind it up. "This festival is a part of our system," he concluded. "That system is being revised. Under the circumstances, it would have been strange indeed, perhaps a miracle, if we had been able to run the best festival in the world . . . I hope we will all meet here again, next year!"

A banquet followed the press conference. A table the length of the Dom Komposoriterov dining room had been set up, complete with a spread — in those lean and perilous times — of tongue with horseradish sauce, pork, cucumbers, pastry filled with paté and cheese, and the inevitable combination of cognac and Pepsi Cola. I was seated beside Irene, Betty next to a young Russian man who insisted on translating for her; the American record producer George Avakian sat across the way, with his own translator; nearby was Saulsky, who I had finally arranged to interview, even though he was fully consumed by his director's chores; and Igor Bril and Tatiana Didenko sat directly across from Irene. On either side of us were about fifty other people, each with an individual interpreter, it seemed, converting this final animated scene into a Tower of Babel.

"We are talking with festival director Yuri Saulsky in a very noisy, crowded room," I told my tape recorder. Irene and the young man next to Betty began translating what I'd just said, their variants nearly as interesting as what I anticipated Saulsky would be saying himself.

Before I could ask him a single question, he stood up and proposed a toast — the first of many. "I am very happy to have seen you all here at this festival. We have waited so long for this occasion. Seventy-three years! Back in the twenties, it was just a matter of whether or not such a festival could even take place; now, happily, the times have changed. . . . I am sure that the people who are gathered here at present are all very devoted to the art of jazz, and they understand that this is a great art. So let's drink to this great art. Because we are all servants of the same art, and have been witnesses to it on the stage — so let us drink to jazz!"

Irene said quickly, as Saulsky sat down, "First question, please!"

I nodded. "In the United States there are, unfortunately, just three books that touch on jazz in the USSR at all. But in each of these the name of Yuri Saulsky is mentioned, and with great respect. You are a very honored figure in

Soviet jazz. Even in a book on rock music, the author, Artemy Troitsky, says, 'Yuri Saulsky is an all-around 'good guy.' "

"When rock was underground music," Saulsky said, "older musicians like myself tried to help the younger. Perhaps that's why he said what he did. I am of the jazz generation, but I always supported whatever was good in rock."

"Perhaps, to take your mind off the festival for just a minute," I suggested, "we can go back in time, be nostalgic about some of the work you've done in the past?"

"It wouldn't just be nostalgic. When I am at home now, writing music, I always play the blues first, for a long time. It's somewhat like . . . like praying, before I start composing. Then I go on to create music of a completely different nature. But I always start with the blues. At a recent jazz festival in Odessa, playing with Kozlov, we played the music of the fifties. To cut a long story short, writing what I write now *keeps* me from repeating what I did in the fifties, but Kozlov and I would like to do a tour, as a duo, and deliberately play the great jazz music that came after the war, the ballads."

I said, "Frederick Starr has written that 'a tour of Moscow restaurants and theaters in the autumn of 1945 would have given the Soviet jazz fans grounds for optimism. Many musicians who had been demobilized at the end of the war quickly regrouped into small bands that were improvisational in personnel as in style.' Alto saxophonist Leonid Geller had such a group at the National Hotel. It included the 'talented and, until then, amateur pianist and arranger Yuri Saulsky.' "

"From a musical standpoint I would like to go back to 1946," he said, "but from a political point of view I would prefer to go back to fifty-six."

It was time for another toast. Saulsky stood up. "I am very happy that the music played at this festival was music that we like so much. Every successful event has its soul, and here you can find that soul in Zhanna. So I would like to propose a toast to a small woman who has been our heart and soul, *our* Zhanna. Let us drink to Zhanna, the heart and soul of Soviet jazz!"

Zhanna began modestly. "There was a moment when the question was 'To be or not to be?' with regard to this festival. It would then have been very easy to say, 'Let's give up!' We had so many commitments but not enough official commitments, so it would have been easy to say, 'Let's forget about this festival.' But that would have been impossible, so we decided to put the burden on our own shoulders, a burden we shared with Yuri Saulsky."

After the toast I slipped in another request. "Let's go back to the fifties, then, 1957. The Sixth World Youth Festival, held in Moscow . . ."

"At that time I had some experience," Saulsky said. "I was musical director of the Russland Orchestra and was invited to become musical director of the

Young Musicians Orchestra. People are apt to remember a time in which they become very active, and this was one of my peaks of activity. This was a time when the iron curtain had been raised, just a little bit. We had our first contact with foreigners, and we became a bit more mature; we started to understand jazz better. We had *heard* a lot of music before, but now we *saw* these musicians from other countries play. We participated in our first jam session at the festival in 1957. To me, these were the formative years of jazz, the beginning of a new period in our development."

"And the vocal-instrumental ensemble VIO-66, with Igor Bril on piano?"

"Yes, it was a blues-vocal group, a male and female octet, not in the spirit of Ray Coniff, no, but a jazz group. I had it for five years. Four trumpets, four saxophones, eight singers. The vocalists sang jazz harmonies."

"Just how old was that young pianist, Igor Bril?" I asked.

"He was a boy! And I wasn't very old either . . . very young."

Bril spoke up. "I was twenty years old."

"He's even younger now," Irene said. "And Yuri is also very young. Everybody is still very young!"

"Jazz doesn't let you grow older!" Saulsky said.

"How do you explain it?" I asked him.

"It has something to do with the life functions. When a man is fond of jazz he somehow stays young."

"I would like to add something," Bril put in. "I think that love is responsible. People *must* show their admiration for jazz."

Saulsky agreed. "Because a man is not ashamed to show his emotions!"

"Dusha naraspashku!" I said.

Saulsky cracked up. "Dusha naraspashku!" he repeated, laughing approvingly. He asked me what city I lived in, and when I said Monterey, he raised his eyebrows, mentioning the jazz festival there.

"Yuri's son lives in L.A.," Irene told me. "He plays in a rock band there. His son is already thirty-eight years old. Maybe you will get together?"

Emboldened by all this goodwill, I attempted a toast in Russian. Irene translated until she realized she didn't have to. ("Wait, you are speaking Russian, why should I translate?") I said I was just a writer, not an orator, and a shy (*zastenchivyi*) person to boot, but I wished to thank the committee, and especially Saulsky and Jeanne d'Arc, for the opportunity to attend the festival. Irene asked if I did not wish to thank the translators as well, then got embarrassed, the others laughing, when I quoted some lines from *Eugene Onegin:* "Maia krasavitsa, moi angel, ia lublu tebia" (My queen, my angel, I love you). After Yuri poured more cognac, she said, "You will get drunk! You will all get drunk!"

I asked Saulsky for his personal response to the festival.

"He prefers to be more objective," Irene translated. "He regretted the festival the moment they decided to have it. No, that's a joke. He is a musician. A connoisseur of art. And he is pleased with the artistic influence the festival will have on people. They have had a chance to hear musicians they have only heard on tapes and records. But jazz should not just be heard; it must also be *seen*. When he got to see the bass player with Branford Marsalis, when he got to hear pianist Benny Green — when you put everything together it shows that this is a humane art, a beautiful art, one which now, in our difficult times, brings people together. . . . This festival was a giant praznik [holiday], a key point in the lives of Soviet musicians because they were communicating with musicians from other countries. And when musicians come together like this, new Soviet musicians will be born! Vot tak! [That's it!]"

"Bravo!" I replied.

Igor Bril smiled and said, "Okay," in English. The banquet was over.

I said goodbye to Zhanna. "We were talking about how expensive everything is in your country," Irene said. "And Zhanna also says that in a couple more days, she will start speaking English, because she has so often been standing next to people speaking it." When Zhanna protested, saying she speaks "so badly," Irene smiled. "Who cares!" she said, nudging me. "Forget about the mistakes. Like him!"


The concert that closed out the First Moscow International Jazz Festival featured Valery Ponomarev, Baku pianist Leonid Ptashko, and, last but never least, Branford Marsalis offering a skillful impersonation of Branford Marsalis. In a *Down Beat* interview later, Marsalis made the same claim that Sydney Bechet had once made: that Russian audiences were his favorite of all, the most serious, thoughtful, about the music.

Jazz this last evening was mixed with lots of tributes and thanks. Great Britain's Mike Hennessey spoke of the festival as "a most moving and memorable experience." The entire festival crew — Zhanna Braginskaya, Yuri Saulsky, Gabriele Kleinschmidt (a German booking agent who had secured many of the performers for the festival), the sound team from Poland, and George Avakian — came onstage for the inevitable end-of-a-festival celebration. Avakian had instructed Saulsky at the banquet that afternoon to tell the crowd that "what is very important for the future of the Moscow jazz festival . . . and I must say it with no false modesty, for America and for Western Europe, for support of what Yuri is doing . . . that *I* am the symbol of the heart of Soviet-American jazz relations. And it's also very important for him to say that if it were not for George Avakian, we would not have Branford Marsalis in the Soviet Union this night."

"*You?*" Irene had interrupted, forced to translate this advice given to Saul-sky at the afternoon's banquet, as incredulous as I was.

"Yes. And Yuri must also add that he feels Valery Ponomarev is the living symbol of what the young Soviet boy should strive for over the years, and *then come back to Russia* to be an inspiration, come back to his home to be an inspiration for all young Soviet musicians."

I held my breath at the last concert, wondering if Saulsky would actually humiliate himself by repeating what he'd been instructed to say, but he did not. That didn't stop Avakian from doing the job himself, but the woman who translated the defection statement on stage that night ("Every young Soviet boy should follow the example of Mr. Ponomarev and come to the United States in order to play *real jazz*") simply said that Mr. Avakian finds Mr. Ponomarev "an inspiration" — a compromise that drew hearty laughter from those in the crowd who understood both languages.

I had arranged to meet Alexei Batashev at the last concert, for he had promised to make copies of albums from his collection, should I supply him with a list and blank tapes. Many of these he had produced himself, and I was especially eager for those of such artists as Mikhail Okun, whose work I would never be able to find in the States. I had managed to meet with Batashev one more time, following that evening at his apartment, in the lobby of the festival hall. He had been in a jaunty mood, showing up in his customary jeans and running shoes, and a checkered sport coat, with his hair slicked back to a ponytail. He obviously enjoyed his celebrity status and the people who came up to our table as we talked. They all greeted him, friends and well-wishers — everybody but the steering committee that, it seemed, had disavowed him.

At this second meeting I'd asked him to explain a curious statement he'd made previously that Russians, in the area of jazz music, had "no original ideas." "Yes," he said, "as a community, the Soviet jazz world is too small. There are very few chances to develop a new style. It has become much easier to adopt a language that appeared somewhere else. But, even given this situation, there has been experimentation in the Soviet musical community. We do have *some* new ideas. We have some attempts that have been very successful. The work of Germann Lukianov and Alexei Zubov, now living in L.A., for example."

When I asked if there was anything technically unique to jazz in the USSR, he mentioned the sharped 4th (Lydean mode) of Ukrainian folklore; the Moldavian cycle of chords (by fours); and the Indian, Tadzhik, Kazakh, Crimean Tatar, and Asian Turk rhythmic elements, 'isomorphic' innovations (some parallel to Flamingo), of the Central-Asian group Boomerang. "The future of jazz in the Soviet Union could be very interesting," he added, "because the USSR — if it still exists! — will be the only nation that belongs to *two* large continents, continents which contain unbelievable diversity of cultures. The previously 'small' jazz universe could become very great, because of the opportunities for dialogue between these cultures. Also, you must remember that, for a long time, our world has been *closed,* locked out of the larger world. Now our jazz world has an impetus to move forward. This is especially important for American jazz, which is experiencing a kind of stagnation. The American disappointment with its own avant-garde has led the nation to embrace 'straight ahead' music."

Now, at the close of the First Moscow International Jazz Festival's last concert, I found Batashev up on the landing by the popular record and poster counter and gave him my stash of blank tapes, thanking him beforehand, for I truly desired recordings of the artists he said he would tape for me. This simple transaction took somewhat longer than it should have, for the money he requested for mailing was far in excess of the actual cost. Betty was amazed and refused to pay it all, so Batashev and I managed to work out a deal that spared us a subtle shakedown at the hands of the foremost jazz critic in the Soviet Union. I had discovered that this wily survivor, whom I admired, was every bit as complex as people had said he was.

Following the final performance of the First Moscow International Jazz Festival, Betty and I parted with Batashev and other friends we had made. Heading for the Lenin Library subway station, crossing the Kammenyi Moct (Great Stone Bridge) for the last time, Betty remembered that Batashev, when she had given him on this last night some fairly elegant soap for his wife, Larisa, had said jokingly, "You should have brought condoms." "Next trip," I said to Betty now, and we stopped to watch the lights dance in the Moscow River. Above the tree-shrouded Kremlin walls, the fine silhouette of the Water Tower stood (the circular structure so named for what it supplies the Kremlin gardens from the river), then the Great Kremlin Palace, and the Annunciation and Archangel Michael cathedrals. Behind them loomed the Ivan the Great Bell Tower, traditionally the tallest structure in the city, but no longer. Enjoying the splendid view, we thought of Moscow and all the fine music we had heard and the many good friends we had made.

## part three

*Leningrad and the Republics*

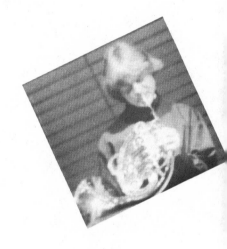

# Peter-the-First
# Stew

Irene had agreed to see us off at the Moscow train station. She told us she would be waiting beneath a giant statue of Lenin that stands smack in the center of a noisy, crowded floor.

"The two of you make a handsome couple," I said, gazing up at the stern underside of Vladimir Ilyich's chin when we arrived.

As usual, I could find no way to curb her generosity. She gave me a volume of Afanasy Fet's poems that opened with the words "Kak beden nash iazyk!" (How poor is our language!) and then demonstrated for thirty-one pages that this was not true. The poems were complemented by watercolors depicting just the sort of landscape we would pass through on our way to Petrozavodsk, north of Leningrad. We parted, Irene stoic as always, me gushing thanks, Betty quietly appreciative.

From our coach car, we watched the giant crumbling twenty-story apartment complexes of Moscow give way to forests of birch and pine. A live talk show blared from speakers. People phoned in on political issues, and the name Yeltsin cropped up often. The talk show yielded to melodic folk songs sung with concert hall aplomb, in turn replaced by a comedian mimicking that succession of infirm leaders who had died in office: Brezhnev, Andropov, Chernenko. The passengers laughed openly, even at references to the poor "Sovetskii liudi" (Soviet people), "Ne livdi . . . sobaki!" (Not people . . . dogs!).

Once out in the country we passed large swamps. Irene had told us a story about how the train line from Moscow to St. Petersburg had originally been conceived: Tsar Alexander had simply slapped a ruler down on a map and drawn a straight line, regardless of the terrain over which the tracks must be laid. When the land grew solid again Betty and I saw dachas with slanted corrugated-tin roofs, the wood stained by harsh weather. Small gardens and hand-somely carved fences, whose patterns resembled linked crosses, surrounded houses topped with TV antennas. The buildings grew more colorful as we progressed north: dark blue, ocher, salmon, crimson, canary yellow, olive with light blue trim. Elegant carving graced the eaves, and each home sported a giant stack of winter wood.

When we arrived in Leningrad an hour late, an Intourist driver whisked us away. "It's costing me money!" he complained. He permitted me a quick trip to the bathroom, where men in their underwear stood brushing their teeth, shaving, and bathing themselves at the sinks for two kopecks. A *babushka* mopped directly beneath my feet as I stood at the urinal, as if I wasn't there. The driver finally deposited us at a fairly classy hotel, compared to what we had encountered in Moscow, but because of broken pipes, it had no water.

During our twenty-four hours in Leningrad, we visited the Peter and Paul Fortress with its impressive gilded spire 120 meters high that to this day limits the height of any building in the city. Artists had set up easels beside the stolid granite walls. Sunbathers lay on the "lazy person's beach," so called because people come here rather than seek out the more spacious venues outside the city. We saw the small, stark quarters that had housed such distinguished political prisoners as Tsar Peter's own son, the unfortunate Alex, tortured to death by decree of his father in 1718; the Decembrists, responsible for an uprising in 1825, five of whom were executed probably not too far from where the artists sketched today; and the Petrashevsky Circle, which included Dostoevsky, Maxim Gorky, and Lenin's oldest brother, Alexander Ulyanov, who was also executed. Their claustrophobic Trubetsky Bastion cells still display a set of manacles, an unsavory cot, one small semicircular window, and a small desk, stool, and lamp. Outside, street musicians played guitars — one a Russian "Gippie" with a brightly colored scarf — even after being chastised by a groundskeeper for collecting rubles in a hat.

We went to the Russian Museum, rich with three hundred thousand items, including fine icons, Repin's famous "Volga Barge Haulers," and Altman's magnificent crystalline blue cubist portrait of poet Anna Akhmatova. I got to savor it all carefully, closely, nose to canvas, much to the chagrin of the vigilant *dezhurniia,* those old women ever on guard, one to a room or, at times it seemed, one to a painting. I also found a record store on Nevsky Prospect, although not much by way of jazz there. I bought two albums: *Dzhaz Vdvoem* (*Two Playing Jazz*) by the fine Estonian saxophonist Lembit Saarsalu, whom I hoped to meet in the Baltics, and pianist Leonid Vintskevich; and *Ten Years After,* the work of two guitarists, Alexei Kuznetsov and Nikolai Gromin. Back in our room at the hotel we heard, on TV, poems set to music, opera, art songs, readings from Pushkin. Culture everywhere, but what a strange country! First they kill these great artists off, then they celebrate the hell out of them: statues, street names, theaters, institutes dedicated to their posthumous honor. My jazz musicians, too, I thought, will just have to wait their day — and statues.


We had traveled to Leningrad by afternoon coach, but for the overnight journey to Petrozavodsk we shared a compartment with two strangers. We had a fortunate draw: a young woman named Irina who worked for Intourist, currently studying Bulgarian; and a young man attending a technological institute in Petrozavodsk. The conversation, in Russian, was awkward at first, but photographs of our *vnuchka* (granddaughter) helped break the ice. We exchanged aphorisms and folk idioms, Irina delighted by her ability to say "You can take horse to water but cannot make the drink." In the morning the *dezhurniia* opened our door and offered us six-kopeck tea at 6:30 as rock music and the day's fresh news poured from the speaker stationed just above my pillowed head.

When the train arrived Betty and I were met by Ludmilla, a rather brisk, gruff blond woman who whisked us off, marching with grand intentionality before us, to a car that would deliver us to the Severnaya (Northern) Hotel. This woman could have played the severe Russian in any of those stereotypical films Americans are all too accustomed to. At the hotel, she suggested we procure tickets for that evening's dinner and variety show. Attempting to do so, I encountered three women who sat at a desk just inside a large dark mauve Victorian dining room, complete with heavy crimson drapes, and thick pillars duplicating the hotel's exterior six fat Corinthian columns.

One of the women asked me where I was from.

"America," I answered.

Another, not having heard this exchange, asked me what I wanted.

"Tickets," I replied to her. "For tonight's dinner and varete" (variety show).

"Net, net, nevushmozhno," she said (No, no, that's impossible). "We have no more tickets for tonight. No tickets."

"He's from America," the girl I had first spoken to whispered to her.

The second woman looked up at me. She immediately filled out a form granting tickets for a meal and variety show — but first she rather saltily asked, "How many do you want?" Betty had by now arrived and was standing by my side.

"Dva, pazhalusta" (Two, please), I replied as icily as I could, sick of these ceaseless games. The tickets were three rubles each, stamped with "Tovarishch, priglashem Bac" (Comrade, we welcome you).

I had come to Petrozavodsk on a hunch centered on a man named Andrei

Kondakov. I had wanted to savor Soviet jazz life in some out-of-the-way spot and, reading the material Michael Dubilet (my Soviet contact from Dnepropetrovsk) had sent me back home, I learned that Kondakov was responsible for a jazz program at Rautio Musical College in Petrozavodsk. On his rather eccentric, highly eclectic rendering on Mobile Fidelity of "Fascinating Rhythm" that liner notes called "a new and fresh interpretation" I heard sax section work reminiscent of Guy Lombardo, which was okay. Charlie Parker himself had approved of Lombardo's tight units. Yet despite some tastefully current piano styling, the music seemed to date Kondakov. I therefore expected to meet a man older than myself, and standing in the lobby of the Severnaya, that's what I searched for. Some kid holding a sack of what looked like phonograph records was waiting also. The two of us glanced at one another from time to time. The lobby was quite small, and I'd been waiting for about fifteen minutes. Finally, this kid strolled over.

"Are you Villiam Mai-nor?" he asked.

"Yes!"

"I am Andrei Kondakov."

Now, in the company of a university student named Igor, whom Ludmilla had assigned me, the young pianist/composer/academician and I discussed how his jazz program came about. In the interview Dubilet had sent me, Kondakov said he was attempting to develop a "backbone" of teachers, a cadre capable of working with students in small improvisational ensembles, producing players who are not merely interested, or knowledgeable, when it comes to jazz, but familiar enough with its principles to perform contemporary music in as effortless a manner as possible. He admitted now that, because the school accepted pupils who did not have a musical background, the college "does have some big problems," although some pianists and guitar players have seven years or so of previous music school training.

The college uses American textbooks, Dan Haerle, but from the first year of study emphasizes ensemble work based on jazz standards, from the most basic to those quite complex harmonically. Kondakov taught a new course, "Jazz Composition," for the first time this past year. "The first program we employed, which came from Moscow," he said, "proved not to be so good, so we are using our own now, one we feel is better. We are independent now. We do what we like. As a teacher, I like to work with rhythm. We have special courses for that. For example, we introduce certain rhythmical structures we feel students need, so that they can grow up *swinging*." He laughs. "*That* is the most difficult thing we have to teach!"

I mentioned the sizable number of fine jazz pianists I had encountered, sprung from a tradition of technical excellence — the Scriabin, Stravinsky, Shostakovich legacy — and, by comparison, the weak inheritance of drummers and rhythm sections in general. "Uh huh," he replied, nodding immediately. "In the Soviet Union there is a great problem with rhythm sections. Especially drummers, but also bass players." He admitted that the classical influence could be salutary for jazz pianists, that they should be familiar with modern classics, but that one's performance must remain "natural"—that being natural was a primary goal. He claims not to have been influenced himself by avant-garde classical composers in the Alfred Schnitke line but acknowledges Prokofiev as a "mentor." He said many jazz composers have impressed him too, beginning with Joe Zawinul and including Nikolai Levinovsky, who helped him "very much in the early stages" when Kondakov started studying music ten years ago. He discovered jazz by way of Erroll Garner. "I was lucky to get a record of his and was shocked by his ability to swing." He tried to play like Garner, preferring him to Oscar Peterson, who he heard next. Then, after some time had passed, came Bill Evans. The next influence was McCoy Tyner, then Chick Corea, Herbie Hancock, Keith Jarrett. Now he likes Marcus Roberts ("very much") and Kenny Kirkland, who I mentioned I'd heard with Branford Marsalas at the First Moscow International Jazz Festival.

"I didn't get to hear him," he replied somewhat wistfully.

Conservatory trained, Andrei Kondakov earned his diploma and graduated three years ago by way of an original composition played in concert, a piece for piano, percussion, and full orchestra.

"How old *are* you, if I may ask?"

"Twenty-seven."

"I think you must be some sort of genius," I said in Russian.

He accepted this compliment graciously, not protesting its implications.

"I also write songs for pop music," he said. "They are mostly 'in mind' now, not down on paper, but I am close to finding time to put them in practice, because I am truly interested in *everything*. I like people who are capable of doing many different things, working with many different musical styles, such as Quincy Jones. They are my ideal as musicians."

"I've heard that Petrozavodsk is a good jazz town," I said. "Eto pravda?" (True?).

"Yes, I think so," he replied. "Because Karelia has some good traditions, although musicians here, I'm afraid, have very weak ties with Moscow and Leningrad. Of course they do take part in some festivals, but not very often, and we don't often go abroad." I said I'd been impressed by the high quality of Karelian visual art I'd seen so far, discovered in a book called *Zhudozhniki Karelii* (*Artists of Karelia*) that I'd picked up at a kiosk. I'd liked Tamara Yufa's interpretations of the Kalavala, found in a museum in Zavodskaya Square, and the work of other graphic artists there. I asked if, in his mind as a musician, there was a distinctly Karelian art.

"Est, est, est, est" (There is, there is, there is, there is), he replied, obviously enthusiastic. "I have compositions which are based on Karelian chastushka [popular songs]. I have recorded these, but unfortunately I have just one copy. Right now, together with the Allegro band [the remnants of the group put together by Levinovsky, which included Igor Butman], I hope to produce a national Karelian composition. One piece is already prepared. It's a combination of jazz and rock. I hope to perform it at the Autumn Rhythm Festival in Leningrad . . . yet the quartet with Leningrad guitarist Andrei Ryabov, that's a different thing. The two are not connected. With Allegro, I use electronic elements, but working with Ryabov, I prefer acoustic jazz."

"Are there specific Karelian elements; that is, specific strictly musical elements, such as Azerbaijanian mugam? Or is what's unique more allied to subject matter, content?"

"It's more a matter of national dukh [spirit], I think," Kondakov said, reminding me of Anatoli Vapirov's similar reply to this question. "Composition based on concrete memories of existing topics. In composition my own feelings must prevail. I use chastushka, but not as ready-made folkloric elements. Karelian folk music doesn't really differ that much from Russian music, yet in some ways it *is* different. But I think it is impossible to say just what that difference consists of, just what is typical of Karelian folk music. I think it could be understood only after listening to a particular arrangement."

When I brought up the issue of current American complacency in jazz — its neoclassical or repertorial fix, just now, on exploring tradition, as opposed to the Soviet trend toward polystylistic experimentation — Kondakov immediately mentioned Sergei Kuryokhin. "I can't say that I like him," he added. "Among the vanguard players, I like Guyvoronsky and Volkov best. Also Arkadi Shilkloper. I like avant-garde music when it comes about through genuine thought, but too often there's more show than music. Of course, the number-one musician in Soviet jazz is Germann Lukianov. He would have achieved great results, excellent marks, if he had only had equal partners. He is a very complicated soul, his nature, and that's why he hasn't achieved all that he might have. I feel for him as a musician. I respect him very much."

"Any others?"

"Mikhail Okun."

"And?"

"Ochen malo" (Very few).

"Do you use polystylistic elements in your own work, or do you like to keep things separate?"

"I do not play polystylistic music yet. I work in many styles, but I do not mix them. Maybe that's the next step. In five years perhaps . . ." He laughs.

"And the future for jazz in the Soviet Union on the whole?"

"I think it's good that so many cities are holding festivals in the USSR."

"About forty a year?"

"Da." Kondakov himself had organized a festival in Petrozavodsk that in 1989 had featured both Richie Cole and Germann Lukianov, plus Kondakov's own quartet with guitarist Andrei Ryabov and twenty-one-year-old bassist Boris Kuzlov. "Unfortunately, the organizers usually are not musicians. That's why they are lacking in knowledge about jazz. They have not been brought up in it, and that is why people are so very often indifferent to this music. But now a new generation of musicians is appearing, people my age. We are not so many, but we will make jazz survive, I think. I believe it would be good if Soviet jazz performers were able to take courses of study at a school like Berklee yet also stay in this country. The only way out now is to leave the country and go abroad, but that is not good for the development of truly Soviet jazz, obviously."

I mentioned that I had been surprised and pleased to see so many younger people at the Moscow festival. "Yes, that *is* very good," he responded. "Although I still think it's not easy to say anything about the future. Once, when Duke Ellington was asked about a future mix of classical music and jazz, he said it was impossible to have any idea of what will happen in twenty years. The only thing I know I am sure of is that jazz will exist. . . . The main thing, the important concept, is the hope that festivals can be offered regularly in this country, because that helps Soviet musicians. Also, that way, jazz critics may look more attentively and be able to distinguish the best among the best in both countries."

"Who do you consider the best Soviet jazz critics?"

"I can say nothing about that because I think jazz players here in the Soviet Union have much more information about jazz than Soviet critics do. That situation doesn't compare to that in the United States. I do respect Vladimir Feyertag as a person, and as a man."

After the interview, Betty and I did enjoy walking about Petrozavodsk, down Lenin Prospect, which leads straight to Lake Onega, and over to Kirov Square, where both the Russian Drama Theater and the Finnish Drama Theater have been erected on the sites of demolished churches. Poor stocky little Kirov stands between the two, very much alone. A large stand not far from Kirov, obviously once used for political rallies, has been dismantled. A large park runs alongside Lake Onega, containing handsome wood-carved selections from the Finnish epic *The Kalavala* in Russian, complete with equally handsome statues representing key figures from that drama, one a mermaid who looked as if she'd make a fine addition to the prow of a ship.

Petrozavodsk contains a provincial charm we had not encountered in Leningrad or Moscow; but this open, natural, friendly woody ambience —

and Andrei Kondakov's taste and intelligence—had not been evident in the *varete* we had witnessed the previous evening. This show proved saxophonist Larry Ochs's words, speaking of the middle-aged clientele for Russian disco: "They're supposed to be there now, but they don't really know why." I'm not sure we knew exactly why we were there ourselves, except that we were discovering it's impossible, in many hotels, to get at the food without also suffering through an attendant variety show. Being American may have served as a password for getting us into this heretofore sold-out affair but also seemed to have mandated—in revenge for my having thrown my California weight, such as it was, around?—our being seated behind an immense column that blocked our view of the stage.

Our tablemates were two dressed-to-kill women in their, perhaps, midthirties. When I looked around I noticed that fairly attractive young women were at just about every table. What was this, girls' night out in Petrozavodsk? Every table also had Karelian lindenberry juice and a full bottle of Stolichnaya. When the two women asked for their own, I realized the bottle that sat before us was intended for Betty and me alone, a more than adequate supply—until I noticed that couples at an adjacent table had polished off two bottles long before the show even began. Russian proof is somewhat lower—38 percent, I believe—than the potent Stoli we get at home, but not that much. We were also well supplied with *zakusky* with which to ground this drink: beef and chicken chunks, the inevitable salami, cucumbers, tomatoes, lindenberries, yogurt, and fine black bread. Then the *varete* began, equally sumptuous: the oddest amalgamation of adopted Americanisms I have ever seen—a travesty that made a Las Vegas review seem like a children's Christmas pageant or a Presbyterian ice cream social.

First came "the girls," all in a bunch, as Mark Twain once said about the way a bucking bronco landed its hooves after it threw him. To this day my wife claims these young women lacked "muscle tone" ("too much salami"), but I can't agree. Flesh, of whatever quality, we got, my favorite dancer a unique blend of Debbie Reynolds and Marilyn Monroe. Wearing an infinitesimal G-string, she was immensely enjoying this opportunity to step out of customary Russian modesty. I indulged a small fantasy: taking her home to the United States and making a star of her, as a jazz singer perhaps, yet as far as I knew she couldn't sing, or play any instrument other than herself—although she was doing a fine job of that.

The music to which the chorus line danced consisted of everything from Georgian folk tunes to an imitation of Smokey Robinson and the Miracles. A rock group—guitar, electric bass, and keyboards buried in a twittering strobe light, plus sudden explosions of ink blue, crimson, pea green, and decibels galore—provided accompaniment, not just for "Smokey," but also for a female singer doing "Send in the Clowns," a scat singer who made hash out of "Just in Time," and an attempted, uplifting version of Bob Dylan's "Knock, Knock, Knocking on Heaven's Door." This was followed by just a snatch of not bad jazz, and various ethnic musical dishes — from Hungary, Bulgaria, Czechoslovakia, and Israel, all delivered in full costume, free-flowing shirts and black boots. We were also treated to violin gypsy music, Latin dancing (two ballroom Terpsichoreans spreading mock elegance throughout the room), and an opera singer, interspersed with more long-legged girls, quick-change artists who appeared in a stunning array of outfits, if and when they wore much of anything at all. A couple in the audience, impatient to dance, stepped out on the floor and had a go at it themselves, to everyone's delight but the half-naked chorus girls on whose toes they were treading. The show, called "Odilon," closed out with a can-can finale.

At first I explained the presence of so many young women in the audience as an opportunity to see this display of clothing not accessible to them in stores — everything from sleek, bright-yellow knit dresses to red velvet strapless evening gowns to tight miniskirts bearing Karelian folk designs — and to admire the bodies of women in various stages of undress not acceptable for themselves. Then I discovered the peanut gallery, a mezzanine balcony loaded with males who, once the *varete* expired and a program of dance music — disco, folk, and rock 'n roll — began, commenced to check out the women, who danced with one another until a man descended from the balcony and stole his selection from her female partner, the other males following suit.

By this time both of the women at our table were tipsy, silly, and friendly, the four of us having survived a series of straight-shot toasts we took turns proposing, they having offered the first — "Znakomnia!" — after we showed them pictures of our sons, whom they found "pretty." The most striking of these two women was soon snagged by a man of such slick looks that he inspired little trust, although she seemed to have taken an instant shine to him. Later, this gentleman asked our room number, saying he had a "most interesting collection of souvenirs" for sale, so my instinct proved true. No one chose the second woman and I felt badly for her, but the evening's conviviality grew, and next thing I knew we all were up dancing, en masse, joined by an old woman who was trying to teach Betty and me Georgian steps to match the beat of Stevie Wonder's "I Just Called to Say I Love You," a tune the band played over and over again while Betty and I shouted the English words.

I had picked the city of Petrozavodsk as one to visit in the USSR largely because of the hunch I mentioned before, gambling that Andrei Kondakov and the program at his jazz college would be interesting in their own right, but I'd also read that the town served as the starting point of an eighty-minute trip, by hydrofoil, to the island of Kizhi, famous for its peasant architecture, its wooden churches dating back to 1390 — a sort of universal navel, a holy site. We met the student Igor, my interpreter from the previous day, at the dock not far from a statue of Peter the Great, who established a foundry in Petrozavodsk. Our boat was filled with chattering schoolchildren, whose teacher was a friendly woman whom Igor told we were Americans. She pointed to me and asked, "Is he the president?" I gave her my best George Bush smile.

As we sped across Lake Onega's huge expanse of flat silver-blue water, Igor supplemented the woman's running commentary on the thirty canals leading to the White Sea (although she didn't mention they had been constructed at a heavy toll of life on the part of convict labor) and another lake, Ladoga, the famous "road of life" during the nine-hundred-day seige of Leningrad. He said the area experienced winter temperatures of below 25° centigrade and that from November to April all lakes in Karelia were frozen.

What impresses one first about the island is the extraordinary light, and then its amazing sense of tranquility — for which the light probably is responsible, to a large degree. We hiked up a rutted walkway straight out of the painter Levitan's "Vladimirka" (those multiple ruts that had puzzled me I now learned are created not for aesthetic delight but as alternate routes once the prevalent slush renders one set inoperable). We hiked alongside fields coated with dandelions rising to uncanny heights of glory on the island, the light infusing everything — opulently thin and diffuse, easy, a substance, ideal, converted to pure *air* and generous to a fault.

One feels bathed in this light, under the rich, blue sky. Against it rise the cupolas of a series of wooden churches erected without nails. One, the Transfiguration, dating to 1714, boasts twenty-two cupolas. The modest 1390 church of St. Lazarus (the oldest wooden church in Russia, according to Igor) is considered sacred and therefore lucky to the touch. A bell tower close to the first church, erected in 1874, affords a splendid view of this wooden church and light-infested island. I felt sorry I had not been able to hear the music that Andrei Kondakov was composing now, for if it reflects the Karelia of Kizhi Island at all, it must be some music indeed.

Down at the dock, waiting for the return trip, teenage girls shivered, embracing one another but turning angry when Igor evoked our *inostranetsy* (foreigner's) privileges to get us on board ahead of them. By way of thanks, we asked him to have a meal with us back at the hotel restaurant — no *varete*, this time, thank God — a meal he attacked eagerly, especially the meat, as if he hadn't eaten for days. I don't think this was the case, although he did say that recently Petrozavodsk had been subjected to rationing, and he admitted to great concern about the price hikes to be imposed on July 1. As so often would prove true on our trip, an interpreter or guide turned out to be nearly as interesting as the places he or she took us to. Igor was well-read. He asked if I could get a copy, in Russian, of Vladimir Voinovich's still forbidden satirical novel *Moscow 2042*. He had read this book in English, a friend having procured a copy in Finland. Igor said he and his buddies attempted to imagine, sentence by sentence, what the original Russian was. He also asked me to send him a copy of George Orwell's *1984*.

Igor confessed he was not all that crazy about jazz, but he had attended a recent concert in Petrozavodsk featuring the Leningrad Dixieland Band and an English singer named Jenny Evans. He liked Evans, but his taste, he told me, runs more toward the Doors. He told me that Jim Morrison was born on the same day Lenin died. Igor was planning a trip to Duluth, Minnesota, for a month, on exchange, during the summer of 1991 — since 1986, Duluth has been the sister city of Petrozavodsk (no wonder, considering the compatibility of weather).

On our last night in Petrozavodsk, a city once considered out in the wilds by sophisticated St. Petersburgers and the "Siberia-near-the-capital" for "minor offenders" sent into exile there, we went to the classiest restaurant we'd been to so far: the Petroshka, housed in what may once have been a monastery, with small cell-like rooms with thick walls, down which, through slanted channels, whatever external light passed. I was pleased to discover that I could read everything on the menu and not so pleased, later — the waiter having nodded at every delicacy I ordered — to discover only one item listed actually available, small N's next to most meaning "no." Peter-the-First stew is a handsome concoction of mushrooms, slices of genuine beef, and a rich gravy. I received two servings of this specialty, because, after consuming one and thinking it my soup, I demanded the rest of the meal I thought I'd ordered — and received a second helping of Peter-the-First stew. A rock band began to play in the cell next to ours, and people in our room, as impatient to dance as all Russians seem to be, got up to do so. We were joined at our table by a former engineer awaiting the arrival of his *dama*. After chatting a bit in Russian and a generous string of straight-shot vodka toasts, he said that Petrozavodsk was "fine, but a bednii gorod" (poor town). He told a long mournful tale of how, because of the current dreadful economic situation, he was now working in an ordinary factory at a laborer's position. That night, Betty and I danced to the Beatles' "Michelle," the band a typical disco aggregate with a very bad drummer.

Igor met us at the train station in the morning. We discovered, to our surprise, that he was the son of Ludmilla, the stoic stereotype who'd met us when we'd first arrived in Petrozavodsk. I hoped Duluth would treat him well.

# The Freedom Monument

Our compartment mates on the trip from Petrozavodsk back to Leningrad had been a grumpy gentleman with an impressive gold emblem in his lapel and his delightful ten-year-old daughter. Sizing us up, and not suspecting that I understood what he was saying, he immediately instructed her not to speak to the *inostranetsy* (foreigners), advice she fortunately didn't take to heart. Each time he felt the compartment to smoke — which was often: "Papa kurit? Da!" (Papa's going to smoke? Yes!) — she and I chatted away furiously about her sixth-grade class in school, her English lessons, the "White Nights," her love of travel, and in general the world of a ten year old.

In the morning, having listened to her father snore, fart, belch, and breathe his way through a bad night's sleep, I was determined to crack his icy facade. I awoke to see the daughter directly across from me, alert and smiling. "Dobroe utro" (Good morning), I said, wiping sleep from my eyes and, noticing the splattered window once the shade had been raised, "Idet dozhd" (It's raining). I turned to her papa with my widest peaceful coexistence smile, but he would turn out to be the only example of the much talked about Russian paranoia, the xenophobia I had anticipated on a large scale.

We found Borodin, Tchaikovsky, and Mussorgsky in the Alexander Nevsky Cemetery, just across the street from the hotel at which we'd been deposited to wait for our train to Tallinn, Estonia. The three great Russian composers were celebrated by massive monuments adorned with flowers: Borodin's appropriately oriental, Tchaikovsky's sentimental and overdone (a winged angel, hand upon heart, perched on the composer's right shoulder), Mussorgsky's stark and black, befitting a brilliant drunk. "We have no culture today," a tour guide was telling a large group of Russians being shunted from tomb to tomb, "only difficulties."

The driver who took us to the train station turned out to be one of the more entertaining characters in the Intourist line I had encountered so far. With the shoulder span of one of the barge haulers who plied the Oka or Volka Rivers in the nineteenth century, a full mustache that emphasized the wide split between his two front teeth, and a head that seemed to grow more bald as the minutes ticked away on our extended ride, he was swept away by his own opinions on everything from God to Gorbachev (the former was okay, but he didn't like the latter). "Tolka slova" (Only words), he said of Gorbachev, missing a turn and driving right past the train station. "Why is he so popular with Americans? I know nothing about foreign politics, but I am much concerned about the fate of the Russian federation, and feel that only Boris Yeltsin can save it." Our driver had been born in Leningrad, which he felt was "just a big village, compared to Moscow." Yet even Leningrad had grown too large, was "difficult" now, because his wife found shopping here "confusing." He asked if we would like to do a little shopping of our own, disclosing contraband treasures in a bag between two front seats: small black lacquer boxes "for the lady," or an overlarge watch "for the gentleman." When we declined, he was puzzled. "Only you Americans and the Italians don't buy my watches. Why?"

I had the answer for myself, but I couldn't speak for all Americans or for the Italians. Just then we passed a church with striking blue cupolas. I asked him its name. "I don't know," he replied. "It was once used by the Whites, but everything changed in 1917." He then asked me how I happened to be in the Soviet Union. When I told him I'd been a guest of the USSR Composers Union at a jazz festival in Moscow, he raised his substantial eyebrows. "When I was a child, I used to play the accordion," he said. "But now I only play this automobile."

Approaching Tallinn, the landscape at first was not all that different from what we'd seen on the road north: flat; pine and birch giving way to craggy evergreens; the customary ocher, blue, green, and canary yellow houses; small garden plots; an ageless woman on her knees scrubbing a large rug; a *dedushka* (grandfather) gripping the handlebars of a new bike while a small girl sat on its high seat, her baby-fat legs dangling far above the pedals. For dinner Betty and I munched on emergency junk food we'd salvaged — a bag of potato chips, a Sprite, a hard-boiled egg, and two pieces of well-traveled black bread. I began to think about what I might find, by way of music, in Tallinn, my hopes high but uncertain.

I had the names of critic Valter Ojakäär, although I never heard from him after writing, and of a woman I'd met in Monterey, Tiia Loitme, a choir director full of Gippie charm. Removed as we were now from the context of a festival, locating or discovering jazz would no longer be easy. I had gambled and won on Petrozavodsk, and on finding Andrei Kondakov in town, but I couldn't count on such luck throughout a place as vast as the Soviet Union.

Back in Moscow, Germann Lukianov had spoken of the first "international" jazz festival (unapproved) held in Tallinn in 1967 and of how such Estonian independence had cost the city's leaders their jobs. But according to Frederick Starr in *Red and Hot*, the city had sponsored a jazz festival as early as May 1948, and Estonians were quick to point out that this festival had been founded six years before the Newport Jazz Festival in the United States. Estonian musicians used the postwar period of repression elsewhere to their own advantage, establishing themselves "as the most active and talented jazzmen in the USSR." Even earlier, the Murphy Band led by drummer Kurt Strobel (what Starr calls "the first quasi-jazz band . . . formed in independent Estonia" in 1918) achieved "colossal success" with arrangements pirated from Paul Whitman and Vincent Lopez. Obviously, jazz in Estonia went back a long way.

Now as we entered what has been described as "the singing nation," this country of two million known for its large choral feasts and progressive promotion of culture, I studied open stretches of healthy farm land and long rows of crops; private greenhouses composed of glass, not plastic; a green soccer field; modern factories and a freeway overpass; tidy plastered homes with a single slant to their roofs and ornate trim around windows and doors; then brick homes set among wild daisies, cars in the driveways. Both Betty and I got the feeling that Estonia was a more prosperous, more tidy place than we'd seen so far.

Yet Tallinn itself turned out to be our first disappointment as far as jazz went. I could not reach either Tiia Loitme or Valter Ojakäär. The music of Lembit Saarsalu ran through my head as Betty and I scaled the heights of Old Town. Saarsalu *was* Estonian jazz for me. Critic Virgil Mihaiu described him as "an energetic, dynamic saxophone player, as well as a composer and arranger, carrying out successful investigations into the heritage of Estonian folklore." As we ambled across a charming medieval square, I imagined Saarsalu's smooth 1983 Getz-like tenor. Gazing up at the gold-capped onion domes of the green Alexander Nevsky Cathedral in Old Town, I heard the rich polyphony and wild dynamics of Saarsalu and pianist Leonid Vintskevich on "Polyn-trava" (literally, "Wormwood Grass").

Tallinn struck me as more Danish than Russian. The name means "Danish castle," although the Estonians might prefer the older name, Koluvan, taken from Kalev, an Estonian folk hero. The fourteenth-century Church of the Holy Spirit houses Estonia's oldest bell, whose democratic inscription reads,

"I chime just as accurately for all, for maid and servant, for mistress and master, and for that I am beyond reproach." But this small area has passed through many hands, with the Russians taking control under Peter the Great in 1710. Estonian independence, proclaimed February 24, 1918, lasted a single day.

In St. Nicholas Church, built between 1316 and 1350 and now a museum, Lembit Saarsalu — who, when not playing jazz, works as a musician in vaudeville theater and also for TV — and West German clarinetist Hans Kumpf once recorded pieces for a Leo Records album called *On a Baltic Trip.* The church holds two large wood-carved altarpieces showing sixteen scenes from the lives of Saint Nicolas and Saint Victor. It also holds a rich display of shields used for epitaphs, and a long fifteenth-century painting of the danse macabre. On the recording, the two reed instruments, the Estonian on soprano sax, seesaw among the marble rafters, notes spare but sustained and reverent. We completed our tour by walking around Stout Margaret, one of Old Town's original towers, out to a sports complex in sad disrepair, shards of cement making it appear more ancient than the towers and churches we'd seen. Betty pranced in the Baltic Sea ("It's cold!"), just for the record.

Dinner that evening consisted of *viuu zakuski* (paté, pickled apples, and cucumbers) and stroganoff with potatoes, and no one kicked us out of the restaurant for not constituting a *firma* or *groupa.* We went to a bar on the hotel's top floor for a nightcap, and a man sat down next to us and said he wished to buy my camera. When I said it was not for sale, he slammed a massive wad of rubles down on the tabletop. "Worthless!" he cried. "I can buy nothing with these!" A Russian Jew, he said he lived in daily despair over the current state of the Soviet Union, even in "gentle" Estonia. "There is no solution," he said. "No solution, except another revolution!"

By contrast, the driver who took us to the station where we would catch our train for Riga, Latvia, and another jazz festival, seemed content with his lot. The ambience of his cab was oddly Western: a photo of Charles Bronson attached to the rearview mirror, a postcard of a scantily clad "girlie" on the dash, McDonald's and Showtime USA Video stickers. "Joshua Fit the Battle of Jericho" was playing on the radio in English. Leaving Tallinn we saw what seemed miles and miles of stacked small birch logs, their cut ends blond and smiling in the rain.

Once settled on our side of the train compartment, reading, we watched a short, shy man enter, dressed in a blue sweatsuit. His hands were charred and gnarled with use. His red-haired wife reclined her splendid bulk the full length of the lower berth. Without having acknowledged our presence in the compartment, she proceeded to peruse the Russian equivalent of an American movie magazine while she munched on assorted chocolates. Her minuscule but sturdy husband did everything within his power to maintain her comfort throughout the trip, fluffing up her pillow, granting her his own, covering her with a blanket when she dozed off. He also struck up a conversation with me, liberally assisted on my side by my small Oxford Russian dictionary.

I learned that he was retired (*na pensii*). He was also immensely curious about American penalties (*nakazanie*) for drunk driving, registering surprise at their laxity compared to those in his country. His curiosity seemed prompted by firsthand experience. He and his wife had two daughters, he said, one a teacher who had graduated from the pedagogical institute, the other a hairdresser. The couple was on their way to Minsk — the sister city, God forbid, of Detroit — to visit his wife's family. We discussed music. "It's the international language," he said, as Roger Miller's "King of the Road" was piped into the compartment. We discussed the environment. He bemoaned the clearing of so much forest land. "All of this will resemble Siberia someday," he said.

We discussed the degree of friendship our two countries seemed to be enjoying just now. He asked what I thought of Russian people, and I said that I liked them for their "unzipped souls," their openness. He smiled broadly and seemed pleased, growing more "unzipped" himself as the train sped along. I mentioned the Leningrad cab driver who thought Gorbachev was "only words." Smiling again, my new friend confessed that he still admired the party secretary. When I mentioned the perpetual American concern about war, he shrugged and said such fears were no longer necessary. However, when the afternoon news broke into the music on the intercom, and the word *kleb* (bread) was mentioned, both he and his wife — who opened her eyes with a start — sat up and listened. The program reported on the shortage of food, and on rationing, in Moscow. His wife muttered something about "more bad news" and turned the sound down.

"No, turn it back up," he said forcefully. "I want to listen."

We talked for the rest of the trip. He leaned forward into my face, asking many questions, anxious for my replies. In contrast his wife seemed suspicious of us and of the conversation her husband was engaged in. Therefore, when the train arrived in Riga, it took us by surprise when this couple going on to Minsk grabbed our luggage and insisted on carting it out to the platform for us, the wife hefting Betty's heavy suitcase as if it were just another bonbon. In a near tearful farewell outside, the husband gave me a hearty handshake, wishing us "Schastlivovo puti!" (Bon voyage!), and his formerly comatose wife was so fully demonstrative now I feared she might maim my own small spouse with the blunt force of her affection, Betty hidden in the woman's substantial arms. I felt as if she had been studying us throughout the trip and had finally decided we were worthy of this stupendous farewell.

We ensconced ourselves in the Latvija Hotel, a twenty-seven-story affair with 365 "well-appointed rooms and suites" that looks straight down Lenin

Street to the Freedom Monument erected in honor of Latvians deported to Siberia when the Soviets took over. Its base, throughout our stay, was heavily adorned with commemorative flowers. I attempted to phone Anthony Marhel, for just as she had been responsible for discovering Aziza Mustafa-Zadeh, Betty had found and made friends with Anthony in Moscow, although in this case we hadn't known who he was beforehand. We hadn't sought him out. Both his person and his position within the USSR jazz world turned out to be a fine surprise, and he had invited us to visit him in Riga. But I had forgotten my miserable record so far with the USSR phone system. After I had spoken with just about everybody in Riga except Anthony, I walked up Komunaru Boulevard in the rain, looking for the firm Kultura of the Latvian Foreign Trade Association, Interlatvija, where he works. If the Soviet phone system is calculated to drive one insane, the system — if there is one — by which buildings are allocated numbers also assists that condition. Number one Komunaru, Anthony's address, sounded accessible enough. However, where it should have been a doorway disclosed a flight of dilapidated stairs leading up to an export company whose doors were being fastened shut, at 4:30, by a woman who told me that Anthony's company could probably be found at the other end of Komunaru Boulevard.

"Nedaleko otciuda?" (Not far from here?) I asked, hoping beyond hope.

"Net, eto daleko" (No, it is far), she replied, her eyes lowered in sympathy.

And it was. I walked the length of Embassy Row, mad as hell and more soaked by the minute. I finally found him, far across town, in a building (the former Japanese embassy) undergoing *v remonte* (repairs), like so much else in the Soviet Union. Anthony greeted me warmly, immediately supplying a hot cup of coffee.

Compared to the First Moscow International Jazz Festival, Riga's Fifteenth International, or Starptautiskais, Festival was a model of order, efficiency, and clarity of intent. On the steps of the Guild Hall in which the festival's organizational committee was housed, I was introduced by Anthony to the producer/director, Leonid Nidbalsky, a handsome silver-haired man, whom I had met earlier in Moscow. I thanked him for securing passes for us at such short notice, and Nibalsky — busy as he must have been at the time — was quite cordial. Betty and I were ushered into a room in which a festival committee member adhered the snapshots we had been asked to bring to our passes (a procedure that would have spared much wasted effort in Moscow), and I was "William Minor/USA" this time, not "Mulgrew Miller."

Inside the cross-vaulted Philharmonic Concert Hall, formerly Great Guild or Virgin's Guild Hall, with chandeliers that date back to the seventeenth century, the stage was spare, "mod." Large dancing orange letters spelled out "JAZZ" above a row of slats that resembled venetian blinds, and an abstract keyboard, tastefully designed. Flags of many nations hung from the balcony, and the lighting was bright and cheerful. A very compatible atmosphere pervaded the hall, conducive to jazz. In the foyer stood a handsome display of photographs by Marek Karewicz. My favorite was a shot of a morose Duke Ellington adorned with jewelry and deep musical concern.

Unfortunately, because our itinerary allotted only two days for Riga, we would miss hearing Lembit Saarsalu, pianist Leonid Vintskevich, and the amazing Tuva throat-singer Sainkho Namchylak, who would perform with Latvian bassist Ivar Galeniks. We would also miss a Jazz Singers Band from Lithuania and, on the last night, the Guyvoronsky/Volkov Duo from Leningrad, a pair much acclaimed by everyone I had talked to so far, plus a noonday "riverboat musical outing" for festival participants and guests that sounded like great fun.

However, for two nights we heard fine music, the ubiquitous master of ceremonies Vladimir Feyertag once again presiding. "He's so cute," Betty said, as the critic launched into one of his witty, charming yet seemingly interminable intros, announcing the "modern Dixieland" efforts of a group from the Riga Jazz Club — the drummer's stilted, sluggish rhythm dragging the pace of "Caravan" down to a camel's crawl. An attractive, very blond vocalist in black Baghdad pajama bottoms, puffy blouse, and stiletto heels, standing a full head above the soprano saxophonist doing obbligato chores, then sang "Running Wild." Immediately after, two young girls in Latvian dress, white stockings, and pill box hats rushed out and handed long-stemmed roses to each member of the band, including the singer, a ritual that would follow each set throughout the night.

The next group, from Kaliningrad, "conducted" by Maxim Piganov and Viktor Avdeyev, consisted of flugelhorn, trombone, soprano sax, electric guitar, electric bass, and drums. Following a mike check — "Gotovyi? Gotovyi?" (Ready? Ready?) — they plunged the small crowd into a comfortable world of swing, Duke Ellington's tune reaffirming that "it don't mean a thing" if you ain't got it, and this group did, a smooth Kansas City Seven style, right down to some surprising evocations of Freddie Green on the part of the young man with shoulder-length hair playing solid body rock guitar. The beat faded, unfortunately, by the time they got to Jimmy Lunceford's "Honey, Keep Your Mind on Me."

The highlight of this first evening, for me, was the extraordinary Arkadi Shilkloper, appearing solo in Riga, dressed, like the Dixieland singer, in black Baghdad pajama bottoms — an "in" thing in Riga? — and black jersey, his handsome face shrouded by a styled page-boy cut. Shilkloper is very much a showman and, armed with just his French horn, achieves effects that seem to betray the slim potential of human breath. His adroitly improvised call-and-response technique suggests that he might be hiding another instrument somewhere, and he actually plays chords, vocal humming in sync with all this. Sitting lotuslike on the floor, he stuck a small globe — the whole world! — in his horn, and, imitating a shepherd's plaintive but primitive cry, let the sound evolve to a simple, masterful moving folk melody, the notes replicating themselves to become a dizzy "Flight of the Bumblebee" succession, intricate but not just show, as the musician managed to keep the memory of the melody firm in one's mind. The piece was a polytechnical marvel, growls and grunts and groans weaving in and out of the core, adding secondary, or even triadic, themes, the whole always dancing. Shilkloper "toweled down" afterward, changed into a waiter's white shirt and black bow tie, and piped a rollicking tune on two small horns, providing his own harmony. By way of an encore, he concluded with a French horn solo comprised of deep bass tones, lightning runs that climaxed with some blues slurs, classic bop invention, and an exquisite fade-out.

Shilkloper was followed by Latvia's Juli Smirnoff Five, a tight ensemble featuring its leader on tenor sax, a man Frederick Starr has called "the best cool saxophone player in the USSR," a contention which, when mentioned by Anthony, was accompanied by a smirk. I felt the group's pianist was the mainstay, with his agile left-hand bop runs. The bass and drummer appeared a bit puzzled over the exact nature of their functions, the drummer's "bombs" turning out to be just that. After "Groovin' High" and "Billie's Bounce," "Alone Together" provided a fine tenor solo in the Zoot Sims / Stan Getz mode, with tasty intervals. Aside from the pianist, though, there didn't seem to be enough to back Smirnoff up.

The evening's last group was the Jari Perä Sextet from Finland, with a hard bop style and close ensemble work, a seasoned gang whose drummer provided driving accents mixed with intricate rhythmic shifts. The leader, on keyboards (a Technic PX7), projected an intriguing marimbalike tone on "Nights in Tunisia," the time wickedly doubled. This was a solid, professional group, a pleasure to hear. This first night's festival fare had provided interesting range, more catholic in that sense than anything offered in Moscow, where the organizers, eager for their first live listen to Americans, had settled for too many of them. Stars, too, can sleep on the job and were bested occasionally, to my mind, by show-stealing Soviets. The Riga program didn't offer Moscow's depth of talent, perhaps, but the menu had more variety.

We spent the next day on a walking tour of Riga conducted by Anthony Marhel. A stone arch you'd never find on any tourist's map led us to a tucked-away outdoor café, a long, narrow, open courtyard where we drank coffee beneath orange-and-green umbrellas. Anthony had frequented this place during his student days, writing his dissertation about Latvian postcards of the 1970s and 1980s, their "semantic" aspects, elements of folk inheritance. He is devoted to Riga, where he grew up, went to school, has worked since, has done "everything." "My whole life has happened here," he said.

Later, we walked past one of those massive faceless structures so popular with the lords of the land. "Communist Party headquarters," he said, offering his wry smile again. "We call this place 'the open book.' But it is not an open book."

Watching the troubles of neighboring Lithuania on TV at home—that republic to which, at the last minute, we had not been allowed to go—I had anticipated that Riga would be a tense city, nerves on edge, as depicted in those clever juxtapositions the U.S. media loves so much: grim-faced Russian soldiers set off against determined Baltic citizens. However, the streets of Riga exuded a summer ease, comfort, and well-dressed pride. An occasional military truck disgorged its load of baby-faced, acne-studded Russian soldiers lugging their machine guns into some government building, but the Latvians—many lovers strolling hand in hand on this pleasant day—seemed to scan the intrusion with near disinterest, as if the soldiers were a nuisance long endured but soon to be disposed of, a fly you would like to brush back to its native habitat.

"If you return in five years," Anthony said, as we walked along cobblestone passageways, "there will be no Russian on these street signs. And no Russians in the streets. We also will have our own currency." The fine old twisting, turning avenues of Riga exuded independence, hope, and confidence. The Anniversary of the Deportations crowd was out, burying the base of the Freedom Monument in brightly colored flowers. We passed the Museum of the Revolution, where no one stood in line, compared to a sizable queue outside the Canadian embassy awaiting visas for permanent departure.

I asked Anthony about his name, unusual in the Soviet Union. "I am Catholic," he said, explaining his Polish ancestry. He talked about life in Latvia up to this time, of friends who'd been denied their diplomas because of their political views, of being followed home himself after attending jazz concerts, of the fear generated by the power of the Leningrad Party with its antijazz attitude and "supervision" of all activities.

We walked past a vacant lot that still displayed the scars of extensive World War II bomb damage. "Nobody knows if the Germans or the Russians did this," Anthony said, again offering an existential shrug of a smile. Our tour took us past the Powder Tower, a medieval dungeon and torture chamber that now forms a portion of the unvisited Museum of the Revolution, and on to the Domkirk, formerly the Cathedral of Our Lady, dating to 1211 and reflecting its incarnations—Romanesque, Gothic, Renaissance, baroque—

under various foreign masters. This church houses one of the largest organs in the world, 6,768 pipes, still used for concerts.

That afternoon, Anthony took us by bus across the modern Gorkovskii Bridge, eager for us to visit his own *dom* (home). By the way he said the word I knew he didn't mean that sort of sanctuary apartment in a rundown building we'd seen in Moscow. After leading us through a vast and somewhat depressing high-rise project, he turned a corner, and there — sequestered among trees, with a front gate and healthy woodpile — stood the home Anthony shares with his wife, Jeanne, their son, Daniel, and his mother. (Another couple lives upstairs.) We entered by way of the garden, a nice-sized lot with a greenhouse for tomatoes, strawberries, and onions and a picnic table for barbecues — all unexpectedly bourgeois. Anthony stood by, obviously proud of this house he can't, and doesn't, own, and of his wife, Jeanne, her face framed in richly tangled auburn hair. Jeanne is a former stage set designer. An artist of considerable merit, she has now retired, at thirty rubles a month (about five dollars at the time) in order to take care of their child.

Jeanne had prepared sandwiches and tea, and we dallied over these, followed by small glasses of Balsam, a Latvian liqueur I guess you would have to call an acquired taste, but one I acquired easily, although Betty found the stuff too "medicinal," too cough syrupy. Anthony and I talked jazz. As with most of the musicians and critics I'd talked to, my initial questions centered on what was unique about jazz in the Soviet Union. I brought up the one element people had emphasized: the success or failure of attempting to incorporate native or folk elements into the music.

"It's not productive," he said flatly, in that manner of plain speaking that had struck me about him from the start. "It's not productive to use elements of folk music in jazz. And not only in Latvia. The Estonians too have tried to use these elements, probably with more success, because they fit with the cool sound they have inherited from Finland and Norway. It works here in classical music, perhaps, employing popular folk songs, a folk ground, melodic themes, the way Tchaikovsky used popular Russian songs. It was a mold for that time, and was very popular with young people. Music from Armenia, Uzbekistan, Japan, India — it was all very popular here at one time. But people did not understand this music, the impulse behind it."

"The music of a group like Boomerang, from Alma Ata, for instance?"

"Well, that just doesn't *mix* in my opinion. Some groups from Africa can bring it off. And Americans like Archie Shepp and Don Cherry, what they learned from Ravi Shankar in India, because that's a compatible improvisational system. It's structured in the same way jazz is."

"How about Vagif Mustafa-Zadeh?"

"He was very interesting for us," Anthony said. "I am an extremist in music, perhaps, but I thought he played for the mass media. Critic Efim Barban called him an 'idol.' Yet Vagif Mustafa-Zadeh was good for Soviet jazz. He opened up something very new. And his bass player became quite popular."

"Tamaz Kurashvili."

"Yes."

Anthony is wholly earnest about music now, strong in his convictions on what passes for merit and what does not, just as he had been about the future of Latvia. Yet he confesses that the origin of his interest in jazz was quite tentative. He recalls the time he first attended concerts of fusion artist Alexei Kozlov, how "exciting" that era was. "We listened only to rock," he says, "and Kozlov did much to introduce us to jazz. We began to attend lectures. In 1975, I returned from military service. I liked King Crimson, Genesis, Cream. But Jeanne helped me. She introduced me to serious music. She'd been sending tapes to me while I was in the army. It was all very hard at the beginning. Such strange music! But I decided I should, and did, acquire more knowledge than our friends who just liked jazz/rock—groups like Soft Machine, Soviet groups. I had two friends—both dead now—with whom I exchanged records. One had relatives in America. We gathered all the information we could on the new music. I began to collect records. I became a specialist in discographies."

As evidence of this, Anthony showed me six extraordinary volumes, complete discographies kept in ordinary schoolboy cardboard copybooks that list not only every conceivable album and front-line contemporary performer alphabetically—"Abercrombie, Abrams, Adams (George), Adams (Pepper), Adderley (Cannonball), Adderley (Nat), 'Air,' Airto, Akiyoshi," and so on— but sidemen as well.

"A labor of love," he said. "See, I checked all the ones I heard."

The checks were many. The amazing books included not just contemporary performers but jazzmen dating back to 1915. "Many people ask me to recommend records." His own collection was extensive, containing albums purchased from European distributors or directly from companies such as Pedro de Freitas's Sound Aspects in West Germany—the sort of material I've been dying to get my hands on, difficult to obtain through American distributors.

"I mostly like serious jazz," Anthony said. "Serious music—composed music with the elements of both structure and improvisation." He spoke of a time when Russian musicians played whatever they thought was "popular": jazz/rock, fusion, free jazz, harmolodic. "Ornette Coleman destroyed many musicians who started to play jazz at that time," he said. "Just as there was a crisis over jazz/rock, there was a crisis in the jazz world of the seventies over 'harmolodic.' Kuryokhin wanted to be like John Zorn, but this was not Kuryokhin's own music, his own input. I like music without postmodern jokes and songs. I like the Guyvoronsky/Volkov Duo from Leningrad. Ganelin.

Petras Vysniauskas. Sergei Letov, Shilkloper, and Arkadi Kirichenko — the group called Tri-O — even though they do try some jokes, insert the blues, sing in an unknown language."

Again I thought of those elements of the 1920s avant-garde I'd thought I had heard in Russian new music and had set out, initially, to corrolate. Yet when I asked Anthony about all this, his response was the familiar one: the correspondence might be there, but he didn't believe the artists were conscious of it.

"Right! Yes," he responded. "Those parallels do exist. But Kuryokhin didn't think about it. Whatever he made was made spontaneously. Oh, he knew; there's no doubt about that. He has a solid knowledge of the history of Soviet literature and art. You know, he lived here, for a month, in 1978. He's my good friend. He wasn't 'popular' then, just a good musician. And I can remember how he prepared — or didn't prepare. He composed at the moment. That's when he would decide to do this, or this, or this. Now, perhaps, he is deliberately trying to make use of those materials from the past — making up stuff especially for foreigners. But he wasn't when he started. And I don't like his joking now. He's got good ideas, but the realization of them can be quite stupid. Bringing on actors and amateur musicians — that sort of thing. He can't realize his ideals that way. I prefer his solo playing."

He commented on the lack of opportunities for major artists to perform together, and the nesting instinct that keeps musicians playing in the same small groups, Moscow artists with Moscovites, Leningraders with Leningraders. "The whole business of the Moscow festival — of inviting guests, of thinking in terms of super stars — that's not typical of Soviet musicians." Before we left for that evening's concert, Jeanne brought out a rich stock of her own highly impressive art work.

Once Anthony discovered I was interested in the visual arts as well as jazz, he supplied me with many monographs and journals on Latvian art. On our walking tour of Riga, we had dropped into a large gallery housing a retrospective showing by several artists and had walked through a charming outdoor sculpture garden, stepping amidst Brancusi-stylized deer and a Maillol-like life-sized bronze reclining nude. Along with the art work I'd discovered in Karelia, in Petrozavodsk, the art of Riga struck me as the most interesting I had seen in the USSR.

However, I don't think I saw any work in Riga more exciting than Jeanne Marhel's. She had several large portraits of stylish women sitting in cafés, but most impressive were her mock-up designs for stage sets for drama as varied as Kabuki, *A Thousand and One Nights,* and Gorky's *Lower Depths,* for which costumed figures executed in cloth and papier-mâché were mounted on boards —

handsome pieces in their own right, regardless of how they had functioned in the play. I was less fond of a new series of abstract art she had set out upon. I find it a painful irony that, although a Russian, Kandinsky, introduced the world to an absolute art that could "approximate the condition of music," after seventy years of cruel history and an uncompromising aesthetic (socialist realism) visual artists in eastern Europe and Russia are attempting to reclaim a form more modern than they are accustomed to. The attempt to make this leap without having gone through the necessary evolutionary stages is not always successful. Yet I found most of Jeanne's work handsomely imagined and dramatically implemented.

The last evening of the Starptautiskais Jazz Festival we attended afforded even more variety than the previous night, although less of it Soviet. The Akira Ito and Ten Te Ko Mai Group from Japan didn't show up, but Peter Shaevli's quintet from Switzerland did, featuring Tom Varner from the United States on French horn. I was impressed by Varner, who had just won the *JazzTimes* "emerging talent" slot for his instrument, and whom I'd met on the previous evening, beginning to speak Russian to him before I realized I didn't need to. I was also impressed by Odessan pianist Yuri Kuznetsov performing the forty-five-minute straight-shot no-chaser suite I described at the beginning of this book.

After the concert, Anthony, Betty, and I walked back in the fine summer night to the smaller Guild House we'd visited to get our festival passes. In a pleasant back-room pub there, with high wooden booths and a bar, we shared several glasses of champagne with Nikolai Dmitriev, the editor of *Dzhaz* magazine in Moscow. Nikolai said he wished to have my *Coda* article on Sergei Kuryokhin translated and included in a future issue, and we discussed the music of the festival so far with this warm, small bearish man — as opposed to Anatoli Vapirov's large bearish manner perhaps — with, behind glasses, somewhat watery affectionate eyes. I enjoyed — in spite of the realization that we had to be up at 5:30 to catch a plane for Kiev — this chance to kick back among newfound friends and celebrate the fact that we'd been lucky enough to catch as much as we had of the Riga festival.

I noticed someone familiar sitting directly behind me in the next booth, and thought for the moment it was the American Tom Varner. When, clicking glasses for the last time, we were finally compelled to leave I asked Anthony, on the way out, who that person was. He said it was Arkadi Shilkloper. To this day, in spite of the early hour for our departure, I wish I'd gone back and talked to this exceptional musician. I'd made the mistake of passing up a chance to nab Petras Vysniauskas back in Moscow, and here I'd gone and committed this sin of omission again. Fate had intervened in the case of a few other unavailable jazz artists perhaps, but these two had been within my range, and I'd let the chance to get their opinions slip by.

Downstairs, we parted with Anthony and Nikolai, who gave me a solid Russian bear hug, seemingly moved by our departure. Anthony, the stoic, the existentialist, shook my hand and smiled one last wry smile.

# The Ukraine,
## in Joy
## and Sorrow

Home of the original Rus, center of "a flourishing Old Russian community," the "rudiments of a State," in Ronald Higley's words, Kiev provided us three days of Sundays, some respite from the quick-change artistry of travel (within a week we had visited Leningrad, Petrozavodsk, Tallinn, and Riga), and a chance for me to think about and synthesize, if I could, all that I'd seen and heard so far on our quest for Soviet jazz.

Unfortunately, I had not been all that impressed by music from Kiev I'd listened to back in Moscow and had made the mistake — also lacking any specific musical contacts in the city — of writing the place off as a source for jazz. The scene here looked about as dead as the reign of Prince (also Saint) Vladimir himself, a man who'd once possessed eight hundred concubines and had selected Christianity as the state religion in 988 because, unlike Islam, it would allow him to continue drinking.

We didn't meet any saints or princes in Kiev. On the walk from our hotel, the Lybed (Swan), past the *tsirk* (circus) closed for repairs and the large and buzzing Ukraine State Department Store, then straight down many blocks to the *rynok* (large market), we did see people either passed out or sleeping on top of or beneath benches along the parkway. Some had no shoes, their feet wrapped in rags. Returning later that afternoon, we were approached by a young man wishing to convert rubles to dollars. Although I denied him that illegal delight, we struck up a conversation, and he accompanied us nearly all the way back to the hotel, shaking his head over the homeless people we passed (the Soviet Union wasn't supposed to have any). In America, he said, we must be fortunate enough to have no *bez dom* or *liudi ylitsy* (street people, or people without homes).

"Vy shutite?" (Are you kidding?), I said.

He seemed shocked. He'd once seen Bush talking about housing problems on TV but hadn't believed him. The Soviet conception is that everyone in America except Blacks is rich. He asked me how it was possible for people in America not to have a nice home.

"Bez dengi, bez dom" (No money, no home), I said.

As we discussed rents, unemployment, and the lack of job opportunities for unskilled persons, his surprise increased with each revelation. He asked me what nationality I was, and I replied, "American."

"Net, net," he cried. "What nationality?"

Unfortunately, at this time, I didn't know the word for *mongrel* (the most curious of which is *nechistokrobnyi,* literally, "dirty-blooded"). But he wouldn't have understood, because on a Soviet passport one has to state ethnic origin or nationality: Russian, Armenian, Azerbaijanian, Jew — the latter not considered a religion. He was amazed by my passport with the word *American* stamped on it.

"We have rich people too," he said somewhat proudly. "In Armenia. In Georgia."

Sticking with the subject of ethnicity, I mentioned that Detroit, where I'd grown up, was home to forty-four different ethnic groups.

"Dee-troit. Eto avtomobilnoe mesto, da?" (This is the automobile place, right?).

"Mo-gorodok" (Mo-little town), I said, and he laughed.

This got us onto the subject of music. He didn't like jazz but did like *dzhaz-rok.* He mentioned the American group Chicago, and the inevitable Beatles. I mentioned Alexei Kozlov's fusion group Arsenal, stating that I'd met Kozlov in Moscow. He didn't seem at all impressed, saying he'd heard the group and they were "okay." Kiev is a great city for walking, and this conversation set the stage for three days of reflection on my part, much of it while strolling. It brought to mind Russian solemnity, resilience, fatalism, and frankness — all of which I'd also found in the music so far. Once this young man had discovered I was no source for dollars, he'd contented himself with conversation, strolling. Nothing to prove and much to know, or perhaps find out.

Betty and I went to the open Central Market, or Krity Rinok, in Bessarabskaya Square, a huge hall loaded with bins of apricots, cherries, cheese, nuts, raisins, oranges, lettuce, strawberries, potatoes, onions, and what looked to be rancid meat — wonderful stuff everybody looked at but few seemed in a position to buy, except in long lines for the inevitable, unvariable, and apparently inedible cut-rate salami. We hiked up Taras Shevchenko Boulevard on our way to Vladimir's Cathedral, graced with seven gilded domes. A choir devulging sumptuous tonalities attracted crowds of old people who crossed themselves fervidly, and young ones who quietly lit candles. I thought of what Anatoli Vapirov had said about the significance of *dukh,* or spirit, in his work; of Leo Feigin's initial concept of the music as an article of faith, Russia itself as a land of jazz (and other) "miracles."

We slid over the fine parquet floors of the Shevchenko Museum's twenty-four rooms in paper slippers, scanning the eight hundred drawings and paintings the famous Ukrainian writer, also an artist, had managed to fit into his life. Sitting on a beautiful blond birchwood bench, gazing at handsome guitars with extended necks, an extraordinary lute inlaid with flowers formed of jewels, content amid this nineteenth-century opulence, I thought of some late-twentieth-century realities: Igor Butman's, and Vapirov's statements about the limited number of "top artists" in the USSR, the isolation and lack of *partnery;* the sometimes slavish adherence to what they thought constituted musical fashion in the West (Shevchenko himself, for all his Ukrainian novelty, seemed Byronic) or the outright mockery on the part of people like Vladimir Chekasin and Sergei Kuryokhin of that to which they seemed unwilling to be in thrall; the fierce desire for independence and national identity on the part of Aziza Mustafa-Zadeh and Anthony Marhel.

I stood outside the Marinsky Palace and St. Sophia's Cathedral, where a man sang medieval ecclesiastical songs, accompanying himself on a magnificent multistringed instrument, a *bandura*. I looked up at the gold baroque extravagance of St. Andrew's Cathedral. I examined the icons of the Novgorod, Moscow, and Stroganov schools in the Museum of Russian Art. And I thought of the paradox of Igor Butman questioning the value of Soviet jazz while discovering his own Russian uniqueness by way of Slavic scales with just four to six notes he first recognized in Boston, at Berklee. "I heard something that was very familiar," he had told me, "and I went, 'Oh, it's *mine.*'"

Strolling in Kiev I also thought of the mythological legacy of place important to Anatoli Vapirov and Andrei Kondakov, of Aziza Mustafa-Zadeh steeped in the tradition of mugam. I realized that this jazz, whatever you wished to call it — Soviet, Russian, Karelian, Azerbaijanian — was vitally connected with larger culture, a wider source, plus a great deal of continuity. Jazz music seemed related to both folk and high arts to a degree unthinkable in the United States. Lacking specific academic evidence — names, dates, places, acknowledged sources, or any direct confessions of influence — I was, nevertheless, feeling this continuity everywhere on the trip: in the Leningrad cemetery that housed Tchaikovsky, Borodin, and Mussorgsky; in the Kalavala panels in the park at Petrozavodsk; in the singing nation of Estonia; in the flowers at the base of the Freedom Monument in Riga; right down to the phone and postal systems, Irene's admonition to never waste two hours of a Moscow woman's time, and the myriad daily frustrations, delays, and disappointments that made up Soviet life. I could hear it all in the music, and I could see it now in Kiev, this still-beautiful city rebuilt from the cruel attempt, on the part of another culture, to remove it from its place in time, and from the face of the earth itself.

A woman working for Intourist in Kiev joined her driver at a table we shared and burst into tears, muttering, "Oi, oi, oi." The task of escorting a large party of Germans in their sixties and seventies around the city was driving her crazy, assailing her *serdtse* (heart), she told him. She'd lost both her parents in World War II. When she realized I understood what she was saying, she told Betty and me that her brothers now lived in Pennsylvania, Florida, and New York; then she went unblithely back to her task of showing her tour group the paradoxically rich legacy of a city that had survived their nation's attempts to destroy it.

We descended Andreevsky Hill, past the new bohemian sector, past the house at number thirteen where Mikhail Bulgakov had lived as a child, the author who, in "silence" for twelve years and with no hope of publication, wrote what I feel is one of the finest novels of the twentieth century, *The Master and Margarita*. Satirical art was now sold on the street: Castro sucking on the naked tit of Mother Russia. We walked out to what remains of the Bratsky Monastery, where nuns carted and stacked recently cut wood. Then we hiked the length of a park beside the Dneiper River out to the Monastery of the Caves, a golden-domed ensemble of ancient buildings, including the Dormition Cathedral, built in 1073. All but a portion was destroyed by the Germans in 1941. Inside the Historical Museum, a girl in Ukrainian costume bent above a display case filled with painted eggs. A room upstairs was devoted to Alexander Solzhenitsyn. The caves themselves led one down into history's depths: seventy-three tombs and three underground churches, mummified bodies with names attached — the most famous that of the chronicler Nestor, who died in 1115.

Out in the open air, drinking beer and eating *piroshki* in the park close by the Dynamo Stadium (six diving boards at the pool, and a fine track), strolling around Kiev drunk on my own Russomania, I realized I was no longer in a position to judge the music and the culture it had sprung from by external standards. I had become a temporary part of the isolation and self-consciousness Westerners attribute to this massive mysterious state of mind called the Soviet Union. All I could hear in my mind were rich "very long melodies," as Igor Butman had described them. "I can remember Russian melodies," he'd said. "They're very simple, but they are strong. That's what I have from Russia. So that's what I am working on."

Yet in all the jazz music I'd devoted this trip to, music sprung from dangerous devotion ("Jazz on Bones" itself a legacy of that crypt of Nester the Chronicler in the Monastery of the Caves?) and courageous creative commitment, was there evidence of Russian uniqueness, of inner freedom, genuine stylistic — polystylistic — rebellion, a fresh context of architectonic and phonic richness based on *umileniye* (deep feeling), a relevant, reverent, imperative need? My answer was yes and no. So much of what I'd discovered was standard, if delightful, repertory stuff, well executed, heartfelt but commonplace. Universal (by desire and design) in its jazz vocabulary, it was music played by very human, admirable musicians like Germann Lukianov and Igor Bril.

In his liner notes to Leo Feigin's eight-CD boxed set *Document: New Music from Russia,* Alexander Kahn expressed his fear that "the Western new music community," caught up in the hype of "Gorbymania," might set aside its "condescending arrogant attitudes to Soviet new jazz" only to set a fresh "trap" for the music: Soviet musicians as "some sort of messiahs, bearers of the eternal flame of Russia's centuries old culture, or mysterious spiritual souls from behind the crumbling relics of the iron curtain." This was an admonition I needed to pay attention to. Yet even Alexander Kahn couldn't avoid a postscript, saying, "Yes, hopefully some are."


Up until the day we left Kiev, we had been spoiled by Intourist. We and our baggage had been shunted from place to place in a seemingly chaotic yet agreeable and ultimately effective fashion. We always got where we wanted to go. Consequently, when our driver ditched us on the front steps of the Kiev train station, we felt lost and abandoned. Inside, a mob of travelers milled about on a huge marble floor. Posted on the walls were arrival and departure times for just about every city and village in the Soviet Union except Odessa, our destination.

Leaving Betty with the luggage, I sprinted to a platform with a train marked "South" but learned it was going to Kishinev. Finally, as our departure time approached and panic set in, the Odessa train was posted. We took off for the track, toting our suitcases heavy with records I had bought. (I had counted on purchasing cassettes, but they didn't exist, aside from homegrown or black-market goods.) We headed up one long flight of stairs, down another, up a third, down a narrow series of steps, and arrived at track ten, along with a host of fellow travelers. The train to Odessa was late by fifteen minutes. When the chafing ride south commenced and we discovered the train carried no form of liquid refreshment other than hot tea, we would understand why people carted not only their own luggage but countless bottles of mineral water. Now we stood among the mob, the Intourist status that had previously whisked us aboard planes and trains ahead of all crowds null and void here. We were just a couple of pathetic Americans who'd been set adrift beside a railroad track. But the train did arrive, our coach locating itself far from where we'd been standing, of course, and another mad rush was on. Finally settled in our compartment, were were joined by two women who chatted so amicably we assumed they were lifelong friends (they'd just met) and, just before the train pulled out, the distraught face of the Intourist employee responsible for our safe delivery, appearing in the doorway. "Mai-nor?"

"Yes?"

"You are here okay?"

"Yes. Everything's fine. Prekrasno."

"Have a pleasant trip."

"Thank you. Do svidaniia."

And off we rolled, back into a fine Ukrainian afternoon, the sights of which were almost immediately expounded upon for me by Nina, the more friendly at first of the two women, both of whom, I believe, were amused by the incident they had just witnessed and — I'd like to think — somewhat impressed by the fact that we'd actually managed to settle in so cozily on our own. Once the train got that way, Nina too grew very animated. Her face contained that amazing Russian capacity to appear by turns girlishly bright, staunch, ungirded, incredibly sad, stoic, infinitely joyous, and long-suffering. She wore a plain dress with red-and-blue striped patterning on somewhat soiled white, a sort of sash thrown over the left shoulder stitched into its design, a long shoelace loop tied at her waist and resting in her lap where, also, throughout most of the trip south, her hands lay, except when deployed for short, sudden bursts of total animation. Her hair was short, brown, frazzled; her arms were plump, although there seemed to be something secretly unhealthy about her, in the most literal sense, as if she harbored, bravely, some dreadful disease. "She's not well," my wife would say later.

But she was, from the start, spirited, and she pointed out to us gypsies (Tsyganky) sleeping on a hill, their extra bedding slung over ropes to make crude tents; the barn-shaped Ukrainian roofs of brick homes, the brick as pale as unfinished pine; and then, to my surprise, growing in rows alongside the railroad tracks, midget stuff, not the tall elephant's-eye variety of the American Midwest, *kukuruza* (a word that's fun to say, and I did, again and again), what my well-worn *Pocket Oxford* translates as "maize" or "Indian corn."

The other woman, Valinsina, or Vala (as she later became), was more reserved but did show an eager, if stealthy, interest in our conversation. Sporting more than a few layers of makeup, she was dressed in a black dress with a flower print. She had boarded with a basket of food, what looked to be a large whole chicken, which she set upon almost immediately with considerable relish. She was large herself, darker and more formidable than Nina. Valinsina then disclosed a kilo of fresh strawberries, which, after departing to that obscene entity that passes, on Soviet trains, for a bathroom, in order to wash them off, she offered us. Later, I asked my wife just how to describe one of these washrooms, and she replied, "One word: indescribable." The strawberries, however, were delicious.

When Betty herself returned from a trip to the bathroom, the two other women regarded her with compassion. Both expressed surprise that we hadn't taken the express to Odessa, which most foreign tourists do ("There is one?" I exclaimed) because it is not only faster but "cleaner" as well. I said I was pleased we were on this train because, that way, we had been fortunate enough to meet the two of them. They seemed to like that.

Night came on. As the *kukuruza* and garden plots dissolved in darkness, the two women chatted. Eavesdropping — the excuse I offered my conscience was that I was practicing my Russian — I learned that Valinsina's husband had died at Chernobyl, that she herself had been relocated in Kiev, and that she was returning now to a town, north of Odessa, in which she and her husband had lived for twenty-five years. Nina's tragedy, whispered, was one so intolerable — from what little I caught it seemed to involve a disease, yes, and also, perhaps, the death of a child — that Vala simply uttered the ejaculation "oi, oi, oi," over and over again, shaking her head in wonder at Nina's ability to bear the pain.

Later, when we succumbed to small talk again, Nina and I discussed the difficulty of learning a foreign language. She knew some French and used what she knew, which was small but more than mine. Vala knew German — but for all the wrong reasons: following the murder of her parents, when the Ukraine was overrun at the start of World War II — a language which, as she found out trying some on me, I do not know at all. I mentioned that songs seemed to help in the process, and they asked me which Russian songs I knew. I sang Bulat Okudzhava's "Blue Balloon," in which he uses four Russian words (*devochka*, young girl; *devushka,* adolescent; *zhenshchina,* young woman; and *starushka,* old lady) to trace the loss of a blue balloon through childish carelessness, teen love, adult marriage and betrayal, and aging), the song happily resolved by the balloon's miraculous return through hope at the end. I showed them the music to some other songs I'd brought with me, and before I knew it, we had a full-scale hootenany on our hands. They sang Andrei Eshpai's lovely "Dva Berega" ("Two Shores:" — "You and I are the two shores of a river") but said they really preferred Ukrainian folk songs, each woman then subsiding into the wall behind her, heads rested contentedly, dreamily as they proceeded to sing, for more than an hour, a medley of pieces they obviously loved, melodies on which they gently, easefully imposed a lovely, natural two-part harmony.

Up to this point, Valinsina had been the more reserved of the two, but with coaxing ("Oh, I don't think I can remember the words") she began to expose vein upon vein of rich oral memory, verse after verse of haunting

Ukrainian folk tunes. When she sang a song that dwelt on both mother and war her handsome voice forced Nina to ask her to stop, "or you will make me cry." Nina had been vigorously rubbing the gooseflesh on her substantial arms.

"Ukrainian songs make you weep," Nina said to my wife and me. "Mnogo" (Much).

My cassette recorder was buried deep in the suitcase lodged in a metal chest below the bed on which the two women sat, so I was not able to preserve this marvelous evening outside of memory, yet I thought at the time, "Memory will be enough." I did not want to spoil the spontaneity with which they had offered these songs, so I might not have used the recorder even if I'd had it on hand. My wife and I also rested our heads against the compartment's quivering wall, looking out on the passing shadows of fields and listening to the two sad and lovely female voices accompanied by the train's rhythmic clacking through the dark.

In the morning, after we'd all sipped six-kopeck tea together, Valinsina got off at her village, toting her cake, strawberries, luggage, and what little was left of the chicken. We waved to her as she stood solitary but substantial, waiting to see who would meet her. No one came. "It's all right," she mouthed through the window, "I'll go call," and she wobbled off toward a phone. In Odessa, martial music and a huge sign that read "Welcome to the Hero City" greeted us on the platform. As we parted with Nina, I told her I would never forget her night of song. And I won't.


One of the more handsome pieces of writing I've read is a seven-page account by the Russian author Konstantin Paustovsky of his meeting with fellow author Yuri Olesha at the beginning of World War II in Odessa. Dead tired, straight from the front, Paustovsky walked along a deserted Pushkin Street at dawn, the city's "old layer of atmosphere, mild, warm" replaced by a "harsh and empty air." He found his friend in the empty Hotel London. Olesha had refused to evacuate — as everyone else had — the city in which he'd grown up and lived when it "whirled for days on end like a merry-go-round, everything galloping before your eyes: ships, thieves, fast talkers, women."

We arrived in Odessa on June 20, the seventh city in our independent jazz tour of the Soviet Union. I'm not an aggressive believer in fate, but there had been something right about my acquaintance with thirty-seven-year-old Odessan pianist Yuri Kuznetsov from the start. I ran into him in Riga, when Betty and I were walking with Anthony Marhel, to whom I had mentioned my desire to meet Kuznetsov. "Here he is now," Anthony said, introducing us to a short, handsome man, alert, cordial, serious, and a shade impish. He put me in mind of qualities Paustovsky had attributed to his friend Olesha, his eyes "ready to blaze instantly with the flame of fancy and inspiration seized on the spur of the moment." That evening in Riga, Kuznetsov had performed with Estonian singer Sergei Manukian, their prolonged suite ending with the sailors' hornpipe that prompted Manukian to shout, "Odessa! Rah, Odessa!" at the finish. The crowd loved it. The young girls in Latvian dress had come out and handed the duo long-stemmed roses, and Manukian and Kuznetsov had exchanged their sweat-soaked t-shirts as a symbol that they were one.

Although I looked forward to meeting with Kuznetsov in Odessa, on my first day in the city I went looking for remnants of Yuri Olesha, who for me was the reigning spirit of the place. I discovered that the Potemkin steps made famous in Eisenstein's movie — those I'd hoped to climb up upon our arrival by boat in the USSR — were cement, not wood as I'd thought. At their top, photographers hawked tourist shots beneath a statue of Richelieu, so I was glad we hadn't arrived this way. I found the stately opera house and acacia tree to which Yuri Olesha had led his friend Paustovsky on their wartime walk, and I worked up the nerve to ask the dignified, elderly porter outside the Krasnaya Hotel, a man who looked as if he might predate Tsar Nicolas II himself, if he knew the Hotel London that Olesha wrote about fifty-five years ago. He immediately pointed out the building that Isaac Babel, another author from Odessa, called "that refuge of all sufferers."

Yuri Kuznetsov and I did not meet at the London, no longer a hotel, but in the lobby of the Chornoye More. Yuri was dressed in a loose green short-sleeved shirt and pegged gray trousers, as exuberant and convivial as I remembered him from Riga, ready for a full day and probably night, for he seemed disappointed when I told him my wife and I had tickets for the opera that evening. We were introduced to his friend Vasya, an architect, and whisked away in Vasya's car down French Boulevard, past once stately, brightly colored homes of the bourgeoisie, past what they jokingly referred to as the Hotel Hollywood (one of many large video palaces springing up), then past Communist Party headquarters. Mock machine-gun fire issued from the car along with laughter and a declaration that, in Odessa, people didn't really care much for politics. They had more important things on their minds.

"Such as?" I asked.

"Life."

"Bureaucrats hate jazz," Yuri added.

"Eshche?" (Still?), I asked.

"Well, it's better now, but . . ."

We stopped south of the city where a giant cement breakwater was being constructed for surfing adjacent to a public beach. Yuri gulped down quantities of fresh sea air, just as exuberantly as he quaffed two pints of *peva,* or beer, and smacked his lips, at the beach we stopped at next, one alive with what Betty described as "chunky little teenagers in bikinis," the fabled Russian modesty thrown to the sea and winds.

Vasya, who originally hails from the more temperate Baltics, kept saying, "Ekzotika, ekzotkia. New freedoms. Perestroika."

Isaac Babel once wrote of singers — not pianists — from the South, from Odessa, that they had "joy, artistically expressed joy in their being, high spirits, lightness of touch, and a charming, sad, and touching feeling for a life which is both good and bad, but extraordinarily . . . interesting." For the second time, I sensed that a writer might have been describing Yuri Kuznetsov.

At Vasya's place, where we were taken next, Yuri and I went upstairs to Vasya's sunlit studio overlooking a garden full of peonies and roses. When I asked if I might take his picture, Yuri snapped to attention, saluting in a manner reminiscent of British comedian Benny Hill (had he ever seen him?); and I photographed him that way. We then sat down to some serious talk about his music.

He preaches what he practices, his cardinal tenet being a belief in *ekspromt,* or creation on the spot, no clearly delineated composition but an open field of improvisation, fully spontaneous, calling on a host of musical sources but not the conscious use of any single one. That ruled out the deliberate use of folk or national material employed by other musicians in the Soviet Union I'd talked to — although some Armenian, Estonian, and Ukrainian elements occur in what Manukian and Kuznetsov do together. In spite of the diversity of folk musics, Kuznetsov feels that they are essentially one, and the goal is to infuse or penetrate folk music with one's own soul, producing what he calls "global jazz."

"Just how do you do that?"

"By speaking directly and sincerely to the audience."

"Nabliudenie," Yuri added, a word Olya, a woman assisting me, said she loved: keeping an eye on, observing people, how they live, and speaking to them about that musically. The means would appear to have a touch of Zen to them, a philosophy that interests Yuri. He says that instruments are not important. They play themselves. Technique is not important. It is something that is "always with me," that exists only to assist in "opening my soul." He told me he feels restricted by sets, that the extended piece I experienced as somewhat too long had not been long enough for him.

How do he and Manukian gain the rapport to speak as one soul, right down to exchanging sweat-soaked t-shirts?

"We are good friends. We meet every day. We watch football matches together, talk, joke. Mutual timing, understanding, trust. One heart, one life. The switching of shirts is a symbol of that unity. Drug druga — friend to friend, for each other."

Whereas so many other musicians in the USSR had complained to me about the difficulty of finding *partnery,* significant others who can play on their level, match their ideas, and speak the same musical language, Yuri feels he's found a solution to that problem in Manukian, just as he says he did while playing with Vilnius saxophonist Vladimir Chekasin, although he claims the musicians he'd truly like to work with in the Soviet Union number about ten. What he truly hungers for, as do so many of the artists I talked to, is the chance to play with jazz greats he has "only heard on record, but not as living contacts." Kuznetsov's isolation is heightened by domicile registration, a Soviet institution that does not allow people to move freely from city to city, town to town. "It's difficult for musicians in smaller towns. We say that Odessa is a city, but it is not a very big city." Yet he feels he, as an individual, has "strength" and original ideas, and he would like to meet and exchange talents with other "global" musicians. When I asked him which American artists he might like to perform with, given a choice, he closed his eyes and shook his head.

"Mnogo musikanty, too many," the interpreter Olya said. "His heart is too full to respond."

"Everyone!" Yuri said finally.

His request is probably the most basic an artist of any sort can make: he wants to bring his talent to the larger world while he's still alive.

After our talk, we went down to a sumptuous Ukrainian meal, an endless array of *zakuski,* or hors d'oeuvre, plus cognac, wine, delicious deep red borscht, a giant salad, strawberries, and *vareniki,* dumplings with potato stuffing, and later, the same filled with cherries for dessert. Dinner was accompanied by a host of toasts, which everybody got in on—Yuri's wife, Lena; Vasya's wife, Luda, and their daughter; the interpreter, Olya; Yuri, Betty, and myself. We toasted friendship, mutual happiness, the universal language of jazz, and just plain *dzhaz* itself. Yuri played a duet with Vasya's eighteen-year-old daughter, Nataly, he at a spinet (which, I was told, received much late-night use), she on flute. Although an amateur, she improvised beautifully, providing a perfect dessert. Yuri then played a tape of his performance with Manukian in Riga, conducting effusively with his soup spoon and explaining by gestures alone the progression from mood to mood. He then lowered his standards long enough to play a blues duet with me—"Goin' to Chicago" ("Sorry I can't take you!")—a journey I could barely believe we were singing about on a superb sunny afternoon following a splendid Ukrainian meal, on the edge of the Black Sea in the city of Odessa. Yuri shouted, often, two of the few English words he knows, "Oh, yeahhhhhh!"

He was growing expansive, the cognac lucrative, Cimarosa's "Secret Marriage" (the evening's opera, and something we could probably have done without anyway) waiting in the wings of time left to us in the city. Yet we did make it. After what seemed a suicidal ride back through Odessa, we parked and hurried up Lenin Street toward the famed opera house with scenes from

Shakespeare painted on its ceiling. Yuri pointed out the apartment in which he was born and where his mother still lives. He and I broke out spontaneously into a scat on "Muskrat Ramble," drawing a look of concern from Vasya, as if we'd suddenly lost our minds — which, delightfully and for the moment, we may have.

When author Yuri Olesha's friend Paustovsky, on their wartime walk, suggested that the city had lost its traditional liveliness, Olesha responded, "Ba-lo-ney! Odessans don't surrender and don't die. Their wit is crossed with fearlessness. Their bravery sharpens on smart remarks . . . even now, during the war, Odessans are just as brave, cheerful, and funny as ever." And even now, no matter what severe changes the former Soviet Union may be going through — "God only knows how the world will turn out; let things be as they are!" Yuri said to me, in a manner that combines Russian fatalism with a touch of Zen — the city's spirit seems to live on in someone like pianist Yuri Kuznetsov.

We stopped on the opera house steps. "Now we must be serious," I said.

Yuri drew himself up to his full short but solid stature, grinning impishly. "Yes," he said. "Here you are at La Scala."

I tried to explain that I had deep rich feelings but too few words, in Russian, to express them. He said he felt the same but was "very bad" (a phrase he pronounced well) at English. We understood each other perfectly, and parted.

Our remaining days in Odessa were pleasantly torrid, the intense heat assuaged by the sea, crowds cruising up and down Deribasovskaya Street, stopping at *bliny* (pancake) or ice cream or fruit juice stands, stripped down to decent — or in some cases, mildly indecent — essentials: shorts, halters, open blouses. The parade got even better at dusk, when the quickening night cast crimson shadows, the women not wearing slips — because they were not available? because they couldn't afford them? — approached us, their bodies handsomely silhouetted in their light dresses.

Evening stayed hot, a New Orleans torpor, what Isaac Babel called "the maternal sexiness of Odessa nights" settling in, sensual, jazzy. Languidly, we returned to a restaurant we'd scouted out that afternoon, the Ukraina, where we found our promised table usurped by the arrival of an entire tour boat, that most common experience in the Soviet Union: two solitary individuals displaced, or bounced, by a *groupa* or firm. In retaliation, we decided to remove our individual desire to the hotel where, after a small meal and a goodly share of lemon-flavored vodka (so cool, luscious, on a hot night), we sat on the bed in one another's arms, sans clothing, my loved one the woman Yuri Kuznetsov had rechristened with the diminutive Betichka. We watched the evening turn the giant dome of the church across the way — now a theater — first pewter, then rose, than a looming but somehow approving shadow of what Babel called "the former God."

On our last day in the city we walked out Chkalova Street past filthy but colorful courtyards — "This is not a toilet!" inscribed on entranceway walls; clothes on a line as varied as a display of United Nations flags; old crones in black; mothers with innumerable babies. "If you want to see something of life, turn into our courtyard; there's something to laugh at," Babel wrote. We walked out to a beach on the Black Sea, the day scorching, the scene lively: sleek young women with thigh-cut bathing suits juxtaposed with veritable tanks, bastions, colossal mounds of white steaming flesh, the fattest human beings I've ever seen in my life, all reposing, roasting, on a narrow strip of sand, the fabled Russian modesty again — just as we'd encountered it at the beach Yuri and Vasya had taken us to — thrown to the sea and winds. Families, lovers, giggling teen girls strutting their unsure stuff, summer stands exhibiting everything from *shashlyk* (shish kebab) to bottled mineral water to soda pop. With this as his milieu, I could see now why Yuri Kuznetsov's music was so lively.

We strolled back up Dzerzhinskovo Boulevard, stopped for delicious vanilla ice cream cones that we paid for by the gram, then over to Deribasovskaya, following, I think, just about the same route a very young Yuri Olesha took to school. At a large finely stocked bookstore I browsed among jazz books — mostly piano instructional material translated from American texts — and somehow managed to arouse the suspicion of a clerk who, although the area was about as large as a university library hall, insisted on kneeling right below me, fastidiously rearranging all the books on the shelves, including those I was about to examine. Why she did this, I will never know.

Our virgin flight on Aeroflot within the USSR had been an uneventful trek from Riga to Kiev, but the inception of our journey east now was worthy of the slightly mad, unpredictable, lively town of Odessa itself: fire — which, fortunately, my wife did not see — shooting past the window as the engines revved up, smoke suddenly filling the plane's interior. This turned out to be dry ice released from khaki bags stored five to a side in the overhead racks running the length of the plane. The temperature plunged toward zero. Children of every age, some apparently in their teens, were commanded to sit on their parents' laps in order to provide space for more passengers. Three people got crammed into a section for two across from us, seatbelts dangling useless, and we received no preflight safety instruction. As one old lady crossed herself with furious abandon, we sped down the runway and took off for Semferopol and Yalta.

# The Healing
# Waters
# of Tbilisi

The now much troubled Georgian city of Tbilisi is set down in mountains, one of which, Kazbek — to the west — rises to fifteen thousand feet. In spite of its elevation, Tbilisi got off to a low, slow start for us, although our sojourn there finally did turn wondrous at the hands of a single man — someone I was put in touch with solely by accident, yet, ironically, one of the musicians who had sparked my interest in this music in the first place.

Before we arrived there, I puzzled over the name *Georgia*. To Russians the former republic is Gruzia, to the Gruzians themselves, Sakartvelo. So why *Georgia?* Starting out, on the ride from Yalta to Semferopol, I was too sick with some bug I'd picked up to ask and find out.

It was a Sunday, and along the road men had dispensed themselves at different leisure stations on chalk-white terraces, stradling cement blocks, drinking pints of *pivo* (beer) to beat the scorching heat. The airport, once we were deposited there, appeared empty, aside from an interesting display of political cartoons, one depicting a "museum of antiquities" that contained "cleansing powder, footwear, soap, meat, cheese, caviar."

We'd gone to Yalta because I had some half-baked notion of interviewing not jazz but resort-area musicians there, for the sake of contrast and maybe for fun. However, the first *varete* (variety show) we were forced to attend brought home the fact that this was a foolish idea. It was no gig I wanted to know much more about, although I'm sure plenty of Soviet musicians spend their time playing them. We had been seated far in the rear of a room as large as a baseball stadium. A couple across from us, who like Betty and I just wanted food and not the naked floor-show garnish, had been waiting for their meal for some time. They were friends or lovers who worked together at a video film studio in Moscow, making documentaries. The woman was svelte and sophisticated, the man short and ruggedly handsome, built like a boxer. They'd been coming to Yalta together on *otpusknoe vremia* (vacation time) for three years. The man was a B. B. King / Santana / Chicago fan whose jazz taste was restricted to Miles Davis and Gerry Mulligan. Neither had ever heard of Andrei Kondakov or Yuri Kuznetsov, with whom I figured they shared approximate age, but they did like Alexei Kozlov's fusion group, Arsenal.

I enjoyed observing Soviets at play. As tourists, they seem to take to their leisure avidly, especially in an attractive — Mediterranean, cypress-spotted — sunny spot like Yalta. We sat on the balcony of our spiffy hotel and drank good *sovinoi* Krymskii wine. Betty swam in the Black Sea, finding the pebbly bottom tricky to walk on. We cruised Yalta. I found copies of the work of Isaac Babel, Yuri Olesha, and Marina Tsvetaeva at a small kiosk, a Russian exclaiming, "This American reads Olesha and Babel" when I extracted the requisite number of rubles — ten per book, about a dollar each — from my wallet. We also made a pilgrimage to the home — and gardens, where he'd once sat chatting with Maxim Gorky — of Anton Chekhov.

Sick as I was, on our snaky, tortuous journey to the airport, I did manage to enjoy the view. Small stalls had been set up along the road, a deep drop to the sea serving as background, people privately selling radishes, potatoes, lettuce, cherries, strawberries, apricots. The flight wasn't bad. The confusion started after we landed in Tbilisi. We had been assigned a room at the Adjaria Hotel — "not well located for tourists," according to *Fodor's*. The city also has an Abkhazia Hotel, to which we were taken by mistake. At the front desk, an attendant who seemed to be doing absolutely nothing but staring into space told us to wait for a second attendant, a man wearing a shirt that read "U.S. Air Force," who was engaged for the next forty-five minutes in passing out keys to a large Greek tour group. When we finally made it up to the desk, he swung into action, our porter standing by with our luggage looking massively confused, and phoned — the second useless attendant actually handed him this device! — the Adjaria. This generous man then rushed out into the street to hail a cab, paying the driver out of his own pocket to take us to the right place.

That night we discovered we couldn't lock the door to our room. The next day we learned that several people on the eighth floor had been robbed — we were on the twelfth. One young American woman had chased a man running off with *all* her luggage, down the hall, but unsuccessfully. A squad of KGB officials had been called into the hotel to reestablish law and order, we were told, but they must have looked much like everybody else, for I failed to recognize them. In spite of the confusion I did manage to call the only musical contact I had in Tbilisi, Gela Charkviani, who worked for the Georgian Society for Friendship and Cultural Relations with Foreign Countries. He had written me just before we left, offering to help me meet "some of our jazz musicians." Now that I was in Tbilisi, Gela was quite friendly but told me that both of his parents were seriously ill, hospitalized, and that he would not be able to get together with me to "discuss other things under the sun," as he'd said in his letter. However, he said he had arranged for me to meet a local musician. "His name is Tamaz Kurashvili," he said.

Tamaz Kurashvili! I was thrilled. Tamaz was where this music had started for me. I'd come halfway around the world to meet, by accident, one of my initial heroes. For some reason, I had not thought of Kurashvili as accessible. Critic Virgil Mihaiu had written that the "Mustafa-Zadeh / Kurashvili collaboration . . . is one of the notable feats of piano / bass since 1965," the keyboard work finding "its adequate, stimulating complement in the springiness and consistency of the bass lines."

Our meeting entailed the same comedy of errors I'd fallen prey to in Petrozavodsk. I'm still not sure what I think a jazz musician is supposed to look like, but the tall, broad-shouldered man who seemed to know everybody in the lobby of our hotel didn't fit the bill. He could have been a friendly business leader, celebrity athlete, or aspiring politician. After about fifteen minutes of scanning the soccer field–sized lobby for a jazz musician, I finally began to suspect that this bald man checking his watch from time to time might be Kurashvili.

We decided to conduct our interview in the hotel room, so he could meet Betty. Tamaz speaks English in a soft meditative manner. He has been to America twice, for three months on the last visit, playing in New York as part of a Georgian / American exchange program in the arts that included a dance troupe and folk musicians. He was part of a three-concert program at twenty-nine-year-old impresario Vartan "Jazznost" Tonoian's reopened Bluebird Club in the city, working with Soviet émigré pianist Nikolai Levinovsky and Alexei Zubov, a Soviet artist who was part of an earlier musical emigration in the sixties. Kurashvili told me that the Bluebird is "nice, big, beautiful, a very big club" holding about four hundred people. He also worked with American pianist Dick Hyman in New York. Since he has been a part of both worlds, what is the difference between Soviet and American jazz?

"Difference? Yes. Very different," he said. "Many different musics in New York—standards, modern, fusion—and many music people. Young! And they can play all instruments. There are many good situations for them, and much communication."

He cited the work being done at Berklee College, which has produced its share of youthful talent, so I asked him if he felt there was a comparable school or program in the USSR.

"No. Berklee is Berklee."

When asked directly about the quality of jazz in the Soviet Union, about the best musicians, he replied that pianist Vagif Mustafa-Zadeh has to be placed at the top of the list. "He was a great poet," Tamaz says. "A very different kind of person, as a man and as a composer. He knew and liked Georgian music. As for today, I don't know many young musicians here. Maybe the Armenian pianist David Azarian. And young reed master Petras Vysniauskas, in Lithuania."

"How about Aziza Mustafa-Zadeh?"

"Yes, Aziza. And in Moscow, many good musicians. Germann Lukianov. Igor Nazaruk is very original. And Mikhail Okun. We have this trio. There is also a college in Moscow, the Gnessin Institute. Igor Bril, Alexander Oseychuk, Okun all teach there."

Asked about the influence of folk music on his own work, what one critic has described as "the contortions of Central-Asian music," its specific harmonic patterns, Tamaz mentioned that American artists Charles Lloyd and Keith Jarrett know Georgian folk music well and incorporate it in their playing — that Georgian music, polyphonic in nature, is quite different than Armenian, Azerbaijanian, or Russian. Its organization is quite different, for a piece might employ anywhere from eight to twelve separate voices simultaneously, each working in its own way. And the folk music of West Georgia — of the Abkhazian and Ajar republics, of Imeretia and Mingrelia, more Mediterranean cultures — is quite different from that of East Georgia, the South Ossetian region, and Kakhetia, which have a dry, continental climate (as I would see, later, reflected in the architecture, when Tamaz drove us to an ethnographic park situated just below a large handsome lake). The rhythms, polyrhythms, and harmonies employed in Georgian music are quite distinct, Tamaz thinks. Asked if he made use of all this in his own music, he said, yes, he does try "to bring all that into jazz."

"My group here, the quintet I have in Tbilisi, we play Georgian folk melodies in a jazz style." He also mentioned the influence of Alex Zachorian, a classical symphonic composer who writes national folk music. Asked if he could describe rhythms unique to Georgian music for me, those not accessible to American musicians, Tamaz said that would be difficult to do, verbally. Fortunately, we were seated at a large circular wooden table that afforded marvelous potential as a drum.

"Could you tap them out for me?" I asked.

He immediately did so: first a fine 7/4 beat, crisp and clear.

"Is there a specific name for that?" I asked when he'd finished.

"Khorumi," he said.

"Any other rhythms?"

"Many rhythms, yes. ⁷⁄4. ⁵⁄4."

"How about a ⁵⁄4?"

A second table-top demonstration ensued, rich with what critic Mihaiu, speaking of the Mustafa-Zadeh/Kurashvili collaboration in general, has described as "sumptuously adorned formulae, a sophisticated sound architecture made up of various touches and contrasting variations, dexterously blended into colorful fabrics . . . full of surprises." This session of rapping was so engaging that I forgot to ask the name of the beat.

Tamaz started listening to jazz at the age of twelve: Lionel Hampton, Erroll Garner, George Shearing. Then came Coltrane and Cannonball Adderley. "After, I studied piano, and guitar. From age twenty-two to twenty-five. Then I begin to study bass. I like bass, its full sound and harmonies. I studied at the conservatory with Sadchenko. I played with a jazz group, but also with the symphony orchestra."

When I asked him my stock question about the possible influence of pre- and postrevolutionary experimentation in all the arts in Russia, Tamaz said he felt that the avant-garde today was largely confined to the Baltic countries, to cities such as Tallinn and Riga. "They have different problems in music there. They like free jazz, the avant-garde. They don't have much traditional jazz. In Moscow, Leningrad, Erevan, Tbilisi, Baku, people study standards, mainstream music, but they are more limited in the Baltics. They are good musicians, but they have not practiced 'big jazz.' They only play free, like saxophonist Vladimir Chekasin. He's a very good composer. But I feel musicians must have strong grounding in harmonics, standards, the fundamentals."

Once again, the trail linking contemporary music to past cultural achievements was eluding me. To Tamaz's mind, the Soviet Union's distorted or denied disruptive history had left only this universal language of "fundamentalist," mostly mainstream, jazz behind. We discussed the other ubiquitous concern, the quest for adequate *partnery* in the USSR's geographically scattered jazz world. Kurashvili seems to feel he has had better luck than most in this area, beginning with his collaborations with Vagif Mustafa-Zadeh and continuing by way of his work with Germann Lukianov. "We have not time to practice together, so for festivals we rehearse over the telephone." (This must be a wild scene, Lukianov in Moscow, Tamaz far South in Georgia.) Tamaz is also very pleased about his association now with pianist Mikhail Okun. In 1987 they performed together in Prague, joining Branford Marsalis there for a three-hour jam session.

"Is Okun as good, do you think, as everyone is telling me he is?"

"Yes! I have two recordings I will play for you in the car. One from a concert hall, the second done in a studio."

How about drummers?

"Yeah, that is the first minus of Soviet jazz. We have not good drummers. Maybe we have not schools to teach them. I know many drummers who have much information, they know many tunes, but they play too heavy, too low class."

And the future here?

"I think the best musicians are in the U.S. — Coltrane and Paul Chambers in the past, and today the Keith Jarrett Trio, Wayne Shorter. They are very different, very interesting. Freddie Hubbard. The Marsalis brothers. Very great musicians."

"Do you think you'll be returning to the States, to play there some more?"

"Yeah, maybe a couple more times. I would like to be recording, with trio and quartet, here. Maybe after we will have a big tour in the United States. I have a good friend in Los Angeles who is with the group Free Flight. And I know Milcho Leviev, a very great musician." (Leviev, a superb Bulgarian pianist, also lives in Los Angeles.)

Apologizing once again for his English, this gentle, thoughtful, mild-voiced man — almost monkish in his deference — rose from his chair, turning into the first-round draft pick for any pro team in the States or that impressive political candidate I had seen strolling the lobby downstairs, saying "I have whole day," and insisted on showing us the sights of Tbilisi. When I commented on his popularity, the number of people who knew him on sight, he said the manager of our hotel was a big jazz fan. He put musicians up there throughout the annual Tbilisi Jazz Festival and allowed jam sessions to be held in the restaurant after the end of each concert.

We took off in a new white car of which he is very proud. Steering it through the insane rush of Tbilisi traffic, he removed the false dashboard and, on the excellent stereo system it had concealed, he now played the elegant Prague festival performance by Mikhail Okun and himself. Is Okun as good as they say? Yes. Tamaz took us to a cooperative restaurant run by a friend, although everybody we came across seemed to be a friend of his: his popularity displayed by way of a hearty handshake matched with a kiss, a custom among men, Georgians living up to their reputation as the most independent, demonstrative, uninhibited, free, Mediterranean peoples in the Soviet Union. I was still feeling a bit uncertain physically (that is, sick), but there was no way I was going to pass up the rich and multifarious array of dishes set down before us, this aspect of Georgian living matching its reputation for taste and abundance.

Taking up all our table's space in this small restaurant of five or six tables sat an exotic onion dish, stuffed eggplant, *karabakh loby* (string beans in sour cream and tomato sauce), *mdzhavai kombosto* (red cabbage salad), meat and mushrooms cooked in spices and olive oil, cucumber-tomato salad, *tavhcuna* (leaves of anise), three kinds of cheese (one from the mountains of East

Georgia, a sort of firm, stony Gouda; the others soft), olives, pickles, crepe pancakes with cheese filling, flat bread and french fries, sweet green water, and "the best" Georgian wine, Makhari.

Back in the car, which I more or less crawled out to, the superb Kurashvili/Okun concert continued at maximum volume as we drove through Old Town, up curved and narrow streets past Armenian and Georgian churches, a mosque, inviting parks, and the Anchiskhati Church dating back to the sixth century. Perched on stern cliffs rising above the Kuva River were homes in colors from salt blue to salmon to brick with noble balconies, fragile railings, circular stairways, semicircular arches, and tiled roofs — ornate and intricate as the music Tamaz made with Zagif Mustafa-Zadeh. Tamaz stopped at a small shop where Betty found handsome hand-decorated purses and a splendid set of dangling silver earrings. After, we headed for the Georgian Art Museum — once an ecclesiastical seminary at which Stalin, one of Gruzia's more ambiguous sons studied — but it was closed. Driving up Rustaveli Boulevard, a favorite promenade spot for the city's inhabitants, Tamaz suddenly squealed to a stop and hopped from the car to talk with a man he later described as "the master photographer." This was Konstantin Kokhreidze, who we would meet later that evening along with his assistant, Konstantin Ketoschivili — "Big" and "Little" Kostya.

Tamaz informed us it was time to eat again (God forbid!). He took us to a popular, contemporary, nearly chic spot, open, sunlit, noted for its Georgian pizza (Khachapuri: an abundant dose of egg and cheese enfolded in dough) and healing waters. Legend has it that in the fifth century, King Vakhtang of Georgia wounded a deer, which fell into a warm sulfur spring and, cured, ran off. Impressed, the king ordered a settlement established in what is now Tbilisi — the name signifying "warm," a town of warm springs. The healing tradition continues, it seems, in this modern-day pizza parlor, for it was jam-packed, Tamaz disappearing for a moment, reappearing with the manager — another friend! — who unlocked a special banquet room for us and then brought the Georgian cheese bread and a tray bearing a variety of Lavigitza sweet waters (as they are called, named for the man who instituted *this* nonsulfurous — as far as I could tell; the waters are delicious — cure): lemon, ginger, anise, even chocolate — the taste somewhat similar to those marvelous pharmacy phosphates I loved as a kid.

That evening both Big and Little Kostya came up to our hotel room with the most extraordinary packet of jazz photos I had seen in the Soviet Union, striking black-and-white shots with superb dramatic lighting. I assumed that Kokhreidze, who speaks excellent English, had brought the photos along to sell, but I was dazzled by the sheer volume of them and wasn't sure just how many I could afford. To my surprise, he gave me the entire batch, a stunning act of generosity. That evening marked the only drunken bout we encountered on our trip. I had been prepared, by all travel accounts previously read, for endless revels, evenings of inebriation that, up to this time, had failed to materialize. But the two Kostyas made up for lost time and effort. The night was roasting hot in Tbilisi, so hot that we repaired to the hotel's vaguely air-conditioned bar, where we were joined by Tamaz. The two Kostyas filled tray after tray with another sort of "healing waters": red Georgian wine, Heinekin's beer, a bottle of vodka, and a fifth of gin for themselves, most of which they would consume before the evening was out.

Tamaz, by contrast, was quite sober and serious. He had to take his son, setting out on a trip to Sweden, to the train station early in the morning. Big Kostya chided him for this, saying that ever since he'd known Tamaz — and apparently they had been friends for quite some time — he "has always been serious, ever since the day he was born!" The bassist seemed to harbor some reservations concerning his companions' behavior, Little Kostya having unleashed a fierce wit and predilection for puns, most of which — not being that sophisticated with the language — I missed. Both photographers told stories of the Tbilisi Jazz Festival, run by a man, manager/director of the state theater, Gayoz Kandelaki, they called "Mr. Cadillac." Their favorite American guest had been jazz organist Jimmy Smith. When Georgians had wished to touch him, incredulous that this musical hero was in Tbilisi, Smith had said, "Yeah, man, go ahead and touch me! Go ahead!" Les McCann, approached by an eager fan who said, "You are my brother," replied (according to Big Kostya), "Not yet! When you are as fat as I am, then we will be brothers, but not yet!" Little Kostya's commentary on a great exterior shot of McCann at the piano was, "You can always tell a great artist from the rear!"

I would like to repeat each and every witticism that passed across that table that night, and later in our hotel room, but the truth is, in spite of Little Kostya's awe over my ability to pocket alcohol without partaking of food, the evening did take its toll on me, and I simply don't remember much of what was being said. Tamaz had sense enough to leave early, but the two Kostyas ended up in our hotel room until 4:30, at which time Betty, I think, must have thrown them out. Her notebook contains the single entry: "Ended up in the room with the men doing their macho number. Bill included, who I could have killed."

I have retained stories from that night about Jimmy Smith's capacity to drink ("A very big lover of vodka," said Big Kostya), of Smith's "vision," impressed by the city's many sweeping vistas, of his playing the organ atop a hill until "people stopped making love" (or "making sex," as Kostya put it) and cried out, "Stop what we are doing; it is Mr. Jimmy Smith, the great American jazz artist, playing! Stop what you are doing, and *listen!*" Big Kostya spoke of jazz musicians as simple, wonderful people — unlike, he felt, rock stars. "Jazz musicians do not wish to be kings," he said, citing, by way of example, Art Blakey's modest surprise that Kostya was "making so many photographs of these black men." And Little Kostya told of his "one desire" that he had waited four years to fulfill, and here he produced the visible evidence from his pocket: a harmonica. He complained that now, his dream fulfilled, he has "no time to practice," and he began to play in our hotel room at 4:30 in the morning. That may have been the reason Betty ran the two photographer friends out.

Tamaz Kurashvili came to say goodbye ("Nakhramdis," in Georgian) to us the next morning. The driver who took us to the airport zigzagged over drenched streets, streets pregnant with puddles he spun through, no lanes designated, cars converging on each other with all the apparent heedlessness of small scarred dodge-ems at a carnival. I had noticed, on the previous day, that even the gentle Tamaz couldn't resist the temptations that seem to beset one, in Tbilisi, behind a wheel, honking with uncustomary imperiousness at some poor father unloading a patient before, I think, a hospital.

Once we were on the plane, a man by the window, next to Betty — no Chaliapin in his sonorous efforts, that celebrity who loved Tbilisi for its beauty, charm and ancient Iberian culture — snored vociferously. I held recordings Tamaz had given to me as gifts, one called "Classical Jazz Ballades," featuring himself, pianist Nikolai Levinovsky, and tenor saxophonist Sergei Gurbeloshvili. Other albums contained Georgian folk music (drinking songs and a Megrelian wedding song on one; the Rustavi Ensemble on the other) and popular singer Gamlet Gonashvili doing folk tunes. Turning down a greasy piroshki and thick coffee offered to us by the stewardess, I sat back, closed my eyes, and thanked fate that the "one of our local musicians" whom Gela Charkviani had arranged for me to meet had turned out to be Tamaz Kurashvili. I held my grand stash of jazz photographs to my chest, that gift from Big and Little Kostya, all the way to Leningrad.

# 16

## *Leningrad Shadows and the Long White Night*

Leningrad proved to be the most frustrating stop on our trip — yet my favorite. The place has been a paradox from its own beginnings, built where no city should be, a shadow-puppet theater set down in a swamp. I had a hard time imagining jazz, or nearly any other form of human activity, taking place behind its handsome but forbidding granite walls and within the maze of its curling rivers. The musicians I had come to contact — Sergei Kuryokhin, bassist Vladimir Volkov and his trumpeter-partner Vyacheslav Guyvoronsky, guitarist Andrei Ryobov and the trad group Nevskaya Vasmoika (with tenor saxophonist Mikhail Kashtushkin, for whom I'd brought reeds) — were all out of town, playing in Moscow (Kashtushkin with Kuryokhin's Pop Mechanics), or at a festival in Murmansk. I did finally manage to fit in two of the best interviews I'd gleaned on the trek — with respected jazz critic Vladimir Feyertag and his younger counterpart, Alex Kahn — and discovered what is perhaps the best genuine jazz club in the former Soviet Union; but the city I initially encountered seemed to have been invented by Franz Kafka. At first I felt like someone accused of having committed an unnamed but heinous crime and being permitted a single essential phone call only to discover that, once I'd made it — and with my very last dime — I had been placed on "hold" for eternity.

A single house we discovered by accident served as a symbol of Leningrad for me. Two stories, it stands behind wrought-iron railings that may have been elegant at one time but are no longer so. The guidebook's "magnificent main gates" were linked shut, but not very effectively, chains sagging to allow just enough space for a mother and her children to slip through, which they had, the kids cavorting now in tall grass and what I thought were sun-spotted wild flowers, but turned out to be *oduvanchiky* (dandelions). These children played

**183**

in the courtyard at the back of which stood number thirty-four, Fountain House, the former Sheremetev Palace, built for a field marshall crony of Peter the Great, and his grandson Nikolai.

To me it was Fontannyi Dom, the "House on the Fontanka" in which the poet Anna Akhmatova had lived, a woman who, born into a distinguished family, had grown up among the lakes and trees of Tsarskoe Selo ("the tsar's village"). The widow of poet Nikolai Gumilev, executed in 1921, Akhmatova was not allowed to publish her work between 1921 and 1940 and was expelled from the Writers Union in 1948. Intermittently ill with tuberculosis, she outlived her accusers, who all died of heart attacks. Except for her reluctant evacuation to Tashkent during the nine-hundred-day seige, Akhmatova was a lifelong resident of this city she celebrated, in poetry, with equal doses of loathing and love.

I had arrived in Petersburg, or Leningrad, with a set intent (to interview jazz musicians), a small amount of luggage, and a heap of ghosts, or shadows, on my back. Akhmatova was just one of them. More would surface as the week we had allotted to the city passed, the living proving not nearly so quick in their presence as the dead. Betty and I are walkers, so we immediately hit the streets, as we had everywhere else. We headed across the Liteiny Bridge and strolled along the Neva embankment. People passed like vapors, indifferent to us, aside from a few who checked out our shoes; one man, wearing a snappy pair of Adidas himself, turned out to be a *fartsovshchiki* (black marketeer), offering me the highest rate of exchange — twenty rubles to a dollar — I'd encountered in the Soviet Union.

The ambience is such that people, real people, don't seem that way, converted by the extraordinary flat spaciousness, no building taller, by decree, than the spire of Peter and Paul, and buildings so intricately artistic even in their decay as to supersede people. I thought of the paintings of de Chirico, those stony plazas in which the laws of perspective don't apply and statues or manikins peer around corners, a young girl's shadow rolls a hoop down the street, or doors of vans stand open, exuding melancholy and eternal patience. In Leningrad, color is provided not by people, who dress pretty much the way city people do throughout the civilized world, but by the buildings, which are painted lime green, rust, ocher, chalk brown, salmon red, carrot, crimson, cabbage white, sand, mauve, smoky sapphire, tawny red — anything to forestall the psychological effects of an inordinately long drab winter, I was told later.

Aside from color, one's eye is drawn to architectural details: intricate latticework, ornate balustrades, colonnades, semicircular triads of windows topped with dancing arabesques, caryatids, enigmatic stone faces, urns on roofs, facades as busy as the music of Vivaldi or Bach. As we ambled along the "black Neva," I tried to imagine which of the buildings we passed might contain the huge bedchamber described by Osip Mandelstam in his richly musical poem "Solominka" (The Straw), one line — "Solomka zvonkaya, Solominka sukaya" — so sonorous I've intoned it as a sleep-inducing mantra at night. While I indulged my fantasy, Betty enjoyed one of her own: simulating suicidal swan dives into Pushkin's Neva, thinking she'd found the spot where Lisa, in the opera version of "Queen of Spades," does herself in because her lover, Germann, is late for a midnight assignation, having wheedled the secret, he thinks, of a winning hand of cards from the old countess, Liza's grandmother.

Men were fishing from the Neva's embankment with agile polystyrene poles, or from rubber rafts out on the river itself. Lovers embraced on the steps that lead down to its very contemporary, murky contents (one does not drink the water in Leningrad). Confused by the juxtaposition of these facts and the broader vision of poets, we took the easy way out and cut up a side street, stopping to take a picture, from afar, of one of the city's long lines — that might, like those in Moscow, have formed for anything from shoes to soap, from cheese to perfume or panty hose.

We checked out Palace Square, the Alexander Column, and the intricate silver gate of the Winter Palace, which once eager Bolshevik hordes scaled in Eisenstein's movie *Ten Days That Shook the World* and, inundated with architecture and history, I thought it was time to head back to the solely contemporary reality of our hotel, for I had an interview later that day with young Soviet jazz critic Alex Kahn. We did wander up Nevsky Prospect where we did discover number ten, the home of Pushkin's old countess, and further along, a canal that turned out to be the Fontanka. There I discovered Akhmatova's former home with a dilapidated sign declaring the former Sheremetev Palace a museum in her name. Like the poet's presence in the city itself throughout her life, it was attended to — if at all — with considerable neglect.

I am sitting on a terrace of the Leningrad Hotel, the stalwart cruiser *Aurora,* which commenced the Revolution, standing guard across the River Neva and converted to a tourist shop. Betty and I are drinking Carlsburg beer served in a small pavilion which, unlike the rest of Leningrad, seems to have been constructed in a single day. We do so with Alex Kahn, a slender, handsome, red-bearded man with no-nonsense eyes. I've asked him to tell me something about Sergei Kuryokhin, his friend, the thirty-seven-year-old — just about Alex's age, I guess correctly — pianist I heard in Santa Cruz but won't get to see on this trip, Kuryokhin on an out-of-town gig (that word still sounding strange to me when Russians use it). Sergei is something of a media darling

just now. His group (*troup* might be a more accurate word), Pop Mechanics —
a ménage of jazz musicians, rock guitarists, amateur poets, acrobats, circus
clowns and animals, gypsies, military bands, you name it — is doing quite well.
Kuryokhin's Leningrad is obviously not the Petersburg of the Winter Palace,
the "black Neva," Mandelstam, Akhmatova, or Pushkin — although Pushkin
does turn up on occasion in his music as parody, a revenge on teachers who
forced their pupils to memorize his poems in school.

Tradition itself is a source of parody for Kuryokhin, handsomely trained
by the many schools he was kicked out of. He once talked with Kahn, in a
serious interview — although his work in this genre, also, leans toward parody — about "the natural feeling of a kind felt by Dostoevsky, questions of
social environment, climatic conditions which in many ways condition our
life," and then broke off, laughing, staring out the window at November's mud
and wet snow. "No sane person could live in this town," he continued.

Kahn told me that Kuryokhin is an extremely cultured person himself,
well-read, erudite in philosophy, literature, history.

"Then he would be likely to know about people I'm interested in, their
possible influence," I said, "those artistic and literary figures of the twenties,
the avant-garde."

"Sure. He knows the history of that. And what he does is, he tries to go
back in his own career, knowing history and trying, in a way, to repeat it."

Kahn claims that artists such as Kuryokhin, aware of the great prestige the
West accords that period and the one that preceded it and the Revolution,
actually exploit this knowledge. "Khlebnikov, Burlyuk, and all those poets,
artists, Rodchenko in a way, Malevich in a way," Kahn continues. "This was
the art of challenge, of the slap in the face." (In 1912, the first two, along
with poets Alexei Kruchenykh and Vladimir Mayakovsky, published the initial
manifesto of Russian futurism, "A Slap in the Face of Public Taste.") Kuryokhin, according to Kahn, has an attitude "very, very close" to theirs. Kahn
described the late seventies scene, on which Kuryokhin first appeared as a rock
musician, as part of "a sort of Leningrad Bohemia," a close, elitist, narrow
circle. A diet of banned books and samizdat led to a solid knowledge of the
previous avant-garde.

"Kuryokhin was sincerely and honestly interested in that. I remember
when we met in 1978. You couldn't help but notice him. He didn't seem to
care about his clothes, his life-style, money, anything." The pianist lived in
his sister's apartment. He had a "teeny-tiny" (that phrase sounds funny in
English, but the Russian — *chut chut* — means business) room of just five
square meters, his piano, his books. Kuryokhin devoured philosophy, literature, American saxophonist Jackie McLean, obscure pop or blues singers, and

his latest craze, Cajun music or Zydeco. "Very eclectic," Kahn admits, and quite often "lacking coherence."

As we sit on the terrace of the Leningrad Hotel, sipping a second draft Carlsburg now, Pushkin, the Neva, the Winter Palace, the bronze horseman in Decembrists' Square, even the Aurora forever in view, seem artifacts from some distant past, true ghosts. Kahn talked about days, not all that long ago, when he first became exposed to jazz, days in which members of "the whole art underground scene" faced a common enemy, "the system we lived in," days when "anything we did was a statement, a very serious political statement" — such as, in his case, bringing the American ROVA Saxophone Quartet to Leningrad, an act for which, officials told members of the group, Kahn and his friends would be sent to jail.

"All these obstacles we had to overcome, all these difficulties; I mean, this was about nothing. A band of Americans had come here to play music, so what the fuck? Why make all this noise, you know? It *was* funny, but the system of values we lived at the time was not."

Kahn spoke of being "initiated," through jazz, into a "totally different world, into a bigger world, a freer world, into a world where everything is possible," and this by way of, at the time, some mediocre Dixieland band of the fifties playing in a dance hall. "It didn't really matter whether they were creative or noncreative, original or inventive. It was a revelation. They were bringing the new life."

That new life, or at least a new reality, had arrived now in Leningrad, though not a stitch of it, so far, seemed reflected in the architecture. The Neva rolls by. The spire of Peter and Paul — beneath which everyone from the Decembrists to Maxim Gorky had been incarcerated for their views — stands tall. One might expect that Alex Kahn, knowing the consequences of the statements he once made, would welcome the change with open arms, but he is cautious, even skeptical. "All this is in a way very painful to realize, to accept. This brings us to a completely new system of values which most of us are not ready to adopt, or at least do not have time to adapt to. . . . This country has never been a democracy. Art in the West has always been mostly entertainment; at best, it was a very sophisticated entertainment, clever, cultural entertainment."

"Duke Ellington?"

"Duke Ellington, or you can take Nabokov, who is a Russian writer but a genius with entertaining words. He is a great, great, great writer, but he is not a writer of ideas. He hated all writers of ideas. He actively hated most of Russian literature just for being so full of ideas. But that's a very Russian trait. People here are big on ideas. A poet in Russia is not a poet. He's a messiah, he's a prophet. Up to now, art in this country was the only way of expressing yourself freely. You could be censored, you could be banned, you could sometimes be put in jail for your art (it happened, more than frequently), but you could still sit at your desk *writing*. Nobody was there at that moment to control what you were doing. You could control yourself. You were doing what you felt like doing, no matter what the consequences might be. And the greater the pressure against your creativity, the more you were willing to oppose."

Everything now, Kahn seems to feel, is up for grabs. "We are in a period where no one can tell you what's going to happen in this country — politically, economically, socially. Of course, jazz is secondary. Anything that's going to happen to culture — musical, jazz in particular — is certainly strongly dependent on what's going to happen to the country."

His own prognosis?

"I think that in the long run the country will get to about — well, of course because it's never been there — a normal life. It won't be easy. It won't be quick. It will be long, painful, and difficult. But it will happen. We have already started to face the risk of the challenge of a consumer society. And most people have already become money oriented, consumer oriented in the arts as well. However, there is going to be an enormous conflict between these people's ideal aspirations as to the kind of culture they should be making and what, on a more primitive level, they can gain or earn. This is a challenge any artist in the West, in a developed country, is facing also, but the situation is going to be much more sharply felt here, the challenges sharper, because, here, nobody has anything, no background, no rear ground to fall back on.

"The choice is not between being a star and making a modest but decent living. This is a choice of *survival,* and therefore even the best of the best and most talented individuals, like Kuryokhin, once they feel, once they see the lure of the West is real, almost inevitably they yield to it. Those who are still very deep in the underground, those who fought, for whom the lure of the dollar is still a little bit far off, is still unobtainable at this particular moment, they are still honest . . . but who knows what's going to happen to them? So it's really difficult to predict."

That evening I sat by the window of our hotel, watching the Neva and the traffic on the street below, waiting for night to fall. It never did. Shadows by day, brightness by night — what a perplexing city! The only link I could find between Pushkin's "green-pale arch of the heavens, / Of boredom, granite and cold," and Kahn and Kuryokhin's "Leningrad Bohemia" of the late seventies and revelation by Dixieland, was the frail thread of art or poetry, that immense, burning desire to express oneself freely, "no matter what the consequences might be." I had the superficial, though influential, historical connection between the avant-garde of the early part of the century and Kuryokhin's own slap in the face of public taste, but I couldn't imagine him sitting down to tea with Osip Mandelstam or Anna Akhmatova, the aristocratic tone of their terms of survival. So I gave up looking for accidental continuity. What they all seemed to share was this sublime city, plunged now in perpetual daylight. I could see why, although I was half in love with the city myself (on compatible summer terms), Sergei Kuryokhin had said you'd have to be insane to live here, where, in Akhmatova's words, "my white nights whisper / About some-one's secret, lofty love."

"Are you coming to bed?" my wife whispered, in the restless daylit room.

"Why?" I replied. "Why bother? I won't be able to sleep."

"What about me?"

"What about you?"

"Why not come to bed for me?" she said, in her best secret, lofty tones.

"Love in the afternoon?" I said.

The next day, on Nevsky Prospect, I discovered that number thirty-four ("one of the largest record stores," according to Fodor's) offered just five jazz recordings, which I promptly bought. The survival law in the USSR is buy it when you see it, for it won't be there tomorrow. I also noticed that the hard-currency, or *beryozka,* stores stood unblazoned by any external advertising. Much of the Soviet Union struck me as a place in which the outside offers absolutely no indication of the inside. Somewhere beneath all these grim granite facades people had to be making art, love, jazz, poems, but you never saw it. In Leningrad, more than any other city I'd been to in the USSR, the visible evidence of active lives escaped me. I even failed, because I miscounted canals, to find the house (104 Griboyedov Canal Embankment) in which Raskolnikov buried his ax in the skulls of the old moneylender and her sister Lizaveta in *Crime and Punishment,* but we did stumble onto the former Hay-market, Dostoevsky's haunt, now Mir (Peace) Square, the area still a bit tawdry, dank, dark—and I did see some brave, or dumb, or desperate souls actually swimming in a rank pond beside the inevitable statue of Lenin. We paused long enough at 12 Naberezhnaya Reki Moyki to pay our respects to Pushkin, who had left his home there on the morning of February 8, 1837, to fight a duel over his pretty, frivolous wife and returned to die two days later of his wounds.

Leningrad can also claim what seems to be the only Western-style jazz club in the USSR (a *dzhaz klub,* in the Soviet past, having been a state-approved social organization set up for players and fans alike). Alex Kahn had told me that David Goloshchekin's Diksi-Sving Klub could be found "somewhere on Zagorodni Prospect." The walls of the club are covered with photos of Armstrong, Basie, Ellington, Parker, Gillespie, Monk, Miles Davis. A ruble bar upstairs serves sandwiches, cognac, and lemonade, all of which people stack, in massive quantities, on their trays. A hard-currency operation just outside the stage offers nearly every sort of alcoholic device the Western imagination might crave.

People were well dressed, and the ambience was loose and sportive. If you dropped two spoons on the floor by accident and they began to clack, I think a Russian would get up to dance. Inside the Diksi Sving Klub, a balcony full of teenagers emptied out onto the floor early, shaking their stuff to the strictly trad Alexei Kanunnikov Jazz Band, playing "Someday Sweetheart," "Savoy Blues," "In the Mood," "After You've Gone," "Alexander's Ragtime Band."

Kanunnikov was obliged to share his stage time with the inevitable *estrada konsert,* or variety show, in this case, girls with that rare combination of balletic rigor and delicacy wearing khaki costumes that included gold-spangled brown ties, executing carefully choreographed can-can kicks, doing a lip sync on "Boogie Woogie Bugle Boy." We had been seated at a table with a young man whose entrepreneurial skills had been brought to bear on this show, who kept leaping up to coach the dancers and to complain to the manager, who came to check our tickets, about our being placed at his rose-studded, love-intended table. The young man grew irritated again when another Russian couple — in spite of the fact that the woman, in a stunning silver brocade dress, knew all the lyrics, in English, to "Red Roses for a Blue Lady" — was seated there. However, Betty won the young man over by offering to slice an apple he'd given his girlfriend with our Swiss Army knife. Cognac seemed to work wonders of détente also.

At the next break I ducked out on the variety show and talked to the band leader, Kanunnikov. He told me he'd once, for the sake of political expediency, had to change the proud name of his group (Jazz Band) to "variety orchestra." He'd started out with Yosif Weinstein's big band ("as a young man"), made records with a Dixieland aggregate, and worked combo gigs in restaurants, playing mostly *estrada* music and "sometimes" jazz. When times changed, Kanunnikov told his own group, "Now, men, let's get down to business" — a solid brand of trad jazz, ungirt, accomplished, swinging. Finding its own jobs, the group seems to have adapted to a new system well, playing anywhere from "two, three, five nights a week," enjoying trips to Helsinki ("We were very proud to be invited"). Like so many Russian jazz musicians of his generation, Kanunnikov discovered the music by way of VOA broadcasts, attracted to the style of Jack Teagarden, whom he calls "the professor, the philosopher." Benny Goodman played in the USSR in 1961, and Kanunnikov comments, "It was unreal; I saw him myself, and I could not believe my eyes, or ears." He experienced the same raptures when Duke Ellington arrived.

Back at our table the woman in the silver brocade dress was experiencing some raptures of her own, recalling — eyes shut, swaying — a tune she wanted her husband to request: "Cha-ta-noo-too-chu-goo." Time came for our *posledni tost* (last toast). Betty and I passed safely hotelward amongst the post-midnight white night architecture of Leningrad, a world that seemed stately, silent, nearly dead, with few people on the streets — just us, the cobblestones, the granite, the canals.

Vladimir Feyertag is a short man of immense national stature. Just about everyone I'd talked to in the Soviet Union agreed that he was the most respected jazz critic of the country. I'd seen him in action, of course, as "Festival Programme Master" (master of ceremonies) in both Moscow and Riga, and he had a gift for bringing a good deal of dignity to what could be a tedious or overly show-busy function. His introductions, delivered in the same tan suit at each festival, the same proud prance on stage and slight lisp, were long, interesting, learned, witty, and just plain good fun.

The Leningrad Hotel lounge was filled with noisy good-time Finns at three in the afternoon, so Feyertag came up to our room, where the sun blistered the windows. Alex Kahn, who was translating, immediately pulled the drapes, closing out the insistent view of the *Aurora* but not the steady noise of traffic. For the sake of some fresh air, we left a window open, which lent the interview some aleatoric effects I had not counted on, Feyertag's statements punctuated by an urgent auto horn or backfiring truck.

Larry Ochs had spoken to me of encounters with musicians who, faced with "the new reality," actually longed for the bad old Brezhnev days when they'd had a "totally defined role, they knew what they were up against, knew just why they were on the planet." Ochs felt that, by comparison with his 1983 trip, considerable confusion existed now. I asked Feyertag about this statement, and he agreed, saying that Ochs had been "very subtle" in his understanding of what he himself saw as a "transition period," a switching over from a "so-called authoritarian system," in which all the arts were state supported or state denied to a "private, capitalist world in which everyone is out for himself." Feyertag feels that, before, musicians banded together because they had to, but that now, adapting to a new world of competition was extremely difficult, "psychologically."

"The Soviet Union is a very different country. People here have never had choices as they do in the West. We have never been able to define our identities as early, or as clearly, as people in the West can. Therefore, the confusion."

When I presented him with Leo Feigin's statement that "the euphoria is over. The musicians have lost their audience. The underground is over. It's overground now, and people understand that what it's all about is simply *music,*" Feyertag simply replied, "I agree." However, throughout my conversations with musicians in the USSR, I had been surprised by the clarity of intent and commitment, nearly to the point of dogma or intolerance, receiving — in many cases — carefully delineated manifestos. How did such intentionality, such lucidity of purpose, fit with a time of obvious confusion in the arts?

"I think it's just a manifestation of our 'planned approach,' the planned systems which have dominated our lives," Feyertag said. "People *have* to be planning ahead. They are thinking and trying to be distinct and precise about their musical futures. Yet sometimes I get the feeling that our musicians are like double-faced Januses. On the one hand they are talented, creative artists looking for better, more innovative ways to express themselves; yet they are also managing themselves, calculating what has to be done in terms of the new market."

Sitting in a padded chair, shaping his hands so that the fingers of each touched in a manner resembling prayer, eyes sparkling as the heavy hotel curtain absorbed and contained the conflagration of afternoon sun, and the fierce traffic continued to make its presence known, Feyertag offered me a number of succinct and restrained responses to my questions. On the nature of "Soviet Jazz" (musicians saying there was no such thing, just the music of separate republics that happened to make up the USSR), Feyertag nodded his head, laughing ("But of course") when I said that one of these musicians had insisted that the music of *her* republic was closest to true American black jazz or the blues. The word *Soviet,* he feels, is no longer appropriate because of its strong political connotations. He prefers a strictly geographical designation, such as "jazz in the USSR." On the deliberate use of ethnic sources, Feyertag feels any art can become "national" if there is a strong individual performer who can arrive at that end "intuitively," but not too consciously. The great Azerbaijani pianist Vagif Mustafa-Zadeh did this, he feels, naturally, but his daughter, Aziza, does not, nor does the group Tri-O, from Lithuania. When I mentioned pianist Andrei Kondakov, who I talked to in Petrozavodsk and who had spoken to me of the Karelian elements in his work, Feyertag again laughed. "But he's not Karelian. He's Ukrainian and has lived in Karelia for only five years."

He made the analogy of an art historian leading you to the Hermitage and explaining the work there in such a thorough and professional manner that "you could paint it," but the act would not be natural, not *yours.*

Yet on the subject of imitation — the accusation, I felt, too often made by Western critics unfamiliar with Russian cultural history, aside from being able to hum a few bars of "Moscow Nights" — Feyertag said, "In our system of training, imitation, or copying a master, plays an important part. Only when a musician has reached a certain level of skill will he be thrown out on his own, left to his own style or devices. And this is not just true in the realm of jazz. Our students are not trained to think individually. They are trained to copy, to imitate."

"Eshche?" (Still?).

"Konechno" (Of course).

Jazz composition is not taught at all, Feyertag claims; the curriculum is still classical. He says he has studied the offerings of the American jazz college Berklee in Boston, and of other schools in the United States, and that he finds them "way, way ahead of us; incomparable, that's all." When I mentioned the intriguing and original compositional techniques of the Ganelin Trio, he said he felt that Vyacheslav Ganelin was truly an "exception," able to master both individual performing skills, with the freedom and imagination that entails, and precise, knowledgeable composition techniques. Unfortunately, he said, many musicians in the USSR have but one side to show. Lukianov, he feels, stifles his improvisational abilities with a rigid structural approach, and on the other hand, you find the loose anything-goes approach of the group Arkhangelsk.

I asked him about an incident I recalled from the Moscow festival. I'd been offended, for the sake of the many Russian musicians on hand, when American trumpeter Freddie Hubbard said, "You guys got classical music, we got jazz." But Feyertag was not at all put out by the statement. "One can't deny the American influence on jazz," he said. "Hubbard has a right to be snobbish about that, and it would be senseless to argue. Besides, we are not that subject to offense."

As to the future of the music in the USSR, he mentioned several limitations that would shape the jazz life there: a "nonexistent club scene" (people would prefer clubs to concert halls but can't have them because of the nation's poverty, the absence of available space, proper equipment, and so on; the dependence on a framework of festivals; restrictions on mobility due to domicile registration (that peculiar Soviet institution that does not allow people to move freely from city to city, a condition Feyertag sees as the source of exaggerated—"our festival is better than your festival"—local pride). Another problem is the "general European weakness of rhythm sections . . . no good drummers." Feyertag feels frontline musicians in the USSR would have sounded much better if they'd been supported by truly fine rhythm players. He feels the recent international Moscow festival may have been beneficial, allowing local musicians a chance to hear good American drummers and rhythm sections that do not merely accompany soloists but actively listen, take part, respond to, relate to them. "Like our own lives," he added. "Our polyphonic lives."

I complimented Feyertag on his fine, intelligent, extended (beyond the capacity of American audiences to endure, I suspect; they probably would have shouted, "Get off the stage and just let these guys *play!*") introductions of musicians at the two festivals I had attended, his role as master of ceremonies. He laughed. "Those introductions are necessary now for purely technical reasons. So much is going wrong backstage that I have to come out and kill time. I suspect that, once we have caught up with you Americans as far as technology goes, there will no longer be any need for my services."

I told him that, in spite of the obviously desired gains to the country as a whole, I hoped that day would not arrive too soon. He had a plane to catch for Murmansk, where, once again, he would kill time as "Festival Programme Master." We shook hands. My wife smiled at this charming man, whom I think she had developed a crush on.

Vladimir Feyertag functioned as something of a missing link for me in Leningrad, allowing me to pass — as much as I was capable of — beyond the limbo of disparities the city presents. After talking to him, savoring his fine manners, his (although this is probably the last word in the world he would use for himself) mild aristocratic demeanor, his dignity, I could feel the gap between Pushkin's, Mandelstam's, and Akhmatova's Petersburg and Kuryokhin's and Alex Kahn's Leningrad closing. And although I had failed to encounter musicians live in Leningrad, I could hear in mind, just as I had in Tallinn, those who represented the city well. Multireedsman Vladimir Tolkachev and fine pianist Yuri Yukechev make up what's left of a group called Homo Liber. They are not from Leningrad but Novosibirsk, more specifically an intellectual enclave known as Akademgorodok ("little town for academics"), where they were allowed to develop their art in relative freedom while Brezhnev was boring the rest of Russia to tears. However, their piece "St. Petersburg" is one of the most handsome evocations I've heard of the "stern, many-watered and dark city" Akhmatova said she could grope her way to in sleep: the vast squares, Neva canals, abundant wrought iron, wild winds, and endless granite. Tolkachev and Yukechev's "Homage to Velemir Khlebnikov" celebrates — with prancing oscilloscope precision and manic polyphonic phrasing, rococo flourishes mixed with radio static and true Russian lyricism — the experimental poet who invented the transmental language of Za-um.

The Guyvoronsky/Volkov Duo consists of two of the most respected musicians in the Soviet Union, a fortunate pairing up. Nearly all the jazz musicians I interviewed expressed their admiration for these two, who, sustaining that rich classical tradition of technical virtuosity converted to pure feeling, are living examples of how fine music can be made from limited means and unlikely instrumentation (a trumpet and bass?). Guyvoronsky and Volkov work with basic themes, understatement, handsome juxtapositions, supple interplay (each player truly listening to the other, a natural counterpart), accretion of mood through subtle tones, figures and patterns as tactile as they are audile. Through intricate rhythms they project a meditative, both velvety and swinging jazz raga, their "set" ending with five short delicious pieces, aptly titled "Fighters," "Tea Addict" (steeped, savored, stoned), "Actors" (clever snippy dialogue), "Futen, God of Wind," and "Poet" (lyric bells, the Miles of Gil Evans days — mood speech), color and statement admirably combined, unrushed, unpretentious.

Leningrad remained enigmatic and historical for me, but at least now I could see how jazz could exist side by side with that architecture, just where among the granite it fit in. Yet Vladimir Feyertag, Alex Kahn, Kununnikov, the dancers at the Diksi Sving Klub, still resembled those small figures in Chinese paintings, stunted by distant mountains and surging waterfalls, dwarfed by rock and sky; and after my loose and open love affair with Odessa, I resented the distance Leningrad seemed to impose on one. Yet Peter (as its inhabitants call it) is still my favorite city in the former Soviet Union.

On our last night there, and in the Soviet Union itself, we booked a boat ride on the Neva. All afternoon puffballs, like light swirling snow, had been blown about the city, their source I know not where. Crossing the Kirovski Moct, the fierce wind stinging my eyes to the point of tears, I thought again of Akhmatova, her poems about the rash, wide, noisy wind slicing through speech itself. Yet our journey up and down the River Neva was calm. We stayed on deck for the most part, going below just long enough to hear a folk troupe play the handsome "Ural Mountain Ash" on a sort of sagging xylophone suspended from the waists of two women.

Walking back across the bridge after, at bright midnight, we passed other lovers — much younger than ourselves — who, or perhaps I imagined this, were not just looking at our shoes but actually smiling at us, although a Leningrad smile is a subtle thing and frequently hard to discern. Strolling by the Naval Academy, I heard, *live,* a twelve-bar piano blues emerging from an open window. I had entered Leningrad — to cite one of Akhmatova's poems again — with a foreigner's curiosity and "been taken prisoner by novelty." And that's just how I would leave the city, amazed by its extraordinary fate, its wonder, mystery, and capacity for survival with style. "You who remained there to perish," Akhmatova wrote after the war, "the desired messengers not arriving, only the charming dance and chorus, of the long white night."

# Coda

"Well, we made it," a young man said to his traveling companion in the Moscow airport, near the duty-free shop that sold china, liquor, and Elizabeth Arden perfume.

"I sure do feel a lot safer now," the other replied.

I didn't necessarily feel safer returning to my homeland. In fact I wasn't sure I was ready to return at all. I'd merely whetted my appetite on the megalithic empire, stunned by the paradox of its diversity. I had a hunger to head east, into the exotic but now dreaded danger zones of Central Asia, sampling whatever jazz I might find along the way. But time and money had run out. Back in Moscow, the driver of a rather ratty car, backbeat rock blaring away all too early, a man with an outrageous plaid cap, sped us past a sign that read "Praise Soviet Science!" The crumbling high-rise apartment complexes once more gave way to the forest in which Sheremetyevo International Airport has been set down. Our conversation went fairly well until I asked him if he liked jazz and he said he didn't care for the stuff at all. He was surprised such a thing even existed in the USSR.

Like dutiful tourists Betty and I turned all our rubles in, as instructed, and then discovered that, beyond the checkpoint, a restaurant we went to for some much needed breakfast took only rubles. This was our last taste of Russian social logic. Fortunately, Betty discovered one last hard-boiled egg in her purse. Once on the plane, I was seated next to an American engineering professor who'd been on a minerals tour of Siberia. Unfortunately, for most of our nine-hour flight home, he slept and snored, leaning over into my seat.

After all the jokes about Soviet inefficiency, we got a solid taste of the U.S. brand at JFK Airport. Our flight to California was delayed for five hours, and mounds of travelers snoozed on the floor, the terminal doing a not-so-funny impersonation of Bombay that day. In Chicago, where we stopped once we got moving again, another two-hour delay was attributed to "cowling problems," the pilot assuring us that "once those mechanic fellas sew this baby back up, we'll be out of town."

In California, the first thing I did was send Anthony Marhel some books and a subscription to a jazz magazine I'd promised. Because of the dramatic turn of events in Latvia, a year and a half would pass before I would hear from him. I certainly wouldn't rate the former Soviet Union postal service the best in the world, but I did manage to hear from a few people I'd met there. And some I had not. Old Dnepropetrovsk faithful Michael Dubilet came alive again now that I was out of his nation, sending me a form letter about the Jazz on the Dnieper Festival and promotional material for Oleg Kireev's group, Orlan: "Each concert of the festival will have two jazz duets to play solo program," Michael wrote, and "music not to be the best mediator but the way of mental development . . . from toneless music primitive to a wise simplicity of genuine art." Once again, he hoped "for a near collaboration."

I would have a full teaching schedule in the fall, so in July I immediately set to work on this book, justifying my inability to contact people I'd met in the USSR — the absence of correspondence — by saying, as I finally told Irene, that I was not writing *to* them because I was busy writing so much *about* them, which was true. And I eagerly, each day, scanned the headlines for news: "Yelstin Quits Party; Exodus May Follow," "Thousands Rally against Communism, March to Kremlin Walls," "Gorbachev Endorses Radical Reforms," "Georgians Turn Out for Multiparty Voting," "Dissidents Win Big in Soviet Vote."

The first musician I heard from was pianist Yuri Kuznetsov, a letter that nearly broke my heart, containing as it did, such wild, unrealistic expectations. He greeted us from the city of Odessa, saying he remembered me and my "wonderful wife Betty" with hope and joy. Then he got down to *delo* (business). Yuri said that nothing had changed much since we'd met. He felt Art and Electronics, the Moscow organization with whom he'd made a recording was acting "incomprehensibly." Yuri had hoped it would get passed on to Mobile Fidelity in the States. Were they trying to cheat him? he wondered, asking my advice. In Odessa, I'd asked Yuri the hypothetical question: Who would you like to play with, if you could, in the United States? At the time he'd been struck blind with limitless possibility and desire, but this is what he wrote now: "You said last summer that you had musical friends with whom I could play spontaneous music. Please send any news of that possibility to me, and I will pass the word on to my partner Manukian. We will be very pleased to meet these musicians from the U.S. and play together." He'd gone on to name Chick

Corea and Herbie Hancock, as if they were best friends of mine, members of some immediate musical circle or family living just up the street.

The letter I wrote back is one of the hardest I've ever had to write. I reminded him that I was *tolko picatel* (only a writer), not a producer, agent, or manager (in his letter he'd asked me to produce a recording or concert for him in the United States). I told him that Mobile Fidelity, as I learned, had put its USSR Jazz Showcase Series on hold indefinitely, which meant forever. Thinking of what Vladimir Feyertag had said about the difficult time Soviet musicians would have "adapting to a new world of competition" psychologically, I came right out and said that probably most of what he'd been told in the past about U.S. capitalism was true: it was nasty *delo,* business. I mentioned that, on radio shows I'd been doing since our trek, I always played his music, so he now had fans in the United States.

Very late at night and in absolute silence, just as he had instructed me in Odessa, I listened to the cassette Yuri had given me. I thought of Tolstoy's *Kreutzer Sonata,* the doubts expressed there about music as "a dreadful thing," the "awful effect," the agitation it produces in the soul without leading to any conclusion whatsoever. Yuri's tape produced the same dread and pity in me. Listening to it now in light of the market economy, I felt this music sounded too wearying, abstract, brooding. I also listened to Yuri performing a bright medley of Gershwin ("Summertime") and Ellington ("Things Ain't What They Used to Be"), perfect for public consumption. He ended with an ironic, bouncing, upbeat version of "Brother, Can You Spare a Dime?"

"Rationing Proposed for Soviet Union's Hungry Winter," "Ethnic Unrest Turns Violent in Moldavia," "Gorbachev Threatens to Impose Emergency Rule in Republics," "Shevardnadze Quits Kremlin Post, Fears Dictatorship." At Christmastime I heard from Igor, our guide in Petrozavodsk. He wrote saying he had received the books by Voinovich and Orwell I'd sent him. "I enjoyed reading the Russian one, and my friends are all reading it now. It is still not published in Russian in the USSR, so there's a line of people who want to have it." The copy of Orwell's *1984* was being used for a seminar on language and style at the institute. Igor also wrote excitedly about a jazz festival held in Petrozavodsk. "Thinking myself, after an hour and a half interpreting your and Kondakov's talk last summer, a specialist in jazz, I could not miss that event." He enclosed the festival program, saying, "Maybe it is of interest for you and you will find players you met," and I did. He also enclosed a New Year's card with a decree by Peter the Great commanding people to be in an "elated mood."

The New Year's news was not good. My own nation had embroiled itself in a Gulf War, which distracted its people from any interest in the Soviet

Union, having found, I suppose, a miniature version of the "evil empire" in Iraq. And, although he vigorously denied it, Gorbachev did not seem disinclined to take advantage of the world's diverted interest, for on January 13, my birthday, the situation exploded. "Soviet Assault Kills Thirteen in Lithuanian Capital," "Latvia Votes to Form Volunteer Home Guard," "Yeltsin Demands Gorbachev Resign; Calls for 'War' against Soviet Leaders," "Latvia, Estonia Choose Independence; Lithuania Votes for Succession," "Pro-Yeltsin Crowd Defies Ban on Rally."

My immediate, selfish concern was for Anthony Marhel and Jeanne. Were they out there on the barricades? Were they all right? In the midst of all this trauma, two letters arrived, from not Anthony but the Lukianovs. The longest, signed "Inna and Germann," was written by Lukianov's wife, grateful for some photos of their apartment I'd sent. She went on to describe a carpenter's bench Germann had built at their dacha; the woodworking tools she'd given him on his birthday; their dog, Ira (who'd given birth to seven puppies, "which brought us much joy, responsibility, and considerable financial assistance"); and a new cat of "excellent pedigree, her parents champions in Belgium, Germany and the USSR." A copy of the Moscow documentary *Dzhazman* was on its way, she said, adding, "You are one of the heroes of the film."

Germann's letter was much shorter. He was pleased I'd undertaken the task of translating his poems, and he hoped that, should the war in the Persian Gulf not damage U.S.-Soviet relations, he might come to the United States ("the homeland of jazz") "to play some sets," not just to travel. "Study the Russian language," he wrote, adding, "We have an interesting but tense life here. I embrace you and send my greetings to your wife."

Shortly after hearing from the Lukianovs, I received a letter from Leo Feigin, enclosing a review of his ambitious CD set *Document,* which had appeared in the *New York Times.* Although I seemed to have been impressed by Russia, he said, he saw it as "one of the most ridiculous countries in the world." For him, the summer trip "was a terrifying experience." However, he would be going again, taking saxophonist Anthony Braxton to Moscow to stage his operas.

I had just finished a review of *Document* myself, for *Jazz Forum,* in which I said the eight-CD boxed set was aptly named. A document it is, weighing in at exactly three pounds on my bathroom scale — the same weight as the human brain. In his lucid intro, Alex Kahn states that jazz-oriented experimental or improvised music from the USSR "defies reduction to any common denominator." One common denominator I found in the pieces in *Document* was a demand that the audience, or listener, truly listen, 100 percent, no holidays, vacations, or domestic sabbaticals allowed. I know of top-notch jazz musicians playing close to the tradition you can nod off on occasionally, probably because you know that when you wake up, the tradition will still be there, but this music affords no such solace. Its demands are large, arduous, ardent. Imagination, genuine invention, even in the arts — where there's supposed to be so much of it — is still a rare quality, and still the standard that must be held up to a form as blatantly open in intent, as relentless, widely assimilating (everything from sonic shadows and atmospheric wisps to ethnic gleanings from Indonesian gamelan and the talking drums and little nature sounds of West Africa), and experimental, even at times indulgent or exquisitely boring, as the music of *Document* is.

Having missed her in Riga, on the CDs I had my first chance to hear the truly astonishing voice of Sainkho Namchylak, eerie, outrageous, otherworldly. I'm not sure twenty minutes of "Transformation of Matters" — and she certainly does that! — is enough to allow one to decide whether she's a dazzling new "expressive vehicle," a singer, or just human oddity (remember Yma Sumac, anyone?), but I could have used more of Namchylak on *Document* in order to find out. Again, the staples — lip pops, glottal clicks, whispers, multiphonics, even singing from the throat with relaxed muscles rather than the diaphragm — have been used by world vocal-instrumentalists from Tibetan Buddhist monks and Mongolian *hoomi* (throat) singers to Bobby McFerrin. Yet there's a quality to Namchylak's voice that is special, deeply moving, as represented in her wonderful "domestic quarrel" with tenor saxophonist Sergei Letov: through bat-wing vibrato, dog-whistle love moans, wordless pop lyricism, a wealth of dynamics, and minaret-tall range.

In his notes to *Document,* Alex Kahn says he hopes that "New Music from Russia: The 1980s" is not a "closed chapter." He goes on to risk that "the music's best time is yet to come," and I hope that proves to be true. For now, this music should be taken as it is, especially in light of the rather extraordinary, at times threatening or prohibitive, circumstances under which much of it was made. It reflects the times, with all their faults: tentative, groping, fragmentary, frustrated, frustrating, even evasive, unable to sustain any given stance or emotion — like Osip Mandelstam's symbolist kettle that refused to boil, demanding an absolute significance, as if boiling, the poet added, had no absolute significance itself.

Spring was long. Was the snow of silence descending again, creating my own personal Gulag as it had before we left on the trip? No, thanks to Pawel Brodowski, who devoted nearly an entire issue of *Jazz Forum* to "New Music from Russia," which included everything from a Singgroup Jazz Festival in Panevezis, Lithuania and Aziza Mustafa-Zadeh's appearance at the thirteenth Jazz-Ost-West Festival in Nuremberg to an account by Valtar Ojakäär of a Days of Jazz and Blues Festival in Tallinn, where Tatar guitarist Enver Izmalov was a "surprising discovery." Pawel wrote me a nice note, saying, "I think that better than anyone else from the West you have grasped the spirit of Russian jazz without making any definite judgements, but rather attempting to find the truth somewhere in between disparate statements by different artists" — so perhaps I hadn't abandoned the principles, setting out on our trip, I'd adopted from John Steinbeck after all.

"Moscow Stores Close on Eve of Price Hikes," "Tension Increases in Armenia Following Bloodshed," "Soviet Georgia Votes for Nationalist Leader," "Yeltsin Elected First President of Russia," "Soviets OK Denationalization of Factories." Then, not eighteen days after President George Bush and Mikhail Gorbachev held a two-day summit meeting and signed their "historic arms treaty": "Gorbachev Ousted in Coup!"

On the night of the takeover I watched the Russian TV program "Vremia," stunned. How could a nation revert to its indecent, self-destructive past so quickly? Would all the magnificent people I'd met be sent packing back to that godawful life they'd known before? I bled for them. Everyone had been so open, so frank, so honest with me. How could I continue my book? How could I, now, should this coup stick and the old horrors return, jeopardize their lives by printing what they'd said to me, no matter how significant such statements might be to the world at large? I sat by the television set for days, watching the events unfold. And then, the miraculous took place (I'd seen my share of miracles that summer of 1990, how had I ever lost faith in them?). I watched, amazed, as the scroll of headlines — and history — unrolled: "Thousands Resist; Yeltsin Calls for Strike," "Gorbachev Retakes Reins; Eight Coup Leaders Arrested," "Gorbachev Quits Party Post; Urges Dissolving Central Committee," "Azerbaijanis Vote to Leave Soviet Union," "Baltics Given Independence," "Republics Declare Soviet Government dead; Last Rites Planned for USSR," "Yeltsin Controls Kremlin; Gorbachev to Make His Exit Today."

Such sudden change left me and a lot of other people dazed. I still hadn't heard from Anthony Marhel in Riga, nor Tamaz Kurashvili in Tbilisi ("Both Sides Warn of Georgia Civil War," then "Rebel Troops Lay Seige to Georgia Capital), but I prayed and hoped for them. I did hear from our translator, the irrepressible Irene. "We are still alive and happy," she wrote, "and hope you are too." She said that life at the time was "full of abrupt turns and unexpected events, but so far, we have managed."

I couldn't go back to the Soviet Union. The place didn't even exist anymore — some poor cosmonaut still floating around out in space without a country! However, I was amazed to discover the number of Russians turning up, sometimes literally, on my doorstep. And true to American commerce, catalogues began to arrive in the mail: "Crafts and Collectibles from the USSR," which contained everything from a Russian salad dressing ("The Party's

Over!") to "Individual Berlin Wall Chunks" and Van Gogh *matryoshka,* or nesting, dolls.

One of the more genuine American discoveries came to me by way of Igor Butman, who was featured prominently on a Walter Davis Jr. CD, *Jazznost: Moscow-Washington Summit,* played at a festival in Moscow (Idaho), and returned to the USSR for a tour set up by Vartan Tonoian and recorded by George Avakian. He told me that pianist David Azarian was now living in Boston also.

David Azarian is a talented instrumentalist/composer afflicted with "the Russian disease" of superb technical facility. He has a unique, slightly filigreed but supple style that converts standard material to his own — Dizzy Gillespie's "Con Alma" transformed to a tune called "With Soul." He also has a host of original tunes with his own signature very much set upon them, along with a unique sense of rhythm. He evokes pictures of his native country, celebrated by poet Osip Mandelstam as a land of "azure and clay," of "snows on rice paper." His tunes are handsomely structured, "octagonal honeycombs" (to call on Mandelstam again), a labyrinth of "moist singing." Literary allusions fit here because another unique quality is his ability to tell stories, to create vignettes, providing extra-musical drama and charm, evoking all-too-human situations without sacrificing anything by way of the music itself. His favorite subject is women: "Martina," delicate yet indelible, "amid earthenware plains"; "Jeanne D'Arc," elegant and processional; and the Joanne of "Joanne's Music Box," sprightly, proud, strutting her stuff.

Over the phone David told me that storytelling as such was, in his case, an intrinsic, deliberate part of the music; that because of the time and circumstance in which he had composed them, each tune did, indeed, have its own "special history." " 'Martina,' " David says, is based on "a love story without a good ending." It's about a girl from West Germany, now married. "Jeanne D'Arc" was written for the theater, the producer having requested music with "very emotional melody, dramatic, tragic" to accompany the last scene. "Joanne's Music Box" is a tribute to a woman who came to Yerevan, visited an art gallery, and fell in love with both the paintings of a friend of David's and that friend himself. "She took my friend from Armenia, as in a dream," David told me. "If you started to love jazz, you also started to love America. I saw this woman as a heroic person, someone who had done a very good thing for my friend. Everybody wants somebody like Joanne, to take us from our life in the Soviet, and so I told my friend's wife how I felt. 'Well, if you think I'm such a great person,' she said, 'how about writing a song for me.' So I did."

A prodigy, David placed number one at the age of twelve in an Armenian music school's piano competition, playing Bach, Prokofiev, and Haydn. I asked him about his classical background. David feels it's an asset. "It helps me very much now," providing a special, and solid, conception of harmony, of possibilities for modulation not customarily used in jazz. Of the deliberate use of "folk" or national elements in jazz in the USSR, he said that not just Armenian but Georgian music as well as that of the Middle Eastern republics in general employ numerous mixed rhythms. David says he now prefers playing, or making, "unusual games" out of strictly ¼ rhythmic structures. "I don't use mixed rhythms now because I am interested to give people rhythm which can take them from their chairs and make them feel like they want to dance — ⁷⁄₄ does not give that chance to the normal listener in the United States."

He enjoys playing what he describes as the "major/minor game," one he feels is typical of Armenian music, which is basically minor but, when it switches to major harmony, opens people up, makes them feel happy. "This is not only from Armenia," he says. "Lots of music plays this game. But Armenians go from happy to sad easily. Happy in the morning, but not in the night. And Armenian music has inside it very deep sadness, because of our history." In Armenia, he noticed that in villages, where people never listened to jazz, the paradiddles employed by percussionists were very close to those of jazz drummers. "Jazz intonation can be very close to that of folk music, but what I play now comes without consciousness. I never think about it. Someone who knew me before recently said, 'You play now more Armenian than before.' Maybe it's nostalgia. I don't know. I never thought I would feel it so strongly."

David has few complaints about his assimilation into the American jazz scene, having found "many teachers and friends," among whom he counts Quincy Jones, "as if I knew him all my life." He did touch on some of the injustices that seem built into a system that, in some ways, he still finds puzzling. "It's very good, and necessary, to find a good agent, but then they say they are already booked up. They don't need to make experiments. They'll do anything for an already-made star, but they don't want to make a star of somebody else. There are so many great musicians around! They play in clubs but nobody knows them except other musicians. Agents aren't interested in people like that. . . . But I am in a good situation in the Boston area. People know and respect what I do."

For the future, David is concentrating on seeking that element he finds missing in other pianists: "to go deep inside much more," to play "not just finger music" but something "very special," every note arising from some deep core inside the soul, until "everything I do must sing. It must be like song."

Another delightful find that occurred right at home was former Leningrad pianist Gennadi Loktionov. We first chatted at the Monterey Jazz Festival, his eyes flashing, an appreciative pixie smile somewhat at odds with a sad and slightly bewildered face. He was struggling then with just about every aspect of America except the superb music of Chick Corea's trio, playing on the main stage. Gennadi is a first-rate musician from St. Petersburg (Leningrad) who possesses all the technical proficiency, verve, imagination, and passion that I found in other Russian jazz pianists. He is equally at ease with Liszt, Chopin, Rachmaninoff, Bud Powell, young pianist Benny Green, or Count Basie's "Shiny Stockings." Because he recently returned from St. Petersburg (caught in the sudden ruble escalation that followed the lifting of price controls, he nearly didn't make it out), I asked him about the jazz scene there. Surprisingly, he said a renaissance of sorts was going on. "Believe it or not!" Gennadi said. "New bands are springing up. For example, Gennadi Garanian, in Moscow, has put together a fine new big band. In Leningrad — or St. Petersburg — David Goloshchekin's Diksi Sving Klub is functioning well, many top Russian musicians playing there. Still, because of skyrocketing prices, travel in the Soviet Union is much more difficult now."

Conducting this interview, I was assisted by another lucky Russian find, writer and musician Marat Akchurin, who was finishing a book, *Red Odyssey*, about his own summer of 1990 journey and his sometimes wild adventures in the Moslem republics. With Marat playing "bass" on a synthesizer keyboard, myself on drums, and Gennadi on piano, we'd managed some grand jam sessions at my house and also at a park near St. Seraphim's Russian Orthodox Church.

"Previously," Marat added now, "a trip from Moscow to Leningrad was as cheap as a bottle of champagne, and a bottle of champagne cost just six rubles, fifty kopecks" — a little over a dollar when Betty and I were there.

"New hotels have opened up," Gennadi continued. "After repairs, renovation. The Europeiskaya. The Astoria. These are five-star hotels. The Europeiskaya, for example, is owned and run by a Swedish company. The manager, the employees are Swedish. It's the same there as it is here. They play light jazz, perhaps. Nothing very fancy or complicated. But it is jazz, and it's being played around the clock. Even breakfast is accompanied sometimes by music." However, a new problem exists now, Gennadi says. Many of these hotels have become hangouts for gangsters. "You know, musicians in Russia are mostly intellectuals," he said. "They are sensitive people. They're not tough guys. Yet these hotels have become contaminated by racketeers who come in around midnight and force musicians to play all kinds of shit. And nobody can do anything about it, because everyone is afraid of these guys. The situation is out of control."

"Sounds like bootleg days in America," I said. "The Jazz Age, the Roaring Twenties."

Gennadi's own jazz past is classic. Hearing the music for the first time in Kursk, his hometown, at the age of sixteen, he had been trained at a *uchilishche* (specialized music school) to play classical music. "Suddenly, here was this strange stuff. So different! I had no concept, then, of improvisation. One night I was walking past one of our Palaces of Culture, and I first heard live jazz. I went in. A quintet was playing, rehearsing. I was shocked. What they were doing was unthinkable for the time. All these guys were in their thirties, and I was just sixteen. Ia mechtal [I was dreaming]. What I heard was the same music I'd heard on VOA. Oi, vot mne by tuda! Vot mne by siuda! Vot mne by siuda! [What had been there was now here!] I said, responding to each instrument. And right then and there I decided that I wanted to be the same. I would simply die if I could not become one of these jazzmen."

Gennadi told me of a time that no one I talked to in the Soviet Union had ever mentioned, when, under seige, "shoved aside by" the Beatles' pop invasion, the jazz circle grew smaller and smaller. Many of the musicians, he said, simply "cracked," drank heavily, "couldn't pass the test," or sold out, including, he confessed on that last score, himself. "I was one of those who didn't pass," he said. "I lost my 'jazz virginity.' I had a family. I was forced to play — well, maybe a slightly better estrada — McCartney, Stevie Wonder, Phil Collins — so that I could feed them. Yet I think I benefited from this experience somehow." He did manage, while playing pop music in Volgograd, to open the first jazz club there.

He feels it's absurd to attempt to compare Russian and American jazz. "That's why my friend Igor Butman is here," he said, laughing softly. "That's why I am here. And Levinovsky. You know, I am the sort of person who is difficult to feed, because I am always hungry, thirsty for better music. After all those years of playing estrada, I have discovered jazz again — and that's made me feel young! I want to play jazz now as often as possible." Asked about his future here, he laughed heartily, then sank into a sort of funk. "Camyi trudnyi vopros!" (That's a difficult question for me!), he said. "I never dreamed, ever, that I would be living in the United States someday. You know, I don't give a damn about supermarkets or overlarge discount stores, any of that. I am interested in other things — such as jazz! Just now I am experiencing a sort of crack up, or breakdown, I suppose, because everything is so different here, so new to me. But jazz is my cross. I must carry it."

"There really is a jazz renaissance going on now in the commonwealth?" I asked.

"Yes! I can sense that as a musician," he replied. "It's just something . . . in the air. I have no solid evidence, I'll confess, to confirm it with. You know, when I was there, winter was ending. Spring was beginning. The heart of every Russian jazz musician I know was responding to this, reacting. We could all smell it . . . the rose, the fresh rose!"

I also received a call from Louis Scherr, a pianist whose appearance with bassist Tommy Cecil at the Moscow festival had made a strong impression on me and the crowd at the State Variety Theater. Sherr and Cecil had stolen the show at one of the evening concerts. Scherr and Soviet bassist Viktor Dvoskin had now put together a group called Jazznost. Times had changed. When Dvoskin got off the plane from his 10,000-ruble Sheremetyevo-to-Dulles airport flight in January 1992 ("Three days later the price went up to 90,000," he said), he was just another bass player arriving for a gig in the United States.

This fine musician, who I thought had stolen the show when I first heard him at Stanford, was setting out on a nine-city East Coast tour with Jazznost, a group that also includes saxophonist Sergei Gurbeloshvili, Dvoskin's former companion in the USSR group Allegro, and Washington, D.C., drummer Tony Martucci. On the night of his arrival, I talked to both Dvoskin and Louis Scherr. Comparing this visit with the other, Dvoskin said, "Before, everything was arranged for us. We just played. This time, Sergei and I had to make it over here ourselves. Of course, now we can deduct what we spend; but I will be more proud of this trip because, if it is successful, it will have been more difficult."

Asked how commonwealth life had affected the forty or so festivals offered each year, Dvoskin said these remain intact, but of the last ten festivals he has attended, most were sponsored by what he calls "appropriators," that rising cadre of entrepreneurs engaged in joint ventures or cooperatives. Hardest hit by change has been the recording business, the previously state-owned monopoly Melodiia Records. "It's not like what it was before," Viktor says, "when you just stood in line to be recorded. Now you have to pay off . . . I don't try to be recorded anymore."

How did two such scene thieves as Louis and Viktor end up together? "Jazznost was really Viktor's idea," Scherr says. The pianist was introduced to the other bassist by Cecil, who'd heard the Russian on his first U.S. tour. "I was curious about Russian musicians," Scherr says. "After the Moscow festival I was set to travel around the USSR for about three weeks. Viktor heard I would be in Kiev and said, 'Would you like to play together there? I can arrange it.' We did perform and the audience loved it."

Given the range of jazz styles in the former Soviet Union, how did Jazznost decide on a common language, a joint sound that would satisfy all four musicians? Both Viktor and Louis agree that a compatible notion of jazz rhythm provided the core. "When I first played with Viktor," Louis says, "I took lots of liberties with time, playing over-the-bar phrases, and I felt free to do just what I wanted because he was always there. Everything was close knit; everything worked. I am now exposing these guys to my harmonic concept. I'm really into the sound of very unorthodox voicings — polytonal harmony —

on a piano." Viktor and Sergei are accustomed to working on "a large stage," knocking crowds over the head with dynamic technical flourish, and unfamiliar with intimate ("club") performances. Louis says, "We are just beginning to discover each other's true musicality."

The lifting of controls in the commonwealth finds musicians' long-desired mobility curtailed not by politics but by economics. However, Viktor seems to be swinging with the new system. "I am playing with two groups, my own quartet and Jazznost," he says, "and I like both. I also play duo with guitarists Alexei Kuznetsov and Andrei Ryabov, and with pianist Igor Bril." Viktor told me Bril has traveled to New Zealand ("some very, very far country," he said) with his saxophonist twin sons. Yet the overall musical situation, according to Viktor, remains "difficult," some performers adapting well (he mentioned Leo Kushmir, the pianist in his own quartet, and Andrei Kondakov), some stagnating. Germann Lukianov, apparently, is having a difficult time adjusting to a new system. Others — for severe reasons — have vanished. I asked Viktor about Tamaz Kurashvili. Georgia, Viktor says, "has disappeared for us Moscovites. I have tried to dial Tamaz but there is no answer. I hope he is in America."

Both Scherr and Dvoskin had high hopes for their own U.S. tour. "There is a good mix in Jazznost, half and half," Viktor says. "We are quite different people, different enough to be interesting together. Life is very different in each of our countries, yet I have never felt so close as I do with Louis. I could never have imagined that before. We speak different languages, and when Louis talks I sometimes miss the words, but I do not miss what he wishes to say. And I hope all this is reflected in our music."

My work was nearly over. I'd heard and gathered a lot of great music made by people I respected and loved, even though I had not blazed many fresh trails as far as my theory of correspondences or influences went. Ted Levin had been correct in his assessment of the situation, his suspicion that ethnic affiliations and sources were casual rather than "carefully conceived and crafted" or even conscious. Roots had certainly been suggested to me by Aziza Mustafa-Zadeh, Anatoli Vapirov, David Azarian; and parallels certainly did exist, the avant-garde showing up in Sergei Kuryokhin, the groups Arkhangelsk and Orkestrion, Igor Nazaruk's links to Alfred Schnitke. Yet most of the artists I'd talked to had denied anything other than "similar cultural conditions."

When I'd set out, I had been looking for a system, a symmetry, a degree of influence or association, a line of sense and coherence that just doesn't seem to exist in actual life. What I had found was the music itself in all its amazing diversity. The continuity, the legacy, might always be "underneath," as Leo Feigin had suggested at the start, but the music itself just is: current, compelling, encouraging me to set aside my own American jazz snobbery and accept the music for itself alone.

I never received the tapes from Alexei Batashev, of course.

I never heard from critic Tatiana Didenko, who'd promised to send material, nor from *Dzhaz* magazine editor Kolya Dmitriev.

I never heard again from Yuri Kuznetsov.

I hadn't heard anything about Tamaz Kurashvili, and I worried, and still do. As I said, I finally did hear from Anthony Marhel a year and a half after our return. "Regards from Latvia!" he wrote, explaining that he'd changed jobs, that his new small nation had suffered through a nine-month "mail blockade," that he was writing regularly for *Rodnik,* a handsome magazine he'd shown me, although they'd had "problems with paper and printing this terrible year."

I also talked with John Orysik, a De Maurier Ltd. International Festival producer. He set me straight on what I'd missed in Kiev: bass guitarist Olexander Nesterov, keyboardist Petrov Torstikha, pianist and vibraharp player Mukolo Zamovoko. Orysik spoke favorably of the Chervonha Ruta Jazz Festival, held annually in different cities throughout the Ukraine, and of musicians from Lviv. Orysik also described, vividly, the frustration of attempting to bring ex-Soviet musical artists to North America just now. "They have no infrastructure with which to bring these things off," John lamented. "Just bureaucratic bungling. It's a horror show." By way of example he said that Olexander Nesterov had spent six months programing his synthesizer, only to have it confiscated at the Moscow airport. Nesterov turned up in Vancouver dejected—to put it mildly—and had to start all over again on a borrowed instrument. This year the Ukrainian Cultural Fund simply couldn't afford a flight price that has increased by 20 percent.

I hear from Leo Feigin fairly frequently. Now nearly the sole producer of Soviet jazz and improvised music, he sends me generous doses of new CDs by Petras Vysniauskas, Keshavan Maslak, Sergei Kuryokhin, Arkhangelsk (which, Leo says, had a "fenomenal tour of Japan — 16 concerts, fantastic reviews, a new CD released by Nippon Crown"), Sainkho Namchylak — even an album called *Astreja — Music from Davos,* the work of a quartet that includes avant-garde classical artist and composer Sofia Gubaidulina performing with Valentina Ponomareva, so the "connection" Laurel Fey had sensed had become actual. American jazz magazines have never been very kind to Leo, but Art Lange did a good review of another boxed set, *Conspiracy:* music from a festival held in Zurich, presenting a "Soviet" all-star big band led by Anatoli Vapirov and an exciting new bassist, Ashkat Sayfoolin. I've run across magazine pieces on Westerners associated with the USSR, everyone from Bobby Previtte to Tom Varner, David Friesen to Mulgrew Miller (I've framed my blue card with his name on it), but little on the Russians themselves. Once I got excited when

I saw that word in a jazz magazine only to find an article about the Russian River Jazz Festival held in California. I read that "Soviet pianist Leonid Chizhik has moved from Moscow to Munich to study," but not much jazz news is making its way out of that large troubled land that no longer has a name aside from "the former Soviet Union."

One night I had a vision of the sort of thing Jazznost is attempting, but on a larger scale. The Monterey Jazz Festival customarily closes with a giant Sunday night jam, the stagefront lined with international artists such as Paquito D'Rivera, Eiji Kitamura, and Scott Hamilton playing beside one another. Each of us has got our own favorite imaginary all-star band, but I envisioned a sax line consisting of Igor Butman, Frank Morgan, Anatoli Vapirov, Lembit Saarsalu, and Joe Henderson; Germann Lukianov paired off with his beloved Dizzy; Arkadi Shilkloper and Tom Varner on French horn; Billy Higgins confiding time-keeping clues to Vladimir Tarasov; David Friesen or Dave Holland standing between Viktor Dvoskin and Tamaz Kurashvili on bass; my favorite American guitarist Bruce Forman dueling with Alexei Kuznetsov; and, on piano, take your pick from the legion of fine artists I have described in this book. As reliable sideman, my vote would probably go to the much respected Mikhail Okun, sharing a stool with Hank Jones or Tommy Flanagan.

When I set off on my jazz journey from London, Leo Feigin commented on the need Soviet musicians had for "allies, congenial musicians," dreaming his own synthesis, saying that Soviet artists had "no idea how good they are." In my vision the fresh rose finally bloomed, and they had a chance to find out.